George Peabody

George Peabody

GEORGE PEABODY

A Biography

REVISED EDITION

FRANKLIN PARKER

Foreword by Merle Curti

Vanderbilt University Press • *Nashville and London*

Copyright © 1971 by Franklin Parker
Copyright © 1995 by Vanderbilt University Press
Nashville, Tennessee 37235

All Rights Reserved

Original edition published 1971 by Vanderbilt University Press

Revised Edition published by Vanderbilt University Press, 1995

95 96 97 98 99   5 4 3 2 1

This publication is made from recycled paper and meets the minimum requirements
of American National Standard for Information Sciences—Permanence of Paper for
Printed Library Materials ∞

Library of Congress Cataloging-in-Publication Data

Parker, Franklin, 1921–
   George Peabody, a biography / Franklin Parker ; foreword by Merle Curti—
Rev. ed.
      p.   cm.
   Includes bibliographical references (p.   ) and index.
   ISBN 0-8265-1255-0 (cloth : acid-free paper) ; —ISBN 0-8265-1256-9
(pbk. :acid-free paper) ;
      1. Peabody, George 1795–1869.   2.Philanthropists—United States—
Biography.   3. Capitalists and financiers—United States—Biography.   I. Title.
HV28.P4P29   1995
361.7'4'092—dc20
[B]   94-24306
                                                                                          CIP

Manufactured in the United States of America

DEDICATION

*To Betty Parker, full partner in this venture, and to the institutions George Peabody founded, aided, or influenced:

Enoch Pratt Free Library, Baltimore

George Peabody Branch of the Thetford Town Library, Post Mills, Vermont

George Peabody House Civic Center, Peabody, Massachusetts

George Peabody Library of The Johns Hopkins University Library, Baltimore

George Peabody Room, Georgetown Regional Branch, District of Columbia Public Library, Washington, D.C.

Georgetown Peabody Library, Georgetown, Massachusetts

J. P. Morgan Information Resource Center (formerly Morgan Guaranty Trust of New York), New York City

The Johns Hopkins University and Medical School, Baltimore

Kenyon College, Gambier, Ohio

Maryland Historical Society, Baltimore

Massachusetts Historical Society, Boston

Morgan, Grenfell and Company, Ltd., London

Peabody Essex Museum, Salem, Massachusetts

Peabody College of Vanderbilt University, Nashville

Peabody Conservatory of Music of The Johns Hopkins University, Baltimore

Peabody Historical Society, Library and Archives, Peabody, Massachusetts

Peabody Institute Library of Danvers, Massachusetts

Peabody Institute Library of Peabody, Massachusetts

Peabody Museum of Archaeology and Ethnology, Harvard University, Cambridge, Massachusetts

Peabody Museum of Natural History, Yale University, New Haven, Connecticut

Peabody Trust (Peabody Homes of London)

Phillips Academy, Andover, Massachusetts

Southern Education Foundation, Atlanta

Washington and Lee University, Lexington, Virginia

Contents

Foreword

GEORGE PEABODY was one of a relatively small number of nineteenth-century Americans who made great fortunes and established impressive reputations by their own efforts and abilities. Lacking family connections or formal education, he achieved success as a merchant banker in Baltimore and as an investment banker in London. His role in mobilizing European resources for American economic development had been thoroughly studied before Professor Franklin Parker began his work; Professor Parker has, while giving a clear and competent account of Peabody's business activities, wisely focused on the less well known story of his philanthropies.

I do not know of any comparably detailed account of an American philanthropist. The research upon which this book rests is, as I can testify from having read the dissertation upon which it is based, staggering in the resourcefulness and thoroughness of its documentation. In the present book we have all the essentials, together with a portrait of the man—a portrait that is sympathetic without being uncritical.

Several factors render Peabody's philanthropies remarkable. Unlike many donors, he does not seem to have been motivated by religious considerations. Nor is there any evidence that a sense of guilt figured in his decisions to give a considerable part of his fortune to philanthropy while he was living. His critics insisted that the vain desire for self-glorification was at the root of his benefactions. Such a motive was indeed present, but it was not the only one. Peabody never married and thus had no immediate heirs to whom to bequeath his wealth. To be sure, he did a good deal for his sisters, brothers, nieces, and nephews, many of whom needed his help. In so doing, he played the role of the patriarchal head of the family and made it clear that he expected the help he gave to be turned to good account. On the positive side, two considerations seem to have been most influential in his philanthropies. One was a deep devotion to the communities in which he was reared or in which he made his money. The other was a secular version of the Puritan doctrine of the stewardship of riches—his desire, in the simplest terms, to be useful to mankind. Having himself been deprived of opportunities for a formal education, he was eager to help others in a similar situation not merely to achieve vocational training but to open the doors to cultural self-improvement.

If Professor Parker does not contend that Peabody was original in developing a philosophy of philanthropy, neither does he claim that he was an outstanding innovator in choosing the things to which he gave his money. Others had given to local institutions for personal improvement and self-education, to colleges, and even to scientific research. Nevertheless, in much that he did Peabody was forwardlooking and statesmanlike. The need for support for scientific research, especially when it held no promise of utilitarian return, was both great and generally neglected. While his gifts to Yale and Harvard for the museums of archaeology and anthropology were the direct result of the influence of his nephew, Othniel Marsh, one of our greatest paleontologists, Peabody's endowment reflected faith in the value of research that promised to throw light on man's origins. Similarly, while the need for adequate and inexpensive housing for the urban working class was widely discussed in England, his decision to make his handsome gift for such an enterprise reflected his sensitive awareness of the blight of slums and his realization of their handicap to hardworking laborers living in them. At the same time, his gift, coming as it did in the midst of strained relations between England and the United States during the Civil War, reflected his long-sustained efforts to improve understanding and co-operation between the two countries. His largest philanthropy, the Peabody Fund for Southern Education, established at the end of the Civil War, reflected his awareness of the great need of the South for help in improving education and his desire to contribute something to the reconciliation of the nominally reunited country.

Professor Parker has described all this and much more. He has also tried to evaluate the long-term significance and influence of Peabody's donations. This is the definitive study of one of the most important chapters in the history of American philanthropy. As one who has worked in this field, I salute the author of this volume.

MERLE CURTI
University of Wisconsin—Madison

Preface to the Revised Edition

On the Trail of George Peabody

My wife, Betty, and I spent the early summers of our marriage (1951 and 1952) studying at George Peabody College for Teachers in Nashville. A small scholarship and a part-time job prompted our move in the fall of 1952 from our teaching jobs in Virginia to Nashville, where we lived until I completed my graduate work in August 1956. Throughout those years, George Peabody College, adjoining Vanderbilt University and Scarritt College, provided a stimulating and challenging academic environment.

We had the good fortune of studying under professors whom we respected as among the best in the world in their respective fields: Harold Benjamin (former education dean at Stanford University and at the University of Maryland, and editor of the McGraw-Hill education series, whose specialties were adult education and comparative education); Willard Goslin (a former school superintendent who, amid much publicity, had been fired in a classic and instructive progressive versus traditional school battle in Pasadena, California); and such stalwarts as William Van Til (curriculum theory), Nicholas Hobbs (psychology), Jack Allen (social studies), Maycie K. Southall (elementary education), Alfred L. Crabb (English education and educational writing), Robert A. Davis (educational psychology), and Clifton L. Hall (history and philosophy of education). All of these professors were well-published authors, frequent speakers at national conferences, skilled researchers, and, above all, outstanding teachers. To our youthful minds, these were sparkling academic giants to learn from and to emulate. I managed to attach myself as advisee to Clifton Hall, a respected and demanding task master—studying under whom, it was said, compelled one to become both a scholar and a gentleman.

One day I mentioned my dissertation topic (already begun) to then Dean of Graduate Instruction Felix C. Robb. He told me that when he was a student at the Harvard Graduate School of Education, historian

Arthur Schlesinger, Sr., had suggested that he write on the life and educational influence of George Peabody. Dean Robb (who would later become president of George Peabody College for Teachers) chose instead to write on school administration. Perhaps regretting a good topic not pursued, he kindly suggested George Peabody to me.

My initial search for basic facts about George Peabody quickly yielded results on the outline of his life: his career as a merchant, broker, and banker turned philanthropist; his poor family origins in Massachusetts; his apprenticeship in a general store; how he helped an older brother in a Newburyport, Massachusetts, drygoods store; the Newburyport fire that led him and his uncle to move south and open a general store in Georgetown, D.C.; his brief military service in the War of 1812; his junior partnership with Elisha Riggs, Sr., in Georgetown and later in Baltimore; his traveling years spent buying and selling drygoods and other wares for Peabody, Riggs & Co.; his five buying trips to Europe between 1827 and 1837; his permanent move to London in 1837; and his founding in London in 1843 of George Peabody & Co., a firm dealing in U.S. mercantile trade and also selling American state bonds abroad.

I learned that George Peabody's bold and prophetic business career had periods of special drama. Peabody pioneered in the sale of American state bonds in Europe to help finance the vast capital-intensive projects, such as canals and railroads, that characterized America's western expansion. Negotiating these sales was often a struggle against enormous odds, especially after some American states suspended their payments of interest following the financial Panic of 1837. Indeed, to express his own faith in such bonds, Peabody made significant purchases himself. In the midst of these tensions came the disappointment of a broken engagement to marry. A happier matter was the favorable international publicity he earned when his timely loan enabled distraught American exhibitors to display their products attractively at the first world's fair (London's 1851 Great Crystal Palace Exhibition). Then there were his celebrated Fourth of July dinners in London, his gift to outfit a U.S. Arctic expedition to search for the heroic missing British explorer Sir John Franklin, his much-praised role in selling Mexican War bonds, and his successful financing of the laying of the trans-Atlantic cable.

One of the primary concerns of this book is Peabody's abiding philanthropic interest in educational and cultural institutions. He founded libraries and lecture halls in the seven cities where he had lived, worked, or had family ties in the United States. These were in Peabody, Danvers,

Georgetown, and Newburyport, Massachusetts; in Baltimore, Maryland (which also included a conservatory of music and art gallery); in Thetford, Vermont (where as a boy he once visited his maternal grandparents); and in Georgetown, D.C. He founded three Peabody museums of science: for anthropology at Harvard, for natural history at Yale, and for maritime history in Salem, Massachusetts. He endowed science and mathematics professorships at Washington and Lee University, Kenyon College, and Andover Academy. Most important was his establishment of the influential Peabody Education Fund for the Southern states (1867–1914), a precedent-setting $2 million foundation whose present descendant is the Peabody College of Vanderbilt University.

The trail of George Peabody led from Nashville archives to depositories in the Library of Congress and the National Archives in Washington, D.C. In Baltimore, Betty and I did research at the Peabody Library, the Peabody Conservatory of Music, the Johns Hopkins University Library, the Maryland Historical Society, the Enoch Pratt Free Library, and the Baltimore *Sun* Archives. In New York City, we read related papers at the New York Public Library Manuscript Department, the New York Historical Society, and the Pierpont Morgan Library. In the Boston area, we did research at the Boston Public Library, at the Peabody Institute Libraries of Peabody and Danvers, at the Massachusetts Historical Society, at Harvard's Widener Library, Peabody Museum Archives, and Special Business Collection, and at what is now the Peabody Essex Museum, which retains the bulk of George Peabody's papers.

In the autumn of 1954, we followed the trail to London, where George Peabody spent the last thirty-two years of his life. We visited the Peabody Trust, which manages the Peabody Homes of London, established in 1862 on the foundations of Peabody's vision and heartfelt desire to provide low-income housing for London's working poor. We searched the archives of Morgan, Grenfell & Co., the descendant of George Peabody & Co., a banking firm established in collaboration with his partner, Junius S. Morgan. J. S. Morgan's son, John Pierpont Morgan, was apprenticed at George Peabody & Co. and began his international banking career as its New York representative.

In the newspaper collection of the British Library, we found accounts of George Peabody's financial affairs and of his grand public dinners that brought together prominent Americans and Britons. The British Library manuscript collection contained Prime Minister William E. Gladstone's cabinet minutes recording plans for Peabody's funeral honors. We visited the exclusive Athenaeum club which George Peabody was invited to join, one of several honors he received in gratitude for his establishment of the Peabody Homes of London. We saw his seated statue near London's Royal Exchange. (Earlier, we had seen its replica near the Peabody Institute of Baltimore.) We also called on the Royal Archives at Windsor Castle, where we read letters between Queen Victoria, her advisers, and George Peabody. In the Admiralty records at the Foreign Office, we found the log of HMS *Monarch*, then Britain's largest warship, describing the transfer of Peabody's remains to the United States. Several British newspaper readers, responding to our request for information, gave us commemorative glassware their forebears had bought in the wake of the widespread public mourning associated with George Peabody's death. (We later donated this glassware to several of the Peabody institutions.)

Back in Nashville, I was honored by an invitation to give the George Peabody College for Teachers Founders Day Address on February 18, 1955. This address was followed by a year and a half of sorting through boxes of notes and documenting the George Peabody story. Throughout subsequent years, while teaching at the universities of Texas, Oklahoma, and West Virginia, we sent versions of our Peabody story to commercial publishers, without success. Then, in May 1970, Peabody College brought together in Nashville many prominent members of the Massachusetts Peabody family for commencement honors. Noting my presence as a speaker at those ceremonies, the Vanderbilt University Press director asked to see the George Peabody manuscript. The eventual result of those encounters was the original edition of *George Peabody, A Biography*, published by Vanderbilt in December 1971.

Later, when the original printings were exhausted and the book went out of print, I urged my publisher to consider a new edition. Finally, as part of a resurgence of publishing activity at Vanderbilt University Press, and in view of impending celebrations of the two-hundredth anniversary of George Peabody's birth, scheduled for February 1995, the new press director expressed interest in this revised edition. The original biographical study is here reissued with a new introduction, an added concluding chapter on "George Peabody's Legacy," updated bibliographical references, and a revised index.

George Peabody richly merits attention at this bicentennial of his birth. Later and vastly wealthier philanthropists such as John D. Rockefeller, Andrew Carnegie, and Henry Ford are better known, but their expressions of largesse were all influenced by Peabody. One must remember that George Peabody's gifts were made before tax laws provided any incentives for charitable giving and that he had few if any precedents to follow. His philanthropies in current dollars seem relatively small, but adjusted for inflation they were significant indeed. Just as important, they were carefully planned and clearly show his detailed concern for the operations and future well-being of those institutions he chose to benefit.

His motives for giving are not easy to document. One important clue is the sentiment he expressed with his 1852 gift that established the Danvers (now Peabody, Massachusetts) institute: "Education, a debt due from present to future generations." Another clue is contained in his May 18, 1831, reply to a nephew who asked his help to attend Yale College: "I can only do to those that come under my care, as I could have wished circumstances had permitted others to have done by me."

Many have directly benefited from George Peabody's institutions in the United States and Britain. His gifts form a goodly heritage. Born poor, he labored long and hard against great odds to win a place for himself in commerce and banking. Simple in his needs and pleasures, he returned to others the benefits that hard work, business acumen, and good fortune had brought him.

When Peabody died, the sorrow was felt equally in both the United States and England. In London, his funeral at Westminster Abbey drew crowds of the rich and the poor alike, and shopkeepers closed their businesses out of respect. In the United States, Peabody biographer Elbert Hubbard wrote: "George Peabody was the world's first philanthropist. . . . [His] life . . . was not in what he gave, but in what he taught. He inspired the millionaires that are to be. He laid hold on the age to come."

Was there nobility and a touch of the heroic in George Peabody? Many in his time thought so. My hope is that the new edition of this book will give new generations cause to reflect on the reasons he was held in such esteem.

FRANKLIN PARKER

George Peabody

Youth

GEORGE PEABODY's family background shaped the values that guided him as an outstanding nineteenth century philanthropist concerned with education, science, and the reform of housing for working-class people. Peabody's aim in all his benefactions was to teach men and women in need to help themselves by hard work and an upright life. This emphasis on the virtues of industry and integrity was perhaps the natural result of the puritan tradition of a New England family.

George Peabody was of old Massachusetts stock. His father's family came originally from Leicestershire in England. The first of them to emigrate to America was Francis Peboddy, as he spelled his name, a dissenter who arrived in Massachusetts in 1635 on the sailing ship *Planter*. Francis was joined a year later by his father, his brother William, and his sister Annis. Francis Peboddy's descendants remained in Massachusetts where George Peabody was born. Francis's brother William and his family later settled in Rhode Island.

The background of George Peabody's mother was similar. Her ancestors, the Spoffords, also dissenters, were from Yorkshire. They came to New England in the middle of the seventeenth century and went to live in Rowley, Massachusetts.

Some of the descendants of these Peabodys and Spoffords had prospered in the New World, but most of George Peabody's immediate forefathers were not well off. His father was always a very poor man with a family too large for his earning capacity.

Perhaps George Peabody was never truly hungry in his childhood, but by modern standards he was undernourished; his belt was always tightened, and his austere New England youth in Danvers, Massachusetts, was frugal and rugged, without security, frills, or comforts. His father, Thomas Peabody, who had been born in Andover, was a casual leather worker and farmer on a small scale. Thomas was not among those shrewd, farsighted citizens of the Commonwealth who made an effort to benefit from the

3

proximity of thriving Boston. Nor was he, harassed by his efforts to earn a living for his wife and growing family, impressed by the fact that Boston, only nineteen miles away, was now not only the great cultural center of America but also a trading center for ships sailing to many distant ports. Thomas, immersed in his family cares, was probably unaware of what it meant to the trade of the United States when, in 1787, the Boston ship *Columbia* set sail for her famous journey around the world, the first such journey of any American vessel.

George Peabody's mother Judith Dodge, whom Thomas had married in Haverhill in 1789, has remained a reserved almost shadowy figure in the records of George Peabody's life. She died in 1830 in Lockport, New York. George built a church and a library in her memory, but nothing is known of his relationship with her in his childhood or of the influence she may have had on his development. Childbearing and never-ending work in the home left her little energy for talk or play with her children. She was undoubtedly a dutiful and devoted mother, but George learned young not to expect demonstrations of affection from her—nor was he himself, except with small infants, a very demonstrative boy. When he grew up and left home, Judith Dodge was, of course, frequently mentioned in his correspondence; he wrote to her, but his somewhat stilted letters rarely betrayed his feelings.

For fifteen years after Judith Dodge Peabody was married, she always had an infant and young children to look after. Two of her children, David and Achsah Spofford, were born in Haverhill. After she and Thomas moved to Danvers in 1794, six more were added. First George, on February 18, 1795, followed by Judith Dodge, Thomas, Jeremiah Dodge, Mary Gaines, and Sophronia Phelps. The last child was born in 1809.

In the frugal, hard-working Peabody home little was known of turmoils in the outside world, though at the turn of the century the Western world was indeed at one of the crossroads of history. Events during the childhood of George Peabody and of his brothers and sisters affected directly or indirectly the lives of everyone in Europe and in America.

It is difficult today to imagine a world without rapid communications in which weeks or months passed before such men as Thomas Peabody heard even vague rumors of startling developments: the ancient monarchy in France irrevocably ended eighteen months before George was born and the King and Queen of France had been executed; Robespierre, the monarchy's ruthless enemy, was himself executed the following year; and England, the late enemy, now in a state of uneasy peace with her former colonies, was at war, from time to time, with various European countries. To such simple people as Thomas Peabody the name of Napoleon Bonaparte was still unknown, though in the middle seventeen nineties he was beginning to make his influence felt, for he had been appointed by the new Directory in France as commander-in-chief of the army in Italy.

Italy, France, even England were only vague place names to the Peabody family in Danvers. One fact of which they were fully aware was that George Washington, the good father of their country, was the President of the United States. In George's boyhood, Danvers with its population of about three thousand, two churches, two district schools, and a few shops was his world.

Thomas had moved with his wife to Danvers, because, as a shoemaker and a maker of other leather goods, he wanted a home near fresh water and oak trees. He needed pure water and the tan made from oak bark to dye his leather before drying it in the sun. Both abounded in Danvers.

Thomas had bought twelve acres of land in Danvers, which he believed would be adequate to provide food for his family. He was obviously optimistic, and he was undeterred when people warned him that the scant top soil in the district produced only a meager harvest at best, and that the severe winters regularly tended to exhaust the small yield from the land won by hard labor during the hot, dry summers.

As the years passed, neither his leather trade nor his rather pathetic efforts as a farmer went well for Thomas Peabody. He was obliged to mortgage more and more of his land, and by the time he died in 1811, after breaking a leg in an accident, the house, too, was heavily mortgaged and his widow was involved in legal difficulties about his little property that remained.

The Peabodys all worked hard even as small children. There were regular chores for each of the Peabody boys and girls. They helped their mother with her housework, they worked on the land, they cared for their younger brothers and sisters. Young George's special responsibility was his sister Judith, four years younger than himself. She and his baby sister Mary Gaines were the two human beings for whom this undemonstrative boy allowed himself to express some affection.

George had little leisure to learn to read, write, or do sums. The Danvers school which he attended for four or five years was a one-room wooden building, and the teaching there was primitive. The school sessions never lasted more than the few months that the children could be spared from work on the land or in the home. George was taught only the rudiments. He did not learn easily. He was a slow-thinking boy, and he found arithmetic particularly hard. He was growing fast, and he was often over tired from physical labors that were too much for a boy of nine or ten. His health, nevertheless, remained good, and the only time he visited a doctor was when a tumor over his left eye had to be removed.

George was largely occupied with his own brothers and sisters and had little opportunity to make friends at school. His one friend among his contemporaries was a boy called John Proctor whose father Captain Sylvester Proctor, a prosperous man, owned the general store in Danvers. John's chances to get an education were greater than George's, and young Proctor went on from the village school to Lancaster Academy. But Proctor never forgot George, and nearly half a century later he remembered him as a manly, well behaved, and honorable boy.

In 1807, when George was only eleven years old, his father could no longer afford to keep him at school. It was time the boy learned a trade so that he could help support the younger members of his family. John Proctor's father, who had often seen George with his son, agreed to take George on as an apprentice in his store. So at the age of eleven George Peabody began his working life as an apprentice in Proctor's general emporium. He was to receive no wages, and his clothing was paid for by his father. Captain Proctor was responsible for his board and lodging.

He had left his parents' house; he was really on his own, though as Proctor's apprentice he lived nearby in the town. Eleven seems very young to make this break, but already George Peabody showed that he had the character to face the world alone. He was fortunate to be working for people as kind as Captain Proctor and his wife, for though George slept in an attic above the shop, he joined the Proctors for meals and was made to feel that he belonged to the family. He found a special companion in the Proctors' three-year-old son Sylvester, who was devoted to George. When he went to see his parents, he often took Sylvester with him. Just as some boys love a puppy, George found in this child an outlet for his affections.

Forty years later, when Peabody was settled in London, Sylvester wrote to him: "Well do I remember the nights in which I nestled in your arms and how vexed my faithful and tender nurse was when I stole from her to sleep with you. And well do I remember how delighted I was when occasionally I accompanied you home to your Father's House and was caressed and petted by your sisters."

Young George Peabody had little time to play with Sylvester. He was working very hard. From Captain Proctor he was learning all the time. He learned to cultivate his neat, clear handwriting, to keep accounts, and to be disciplined and organized in his daily activities. George Peabody was always grateful to Proctor, to whom, as he frequently said in later life, he attributed much of his success.

The apprenticeship was arduous. George opened up the store soon after dawn, swept the floors and kept the shelves clean, rolled out the barrels and other supplies for the day's sales, then waited patiently on the customers no matter how difficult or hard to please they might be. He learned young how to deal with people, for a store of this kind was the village center, and the owner and his apprentice had to be aware of the customers' needs and their ability to pay.

Often by evening the growing boy was very tired, but he closed the shop and performed his morning tasks in reverse. He then sat down at a table and began copying the day's rough accounts into the permanent ledger books. Through these strenuous days the boy gained self-assurance, self-control, and initiative. He was maturing at a very early age.

When he ended his apprenticeship at the age of fifteen, George had earned his keep for four years, and Proctor gave him five dollars and a new suit of clothes. George was now ready to face the world as an adult. The world of 1810 was not a secure one. England was at war with Napoleon's France. Each country was limiting the trade of the other and, caught in the middle of this blockade, American trade and shipping were hampered. The resulting economic depression in New England and elsewhere made it difficult for young men to find employment.

Captain Proctor offered George a job (with wages this time) in the store, but already George was aware that his talents were worthy of a wider scope. He resolved to get away from the narrow life of Danvers. His wanderlust took him first to visit his maternal grandparents who had a farm in Thetford in Vermont. Here, instructed by his quiet, shrewd, and often witty grandfather, Jeremiah Dodge, George worked on the land. Soon he did not wait to be told what to do. If a tree needed felling, he went out and felled it; if his grandmother required help in the house, he saw what she needed done and did it on his own.

George acquired a horse, perhaps a gift from his grandparents, and after leaving Thetford, he continued his travels on horseback. He stopped in Concord, New Hampshire, where he sawed and split wood for his keep at a tavern. He then rode on to Barnstead to stay with his mother's sister, Mrs. Jeremiah Jewett, whose husband was a doctor. Here, during the stormy winter of 1810, when the doctor was away from home visiting patients, George took care of the stable stock, broke paths from the house to the barn and the road, cut wood for the fires, and made himself generally useful. These physical exertions in the open air were good for his health, but he soon realized that physical work was not enough. He wanted to use his brain and his wits.

Early in 1811 he returned to Danvers to decide what to do. For a New England youth of his background, fifteen was not too young to make independent decisions nor to contemplate going into some business on his own or with his brother David who was five years older.

David had opened a drapery shop in Newburyport, a larger town than Danvers, about twenty miles to the north. David Peabody and Company was doing quite well despite the embargo. David had built up connections with merchants in Boston and was sufficiently successful to need George's clerical assistance. George joined his brother in return for a small wage. He earned extra money at election time by writing ballots for the Federalist Party.

The two brothers had an influential relative in Newburyport, Colonel John Peabody, who came from the more affluent branch of the family and was one of the important merchants in the town. John Peabody enjoyed one of the coveted status symbols of the period: he had a front pew in the Congregational Church on Federal Street where the sermons were preached by a famous pastor, Dr. Daniel Dana. George sat in this pew on Sundays, a tall, broad-shouldered youth of fifteen with a straight back, light hair, and blue eyes, wearing his best grey suit with bright, shining buttons.

Everything was going well for George, and he might perhaps have stayed in Newburyport, helped expand his brother's business or started some venture of his own. But his father's unexpected death on May 11, 1811, intervened. His mother's financial position was desperate, and she and George's small brothers and sisters urgently needed help.

Traditionally David, as the eldest son, was expected to look after the orphaned family. David, however, was never a very competent man, and later he was to cause George Peabody great anxiety. George, therefore, at the age of sixteen, assumed the responsibility for the support of his mother and her small children.

After Thomas Peabody's death, in the settling of his tangled affairs, the Danvers home had to be given up temporarily. The family separated, and the children and their mother went to live with Mrs. Peabody's numerous relatives. It was not until 1817 that George Peabody was in a position to pay off the mortgages on the Danvers homestead so that his mother could again have a home of her own.

In 1811, soon after their father's death, George and David confronted a new and unexpected crisis. At half-past nine, on the evening of May 31, when George was putting up the shutters in the store for the night, he saw smoke over the town. He ran to give the alarm, but in a very few minutes fire was making its way through 250 buildings in Newburyport.

George quickly helped to organize the chain of men, women, and children who passed along buckets filled with water to fight the flames. But it was a losing battle. In a short while much of the flourishing town was in ashes. Old people in Newburyport recalled the terrible Boston fire of 1772.

David's store was miraculously spared, but the fire ruined all business in the town. More than ninety families were homeless, most of them reduced in one stroke from financial security to poverty. Relief came from nearby cities—Boston alone sent the stricken town more than twenty-five thousand dollars—but the Great Fire of Newburyport, as it was known in the history of Massachusetts, greatly diminished the purchasing power of David's customers. Though his stock was intact, he realized that he would be out of business for a very long time. It would be impossible, in the foreseeable future, for him to earn enough to send money to his mother and the children still at home in Danvers. Certainly the business could no longer afford even George's small salary.

The Newburyport fire was a turning point in the career of George Peabody. Fate seemed to have made it necessary for him, young as he was, to leave his small-town surroundings to make a life for himself in a larger and more challenging place. The man who helped him achieve this radical change was his uncle, Colonel John Peabody.

John Peabody had lost his store and his stock in the fire, but he was an adventurous man who never minded beginning his career anew. In his younger days he had prospered in the shipping trade, had made and lost small fortunes, and had learned to recover from disasters. He was a born gambler. Now, after the fire, his credit was shaky and he was looking for new connections to enable him to start afresh. Above all, he needed a young and enthusiastic partner who would help him get credit for new ventures. John Peabody felt instinctively that his nephew was not only keen but reliable. He invited the lad to come with him to Georgetown, District of Columbia (near Washington), to open up a store. John Peabody, whose optimism was not dampened by his losses in the fire, firmly believed that all he needed for this Georgetown venture was to obtain credit for consignments of goods from merchants in Boston and other New England towns.

George's self-assurance at this time was quite remarkable in a youth of his age. He handled the whole situation more like a banker than like a would-be merchant. He approached a prominent businessman in Newburyport, Prescott Spaulding, and explained his need for credit. George was so persuasive that Spalding gave him letters of credit to Boston merchants, recommending James Reed in particular.

George traveled to Boston to see Reed, who was as impressed by the young man from Newburyport as Spalding had been. Reed did not hesitate to extend to George credit for about $2,000 worth of merchandise. The sum was more than he had hoped for or requested; it was apparent that he had somehow inspired confidence when he negotiated this credit. He probably did not foresee that this successful interview with James Reed marked the beginning of his great career as a merchant banker. Years later, George Peabody referred to Reed as "my first patron; the man who sold me my first bill of goods."

George Peabody was in an optimistic mood when, on May 4, 1812, he and John Peabody sailed on the brig *Fame* from Newburyport for Georgetown. The *Fame* sailed down the Atlantic Coast to the mouth of the Potomac then up to Washington. A few weeks later the stock came from Reed and the new store opened for business in Georgetown on May 15.

Soon, however, George Peabody was plunged into a situation even stranger to him than Georgetown. He was, in fact, suddenly made aware that events in distant countries could affect him and other individuals who had nothing to do with these events—a lesson thousands of young men have been forced to learn throughout the ages. When the Georgetown store had been opened for business only two weeks, on June 1, 1812, President James Madison sent his famous war message to Congress. The President cited developments of which George Peabody had heard only vaguely: England's impressment of American seamen, her abridgment of neutral rights, the inciting of Indians to hostilities. Three days later the House of Representatives passed a war resolution, and on June 17 the Senate narrowly voted approval. The United States was at war with England. History had caught up with young George Peabody, and he enlisted as a volunteer in an artillery regiment.

Georgetown and Baltimore

TIMES were tense and uncertain, especially in Washington. The Government feared that the British fleet might momentarily sail up the Potomac and attack the Capital. The attack did not come until 1813, but able-bodied men meanwhile were conscripted and trained to defend the Capital.

Young George Peabody had enlisted as a volunteer in the artillery before he was called up. He was assigned to the company commanded by Captain George Peter. George Peabody marched, drilled, and stood duty, but, as it happened, he saw no combat service in the War of 1812. When Washington was attacked and burned, he was visiting relatives in Newburyport. Later, when he had moved to Baltimore, he was a member of the "United Volunteers" under Captain William Cooke and was stationed at Fort Warburton with Francis Scott Key, the composer of "The Star Spangled Banner."

While he lived in Georgetown, quite apart from the national emergency, Peabody had many personal worries. His uncle John Peabody was deeply in debt; thus the responsibility for the new Georgetown business on Bridge Street devolved largely upon him. John tried to help his nephew and struggled along for some years but was never able to meet his financial obligations. When he died in 1820, he left his widow and children penniless. George was always loyal to his uncle, and after the death he undertook the support of his aunt and cousins.

George might easily have been impatient with John Peabody; after all, he was only seventeen years old and was faced with the formidable task of building up this new Georgetown venture virtually alone. He had to arrange the transportation of shipments from Newburyport and Boston, have them carried from the receiving depots in Washington to the store in Georgetown, unload the goods, make them ready for sale, and often deliver them himself to his customers. He had to decide how and in what newssheets to advertise, and he was obliged to devote long hours to his business correspondence. Selling the goods often meant miles of walking with a pack on his back. He worried constantly that he might be held responsible for his uncle's debts.

But George never regretted this arduous commercial apprenticeship in Georgetown. It taught him to deal with all sorts of people, either when they came to the store or when he went out to sell his goods in surrounding districts. His customers, in simple shacks or on fine plantations, learned in turn to trust him and his business integrity.

He had little time for pleasure or sociability; he did not even have the leisure to write to his family frequently, though he regularly sent what money, food, or clothes he could spare.

At this time he formed the habit of sending the newspaper of the town where he was working, so that his family could follow his travels. One letter to his sister Judith, who was with her grandparents in Thetford, is the earliest letter preserved from George to a member of his family. This letter reflects the strain under which he was living during the War. It is from Georgetown on June 28, 1813, and shows that the youth had not yet been able to catch up on his education or spelling.

"Miss J. Peabody," he headed the letter, and continued,

Amagion not dear Sister that two years absence has eras[ed] you from my memory. Nor impute my remissness in not before answering you Interesting letter of the 9th April, to any diminution of love, when I assure you not a day passes but what brings you and the rest of my friends to my memory, and makes me more and more regret the loss of their Society. I however pass my time as pleasantly as can be expected so far from them.

The acquaintances I have found are not very numerous, but agreable, most particularly the society of some young Laidies which can only be exceeded by that of my distant friends, which I expect to have enjoyed . . . before this, but owing to the situation of our business, I regret to say it will be impossible for me to leave till next Spring, at which time I anticipate with Pleasure a short visit to Thetford where I have spent some of my pleasantest days and on which I often derive pleasure in ruminating and at which place I think with your Thetford friends, you cannot but pass your time agreeably.

But in my Situation I cannot feel that ease and tranquility I should wish as the management of the business in which I am engaged entirely devolves on me, and subjects me to all the cares and anxieties that generally attends it. We are also under considerable apprehensions of an attack from the British upon this district, So much so that the President has made a requisition of 500 men which have been ordered on duty and are now encamp.d within sight of this place. I was one of the detach.d members, but fortunately the day previous to the draft attach.d myself to a choir of Artillery, otherwise it would have cost me 50 to 75$ for a Substitute. My duty however now is not the easyest having to meet every other day for the purpose of drill exercise and which is the case with every person cabable of military duty in the district.

Almost every mail from the southward brings accounts of some new depradations committed in the Chesapeake Bay. . . . The President is dangerously sick, he has sent 50 miles for a physitian. My last letters from Achsah [his oldest sister] was in May, the family was in good health. Achsah Informed me that Uncle D was in N.Y. I wish you to Inform me In what part of the city he resides, as should I go there this fall I should like to call on him. I hope Uncle Elipholet has recovered his health before this, my respects to him and all the rest of the folk and Remain your Affe. Brother Geo. Peabody.

The stilted language, typical of a young man with little formal education, does not reveal George Peabody's deep and lasting affection for his brothers and sisters. He already considered himself the head of the family, and any interest he may have had in the "laidies" he met was unimportant compared with his feeling of responsibility for his family. He made all important decisions affecting not only his brothers and sisters but his cousins as well. As he prospered, he arranged and paid for a better education for them than he himself had enjoyed. He gave employment to his brothers and their sons or found jobs for them whenever they needed such help.

He faced family difficulties calmly—and there were many. Thomas, one of his younger brothers whom George had employed as a clerk, was irresponsible: he drank, gambled, and borrowed money frequently. Thomas went off to South America where he became ill and lost his job. He managed to return to America as a ship's clerk. He drifted from job to job, got into debt again, was dishonest in business matters even with his brother David, and finally died in April 1835 in his early thirties. It is not known whether he took his own life or died of drunkenness.

David, too, was now often in debt; while employed by George in New York, he was often unable to pay his rent.

Achsah, the oldest girl in the family, unmarried at twenty-eight, was mentally unbalanced and physically frail. She died at an early age. Caleb Marsh, who married George's sister Mary Gaines, fancied himself a businessman. After much persuading from George, he gave up a commercial career and settled down as a farmer in Lockport, New York. The farm was, of course, purchased for Caleb and Mary Gaines by George.

In fact, George's family was quite an expense for him; it was fortunate that he succeeded in business while still a young man. By 1817 he was able to pay off the outstanding mortgages on the family farm in Danvers and his mother moved back there. By this time, though only in his early twenties, he was a relatively wealthy man; he told one of his uncles that his assets were between $40,000 and $50,000, a considerable fortune at the time for a young man.

As he became more and more successful, George Peabody seemed to grow in stature and self-assurance. He took great care of his appearance. As with many men who experienced a poor childhood and wore the hand-me-down garments of older brothers, George loved fine clothes. When he was a soldier-volunteer, for example, he favored flashy uniforms of blue and scarlet with crossed belts and a hat with waving plumes. When he wore his civilian dress, too, he was well groomed and carefully turned out. His upright carriage, clear blue eyes, and healthy complexion inspired confidence wherever he went—confidence justifiably heightened on further acquaintance.

Not surprisingly, George Peabody, even before the age of twenty, was noticed by the older, established merchants and bankers in the District of Columbia. Here, in 1814 he met the man who was to be his first partner, Elisha Riggs. Originally from Montgomery County in Maryland, Riggs, then a man of thirty-five, was willing to invest $5,000 in a partnership with young Peabody. Riggs was impressed when his youthful partner was able to raise $1,650.40 for the firm. Peabody's Georgetown premises, too, were an asset, and during the first period of the partnership these offices were used as the base for their operations.

The partnership of Riggs and Peabody was formed in 1815 and continued until 1829, when the firm was reorganized by Peabody with Elisha's son, Elisha Jr., and Elisha's nephew, Samuel Riggs. Elisha Riggs Sr., too, had a strong personality, and the relationship of the two partners was at times somewhat strained. Peabody had so much drive and indefatigable energy that it was difficult to keep up with him, and he occasionally irritated the older man. Besides, Riggs, not without reason, was frequently exasperated by the ineffectiveness and carelessness of Thomas and David, George's brothers, whom he had insisted on employing in the firm. However, as a rule, through the years of their association, Peabody and Riggs felt great respect and liking for each other, and when Riggs retired from the business his son and nephew were glad to follow him in the partnership.

In 1852, nearly half a century after Elisha Riggs and George Peabody had met, Elisha Riggs wrote to Peabody, then in London:

Few men can look back for as many years as we both can and examine over all our business transactions and friendly intercourse with as much pride and satisfaction as we can. You always had the faculty of an extraordinary memory and strong mind which enabled you to carry out your plans better than almost any other man I ever knew, and to these I attribute much of your prosperity with extraordinary perseverance. . . .

It had been obvious almost from the start that Riggs and Peabody would flourish. The success of the original partnership becomes clear when one observes that after the first five years of the venture the total earnings amounted to $70,709.24. (It is interesting to note those 24 cents; Peabody always kept precise accounts.)

The firm of Riggs and Peabody bought and sold consignments of goods from American merchants in the North, who, in turn, imported much of their stock from England and the Continent. One of the early notices of Riggs and Peabody in the press reflected the range of commodities they carried. This advertisement announced that "Riggs and Peabody . . . just received French and German goods, viz:

Black, white, and assorted crapes
Assorted double Florences
Double Levantine and Gauze Shawls
Beaver, Silk and Kid Gloves
An elegant assortment of plain and figured ribbands
Fine Twist coat buttons
Thule Lace and cotton gauze
German hat crapes
Ticklingburgs
Burlap

The advertisement closed with a statement that the firm also had in stock "A Genl. Asst. of Canton, Calcutta & British Dry Goods which they offer for sale by the piece or package, at the lowest market price."

Peabody, as the much younger partner, was, of course, expected to undertake some of the more tiring and less interesting tasks for the firm. One of his jobs was the arduous one of collecting bad debts of long standing. In this disagreeable duty he showed how quickly he was learning the importance of diplomacy and patience to the building up of any business. In a letter to Riggs from Fredericksburg, Virginia, written in 1821, Peabody mentioned that he had spent three hours with a reluctant debtor before receiving settlement. Peabody was always encouraged by Riggs, who wrote in reply, "I am highly gratified at all you have done," and that the work "could not be better."

Soon the premises in Georgetown were too small for Riggs and Peabody, and the location of Georgetown was not central enough for the headquarters of this growing concern. In 1816 the partners decided to move to Baltimore and they took a place known as Old Congress Hall on the corner of Baltimore and Sharpe Streets. Baltimore was a thriving center of trade with splendid shipping facilities. The city had experienced a phenomenal growth. In 1800 the population was 26,714; thirty years later it had increased to 80,625, outstripping Boston and Philadelphia, and standing in second place to New York as a great commercial city.

After the move to Baltimore, Peabody traveled even more widely, but for twenty years he considered Baltimore his home, even when Riggs and Peabody, or Riggs, Peabody and Company as the partnership was soon to be called, had opened branches in New York and Philadelphia. It was in Baltimore that Peabody, helped by his association with businessmen of wide interests, developed into an international merchant and financier.

He assiduously cultivated the acquaintance of older men from whom he could learn about world trade. He worked harder than ever after the firm moved to Baltimore, but for the first time in his life he seemed to allow himself to relax occasionally with friends. He and three other young business bachelors, Richard Bell, William Bend, and Horatio G. Ward, exchanged confidences which had nothing to do with business and, judging by their letters to each other when they were separated, these confidences, often rather bawdy, frequently concerned their associations with women.

A typical letter from Richard Bell, a happy-go-lucky young Irishman, to Peabody (Bell was then in London) reflects the tone of their conversations when they met:

"I am glad to find you are passing your time so agreeably. . . . And what are you about? How is all this flirtation to end?" Here Bell mentioned the name of an American lady and then continued: "If *you* bring over such a wife to England, you cannot love her by daylight, along side of our ripe, plump . . . girls.—remember that and don't risque it."

Bell could never resist teasing Peabody about his spelling which continued to be inaccurate. "Will you excuse me," he added, "for telling you you spell opportunity with two p's—and in speaking of the Balto [Baltimore] girls, you say their 'statue' as small meaning stature. This [is] a liberty I would only take with a friend & a man of sense. . . ."

There was no such informality in George Peabody's correspondence with his brothers and sisters. In a proper, very older-brother style, he wrote to Mary Gaines or the other members of his family. When he visited them, George did not, of course, refer to the gay banter he exchanged with his bachelor friends. In fact, he was always, as long as he lived, successfully able to separate his private life from the staid public image he presented to the world and, as a rule, to his family as well.

In his business associations, too, from an early age, he maintained an equally consistent reserve. He preferred to discuss his plans after he had made up his own mind what action would be best. He thought carefully before he spoke. And so, when he decided in the autumn of 1827 to go to Europe, the decision came as a surprise to his family and to most of his business acquaintances. The affairs of Riggs, Peabody, and Company were doing well, and many men would have been content to let them go on as they were. George Peabody, however, at every stage of his career, sought wider and wider opportunities.

He was to travel five times to Europe before he finally settled in England in 1837. Now, in 1827, he went abroad because he realized that there was an opportunity for his firm to negotiate the sale of American cotton in Lancashire. He knew that personal contacts in England were essential, and it would be profitable if he could personally locate, purchase, and ship prints, woolens, linen, and other dry goods. Increasing trade had made it worth-while for Riggs, Peabody, and Company to move from Georgetown to Baltimore. Now, Peabody was sure, the time had come to expand the firm's business to agencies in Europe.

Peabody required a passport for the journey to Liverpool, and this document, signed by Henry Clay, then Secretary of State, gives an accurate picture of his physical appearance at the time.

In this document dated October 22, 1827, Peabody was described as follows:

Age	32
Stature	6 feet 1 inch
Forehead	low
Eyes	light blue
Nose	rather large
Mouth	small
Chin	pointed
Hair	dark brown
Complexion	dark
Face	round

The will George Peabody made before sailing for Liverpool showed that, apart from the responsibility he felt for his family, he was already concerned with gifts to charity. This will, leaving a total of $85,000, and reflecting the financial success he had achieved in thirteen years of hard work, is worth quoting in full.

In the name of God Amen. I George Peabody of the City of Baltimore, knowing the uncertainty of life, and the necessity for being prepared for death, do make and declare to be my last will and testament.

He then made the following bequests:

Mother:
    House and lot valued at $ 2,000
    Annuity of $500   10,000
Judith:
    Cash and stock   10,000
Mary Gaines:
    Bond of Caleb Marsh   1,500
    Cash in bank   8,500
Sophronia Phelps:
    Cash etc.   10,000
Jeremiah: 15,000
Thomas: 7,000
George [nephew, son of David Peabody]:   15,000
Sophronia [cousin, daughter of Uncle John Peabody]:   2,000

After these family bequests came those to charity:

Orphaline Female School   2,000
Baltimore General Dispensary   2,000
Total $85,000

No reason was given for the omission of George's elder brother David from this will. Probably George resented his older brother's unwillingness to share at least part of the financial responsibility for the family.

When Peabody made this first will in 1827, he settled his affairs in Baltimore and New York for an absence of ten months. He had overworked and felt strained and ill. He tended to worry about his health, and in his correspondence, even when he was a young and vigorous man, there are frequent references to his physical disorders. He had, as he himself called his trouble, a "disposition to Bilious Fevers." Now, however, as he wrote to his sister Mary before sailing, "his health that fall had been very good." "I trust," he added, "my voyage will have an effect to completely restore me." He was thus looking forward eagerly to his first and exciting journey to Europe and to a widening of his personal and business experiences. He left New York on the packet *Florida* on November 1, 1827.

He was a very dignified man of thirty-two. He continued to dress with great care and never economized when he bought clothes. He was increasingly conscious of the impression he made on other people. His manner toward everyone was cordial, but he discouraged familiarity, and, as he grew older, he often avoided close friendships. No one, not even, perhaps, the members of his own family, really knew him intimately. George Peabody always remained a man very much on his own.

The International Scene

THE crossing on the *Florida* was to be the first of five such journeys which George Peabody undertook in the next decade. After 1837, the crossing was, for him, the other way round: for he then made England his permanent home except for three visits to the United States.

Peabody's twenty-five days in a small cabin aboard the *Florida* were not an auspicious beginning of his European adventure. The *Florida*'s skipper, Captain Tinkham, who had crossed the Atlantic one hundred times, admitted that this was one of the stormiest passages he had ever experienced. George Peabody suffered intensely from seasickness, and until the last day of the voyage he was unable to join the other passengers in the dining saloon. Broth or gruel were brought to him in his cabin, and when the ship docked in Liverpool on November 25, 1827, he was pale and exhausted and had lost fifteen pounds.

He felt depleted of energy and was not yet used to the unpleasant fact that he was a very poor sailor. He was able, however, after his return journey to America in the following September, to accept his seasickness as the price he had to pay for being an international merchant. In fact, in a rare expression of humor in his letters, he reminded his sister Mary, who was living with her husband Caleb Marsh on their farm in Lockport that, as a lad, he had actually wanted to be a sailor.

"I have written mother to-day," he wrote to Mary, "that I have given up all intentions of being a sailor as I used to threaten as a boy."

During his first few days in Liverpool, in that cold November of 1827, he can hardly have found his thin, tired body anything to laugh about, but he did not allow this indisposition to curtail his activities. Soon he had regained his usual energy and determination, and, strange as it may seem, the English climate agreed with him. He wrote to Riggs that he could work twice as hard as in America without fatigue, "perhaps due to the English climate."

Peabody called upon William and James Brown, a firm well known to him. The Brown brothers had often been in Baltimore where their father was a prominent merchant. The Browns in Liverpool gave Peabody introductions to firms in Manchester, Leeds, and other centers of trade in the north of England and in Scotland. Peabody traveled and worked indefatigably for three months, selecting merchants who could act as his agents. He also obtained orders for southern American cotton and purchased English goods which he sent to Baltimore for sale there.

By the middle of January 1828 he wrote to Riggs that he was shipping thirty-eight packages of goods to Baltimore. He also asked Riggs for the next statement of Riggs, Peabody, and Company's profits, saying he expected it to be about $23,000.

England and Scotland were not the only trading centers with which George Peabody was concerned. Early in his career as an international merchant he was interested in markets all over Europe. And though he was trading on a very large scale, nothing was too small to escape his notice. He would point out to his associates that printed goods mounted on handsome pattern cards sold better than unmounted ones, or that dark blue cloth looked richer when mounted on black paper. This attention to detail was soon apparent to the merchants with whom he dealt. They appreciated his suggestions and welcomed the business he brought them. It was not surprising, therefore, that during each of his five European tours from 1827 to 1837 he purchased and sold goods in an increasing number of markets.

In Manchester and in the County of Yorkshire he bought cottons and woolens. In Glasgow and Dundee, Scotland, he purchased worsted shawls, thread, tablecloth, and pins. From Dublin he got fine linens. And in France—Paris, Lyons, St. Etienne—he purchased luxury items such as fine silks, linen handkerchiefs, collars, gloves, and veils. He appointed agents as far away as Russia who bought for him in St. Petersburg superior sheeting, flems, diapers, and sail cloth. From Florence, Italy, came lustrings, glossy silk fabrics, and thread. In the Kingdom of Saxony he bought fine merinos.

George Peabody's European journeys always followed the same pattern. After finishing his business in England and Scotland, he traveled extensively on the Continent, seeking business opportunities wherever he went. He was less interested in the history of the cities he visited. He was not known to spend any time in museums or art galleries, but he was profoundly concerned with the people, the ordinary people, in the countries through which he traveled. He was shocked by the poverty and the slums he saw in many capitals; he viewed poverty with the deep sadness of a humanitarian who has known in his own youth what it means to be poor and anxious about the support of a large family.

Yet Peabody, even as a young man, was never sentimental; he was beginning to realize that charity alone was never enough. People, he believed, must learn how to help themselves: he was already conscious of the fact that education is the most effective defense against poverty. His growing concern with education became apparent when, in 1832, before his second trip to Europe, he amended his will. In his 1827 will he had left about one-twentieth of his estate to philanthropy, while in 1832, five years later, one-quarter of his increasing wealth (estimated at $135,000) was bequeathed to philanthropic institutions. The largest sum was for education in Baltimore, but schools in his home town of Danvers were also remembered, as were an orphans' home and a hospital.

On his first European journey he was reminded everywhere how poverty can degrade human beings. From Dublin he wrote to his sister Sophronia Phelps, now married to a physician, Dr. Eldridge Gerry Little:

As soon as you leave this city [Dublin] the inhabitants of the smaller towns and villages are in the most deplorable state of Poverty and wretchedness. It was not unusual, on leaving a public house in a country town, to be [surrounded] by 20 or 30 beggars at a time, which always excited in my mind feelings of congratulations, that I lived in a country where such things are unknown, but where industry and economy never fail to procure the comforts of life.

Considering the ground Peabody covered when he traveled, it was surprising that he saw anything but the inside of his carriage. He had an innate revulsion to wasting time. After attending to his affairs in the British Isles in a hectic few months, he would plunge into extended tours of the Continent, often at great speed. During his second journey to Europe, for example, with "an American friend," whose name is not known, he traveled by carriage 10,000 miles in England, France, Italy, and Switzerland. This tour, as Peabody wrote to his sister Judith, who had in September 1831 married Jeremiah Russell, a lawyer, was for "business & amusement," and he also hoped the travel and a change of environment would "eradicate from my system all disposition to Bilious Fevers to which I was a few years since very subject."

On this second European trip he left England in February 1831 for Paris and the south of France. Then he and his companion crossed the Alps to Turin in Italy. Visits to Genoa, Lucca, Pisa, Leghorn, Rome, Naples, and Pompeii followed; then back to Rome, then Florence, Bologna, Venice, Padua, Verona, and Milan before, as he wrote, "crossing the Simplon (one of the highest of the Alps on snow 40′ deep on May 1) into Switzerland." Here they "descended the valley of the Rhone to Geneva and passed near Mont Blanc to Lyons, Paris etc."

In about eight short weeks, Peabody and his friend had seen a great deal. Their travel seems extraordinarily hurried for a trip which was partly for pleasure. Peabody was proud of the speed with which they moved about Europe.

Peabody wrote to Judith,

We travelled in our own carriage, drawn by from 2 to 4 horses which we changed every 10–15 miles and by paying the postillions liberally we travelled very rapidly and were able to see as much of the countries in 2 months as most persons would have done in four besides attending to business—Whenever the country was interesting we travelled night as well as day, & eat our meals in our carriage without stopping—during the fifteen months of my absence [from the United States] I have travelled nearly 10,000 miles by *land* without the slightest accident having occurred—have purchased goods in England—Ireland—Scotland—France & Italy & shipped to this country [United States] to amount to $400,000.

This sum indicates the extent to which Peabody's business affairs were flourishing. By the time he went to Europe in 1832 and again in 1834, he was buying and shipping goods not only to New York, Baltimore, New Orleans, and Savannah but to "Pacific Ocean China" as well, and he estimated the "amount of goods shipped to be nearly $700,000."

Peabody's first European successes had made it clear that he would be a most efficient successor as head of the firm. When Elisha Riggs had retired in 1829, Peabody had welcomed Riggs's nephew Samuel to the business but had changed the name of the firm to Peabody, Riggs, and Company; there was no doubt who was now the senior partner.

After Elisha Riggs Sr., had left the firm, Peabody's relations with him remained friendly, and Peabody never forgot how much he owed the older man. For Peabody was one of those rare people capable of deep and lasting gratitude. Twenty years after Elisha Riggs's retirement from the firm, Peabody wrote to him in 1849, from London that "my feelings of gratitude will ever lead me to consider your friendly aid given me thirty-six years ago. . . ." Peabody considered this aid "as having laid the foundation of my present position and fortune, and it is a source of great satisfaction to me to reflect that your own prosperity has gone hand in hand with my own, and that our interests have been mutually promoted by each other."

Peabody's co-operation with the nephew Samuel Riggs was successful from the start, but rapidly expanding business interests and activities never caused Peabody to neglect his family duties, which he continued to take very seriously. And these responsibilities were increasing now that his sisters' husbands and children, as well as his younger cousins, were accepted by him as part of his financial and moral obligation.

He was informed by letter, or when he visited them, of all family events, no matter how trivial. He was becoming patriarchal and expected his relatives to observe his own standards of values and behavior. It was typical of him to write and advise his cousin Adolphus Peabody "to be friendly with selected people but not intimate with anyone," and that he was to dress "respectably." "I spend as occasion requires," Adolphus replied to his cousin, "and appear as to reflect *your* position of wealth and respectability *without* extravagance . . . keeping your view, and feelings, rather than my means, in mind."

George Peabody was disturbed when younger members of the family disappointed him, and he was deeply saddened when there was a death in the family. In 1830 his mother's death—she was sixty years old—must have recalled sharply to him her difficult life and his own harsh youth in Danvers. None of the family letters at the time mentions George's personal feelings when his mother died, but he had become so reserved that his emotions, whether of sorrow or joy, were rarely obvious.

Nor did he express, except in the most objective terms, his continuous anxieties about his brothers Thomas and David. Thomas remained a cause of worry until his death in 1835. George's younger brother Jeremiah was now farming near Zanesville, Ohio, and his wife Ellen referred to Thomas as "their poor misguided brother." David, too, was never, until his death in 1841, able to cope with life. He lived in New York and was frequently in debt. He never learned to manage his financial affairs and never overcame a haunting feeling of his own inferiority when he compared himself with his outstanding younger brother George.

George Peabody had obviously been so sorely disappointed with David that, as has been noted, he was not mentioned in George's will of 1827. A new will, however, made in 1832, left David $7,000 with the definite proviso that this sum could not be attached by his creditors. To David's son George, however, George Peabody bequeathed a small fortune of $32,000, the greater part of his estate.

Members of his family knew that David had been reinstated in George Peabody's favor because George had grown very fond of his nephew,

David's son George, then an attractive, intelligent lad of seventeen. George Peabody's relationship to this nephew was like that of a father to a favorite son. He wanted young George to have the educational opportunities he himself had missed. George Peabody had always planned a good education for all of his nephews, but he took a special interest in George. Besides, Peabody had now learned at first hand what a disadvantage it was not to be well educated. His travels in Europe and his meetings with well-informed and cultured men had made him very conscious of his own lack of knowledge and intellectual development. Peabody kept in touch with young George's teachers at Bradford Academy and received regular reports from his headmaster, Mr. Dwight. George Peabody's last letter to his mother, written shortly before her death, reflected his great pride in this particular nephew. George Peabody wrote,

George was well a few days ago & I have a letter from Mr. Dwight which speaks of him in the most flattering manner and I shall probably let him take college in about two years.—Mr. Dwight says George is in a class of 18 or 19 in the languages and is decidedly the *best scholar in it* and discovers most promising & assiduous application, & if he should go to college he would be one of the best scholars in his class.—He further states that George's whole deportment is perfectly commendable & such as I should wholly approve of.—The expense including clothes, board, tuition, etc. will be nearly 500$ a year but if he continues to make as good use of his time as he now promises it will be money well laid out.

Young George had written asking his uncle whether he could go to Yale College, and George Peabody's answer from London, dated May 18, 1831, is one of the most revealing documents in his entire correspondence, for it clearly shows the extent to which he had now learned to respect learning for its own sake. He gladly gave his consent to his nephew's entrance into Yale, and added,

Deprived as I was, of the opportunity of obtaining anything more than the most *common education* I am *well* qualified to estimate its value by the *disadvantages* I labour under in the society [in] which my business and situation in life frequently throws me, and willingly would I now give *twenty times* the expense attending a good education could I possess it, but it is now too late for *me* to learn and I can only do to those that come under my care, as I could have wished circumstances had permitted others to have done by me.

George Peabody, in common with many men and women who learn young to keep their emotions under control, apparently found it impossible to express in words the affection and hopes he had for this nephew.

Touring Europe in the summer and autumn of 1832 he often thought of the boy, and looked forward eagerly to news of his progress in the family letters which he would find on his return to London in November of that year.

A great shock awaited him: he learned that on September 24 (1832) at the age of seventeen, young George had died of scarlet fever. George Peabody kept his grief to himself, and he managed to write a calm and quiet letter to his brother David, the boy's father, who had asked George what he wanted done with young George's belongings.

When George was in Baltimore, in the autumn of 1831, I gave him a watch worth 50$.—It has occurred to me as his Aunt Ellen was much attached to him this better be given to her, particularly if she did not receive any compensation for the time he was sick in her house—All his books you will send to Judith— I have wrote her that you would do so.—There was a variety of Bedding etc. bought for him while at Dwights & after he entered College which with every thing else left by him are entirely at your disposal.—

George Peabody ended this letter without any special mark of affection for his brother and signed it simply, "Yours truly, George Peabody."

The death of his favorite nephew was not the only personal loss George Peabody suffered in the eighteen-thirties. His sister Mary Gaines Marsh died in Lockport, New York, of cholera in August 1834 at the age of twenty-seven. His many letters to her are an indication of the closeness of their relationship. She was twelve years younger than he was, and in his early teens she had often been in his care and was one of the children he loved best. After her death his sister Judith became George Peabody's chief correspondent in the family.

Less than two weeks before her death, Mary had given birth to a son named George after her brother. She was apparently making a normal recovery after her confinement when she suddenly became ill with cholera, and the efforts of two physicians could not save her. Mary Gaines Marsh left three young children: the newborn baby, George, who died when he was only a year old; a daughter Mary, five years old; and a three-year-old son, Othniel Charles Marsh. Mary's unhappy husband Caleb Marsh married again two years later, moved for a time to Bradford, Massachusetts, but then returned for the rest of his life to Lockport.

By a strange quirk of fate, the child Othniel was to fulfill the hopes George Peabody had centered on his late nephew George. For Othniel grew up to become America's first paleontologist and a great scientist of the nineteenth century. Othniel Charles Marsh's scientific career, made possible by Peabody's support, led to the founding of the Peabody Museums at Harvard and Yale.

At the time of his sister's death, and for many months afterwards, George Peabody was fortunately so occupied with affairs that his mind was distracted from his sorrow. Maryland, in common with some other states in the Union, was entering a period of remarkable commercial and domestic expansion. Canals, railroads, the sale of lands in the West were moving rapidly, and manufacturing was increasing. Money and goods were in great demand, and Baltimore's growing population and expanding public works provided promising markets for Peabody, Riggs, and Company.

To finance the Chesapeake and Ohio Canal and the Baltimore and Ohio Railroad, Maryland's legislature in 1835 authorized an eight million dollar bond issue and appointed three commissioners to market it abroad. Peabody had heard in 1836 that one of these commissioners, Samuel Jones, Jr., had resigned, and a new commissioner was to be appointed in his place. When some of Peabody's friends urged him to seek this appointment, he had already established such valuable contacts abroad that his position seemed most suitable to sell the Maryland bonds in foreign countries. There was some opposition to his appointment, but finally, in the fall of 1837, he was chosen as one of the Maryland commissioners. He could not, however, devote himself wholeheartedly to this task until some time later.

For in 1836 and 1837 businessmen in Maryland and elsewhere were facing a grave financial crisis. Enthusiasm for the rapidly expanding markets had resulted in overbuying at high prices on extended European credits, and by June 1836 when Peabody returned to the United States after his fourth trip abroad, there was great uneasiness in financial circles. The Bank of England was alarmed by the outflow of gold to America, and in October there was a run on the banks in Ireland with a further demand for gold. Bank failures on both sides of the Atlantic increased in number; the Panic of 1837 was disrupting business.

By early 1837 the credit of American firms in London was dangerously tight. Richard Bell, who looked after Peabody's financial affairs, warned him "to prepare for a gale . . . as sure as fate evil times are coming on us." In America Peabody therefore made a great effort to collect debts owed him as well as gain credits, and he was thus able to remit to Bell £20,000 to cover outstanding debts in England.

In February 1837, Peabody sailed again for England to study the situation. He planned to stay in London for a long time. He found that his own affairs were relatively stable, but the firm of William and James Brown of Liverpool, the chief source of his own early credit in England, was in serious trouble. The Brown brothers appealed to the Bank of England for assistance and the directors of the Bank agreed to help the firm on condition that other firms guaranteed a loan from the Bank. Few firms were willing to risk assisting the Browns, for money was extremely scarce, credit not available, and the future too uncertain to warrant the support of a business in such obvious financial distress as the Browns'.

Peabody, however, remembering that William and James Brown had been his good friends when he first came to England, decided to go all out to help them now. He recommended the Browns to Denison and Company, the London bankers:

"I know," Peabody wrote to Denison, "that they have heretofore been proverbial for prudence and foresight and for requiring of all houses to whom they extended their credit the most undoubted security."

Beyond this recommendation, Peabody himself subscribed £5,000 toward the guarantee demanded by the Bank of England. He also traveled five hundred miles all over England in less than five days to interest other potential guarantors. It was entirely a result of Peabody's genius as a negotiator, his persuasiveness, and his reputation for business integrity that finally, on June 22, 1837, more than the amount required by the Bank of England had been secured, and the Browns' firm was saved. With typical British understatement, but with equal sincerity, William Brown wrote to George Peabody when the strain was over: "To you, my dear Sir, I feel much indebted for the lively interest you have taken and Friendship you have shown throughout the Crisis that has almost killed me with anxiety."

By coming to the aid of this Liverpool firm, Peabody had done more than stand by old friends in times of trouble; he had established his own reputation as an outstanding, courageous, and utterly reliable merchant and financier. And he had also saved the firm of Peabody, Riggs, and Company from danger, for had William and James Brown of Liverpool gone under, Peabody, Riggs, and Company might well have been pulled down with them.

With justifiable pride Peabody wrote to Samuel Riggs from London: "With respect to the standing of our house . . . I believe we are almost the *only* American importers of European goods that have met every engagement on both sides of the Atlantic with punctuality. . . . We are almost the only American house that has not had their credits mostly if not altogether cut off."

Esther Elizabeth Hoppin

GEORGE PEABODY was now a dignified bachelor of forty-three, tall, upright and sure of himself. In the language of the Victorians, he was a "fine figure of a man." Not unreasonably, he was pleased with his appearance and determined to preserve his good looks as long as possible. People he met were struck by his clear blue eyes and his black, well-tended hair. Only to his most intimate associates, men with whom he had spent his youth, did he confess that his hair was dyed. William Bend, for example, was amused by this harmless vanity. "Your confession about African balm," he once wrote to Peabody, "goes to the full extent of all I have heard about your hair."

With or without this "African balm," Peabody would have been an outstanding personality wherever he went in London. He was a most eligible bachelor: a man of the utmost respectability, wealthy, and obviously kind and eager to help others. For many years, however, he was so occupied with affairs that he had little time for sociability purely for the sake of sociability. He did not fit easily into lighthearted and frivolous gatherings at which hopeful mothers introduced him to their daughters.

At this stage in his career, his social engagements were usually with business friends whose interests coincided with his own. W. S. Albert, a Baltimore friend recalled,

In 1838, when on a visit to London, I lodged in the same house with him [George Peabody] for several weeks. Under the same roof were assembled mutual friends from the city of his adoption, upon whom he took pleasure in bestowing those marks of attention so grateful in a foreign land, making the house a home to us all.

At this time many other Americans came to Peabody's home. London was full of visitors from abroad. For it was coronation year; there was anticipation in the air. Everyone was eager to see a London gaily decorated and beflagged for the great occasion and hoped to see the romantic young Queen who was succeeding her dreary uncle.

In this atmosphere of lighthearted celebrations, George Peabody met a pretty young American girl, Esther Elizabeth Hoppin, who came of a prominent family in Providence, Rhode Island. Esther had only recently finished her education at the academy of John Kingsbury, who conducted the first Rhode Island high school entirely devoted to the higher education of women. Now Esther was traveling in Europe and had come to London to see the coronation. This visit to England, and Esther's first European experience, was naturally a source of pleasure and great excitement for her. She was in a receptive mood for new impressions and adventures.

She had already traveled a little in the United States, but these short journeys were nothing compared with this trip to Europe. She almost forgot that, three years before, in Philadelphia, when she was only a schoolgirl of sixteen, she had been in love with Alexander Lardner, a young bank clerk. He was already established in the bank—he was ten years older than Esther—and eager to marry her as soon as she left school. Esther and Alexander had what was called an "understanding," and before she came to London she had considered herself engaged to him.

In London, in this exhilarating and novel world, Esther met George Peabody. He was distinguished, handsome, sought after, everyone spoke of him with respect, and he was apparently in love with her. It is not surprising that Esther was carried away by Peabody's attentions. Any young girl would have been flattered and then attracted by the obvious kindness and generosity of this much older man. The difference in age—twenty-four years—seemed not to matter, and Esther gladly accepted Peabody's invitations to dine or to go to the opera.

George Peabody was very serious about his wish to marry Esther Hoppin. He had fallen in love for the first time with a girl whom he wanted as his wife, and he longed to settle down and found a family of his own. Some of his friends believed that so far he had remained a bachelor because of his family responsibilities and ties, but this seems improbable. For, in fact, he always remained curiously aloof from his parents and his brothers and sisters; never since his teens had he asked or wanted any of them to live with him or share his home. He was not in the least emotionally dependent upon them. When he was younger, his financial obligations to his family would have made marriage difficult, but for years now he had been financially more than able to support his family as well as a wife and children of his own. It is difficult to imagine George Peabody as the suitor of a young and vivacious girl. He had never had the leisure or inclination to learn how to be casual or gay, and he must have seemed to Esther serious minded, sedate, and very middle aged. Nevertheless, his obvious sincerity and his feeling for her, though expressed in a dignified and restrained manner, finally persuaded Esther that she wanted to marry him and they became engaged.

In those of Peabody's letters that have been preserved, no reference is made to his feelings at the time of this engagement or what he may have suffered when, some months later, Esther broke off the engagement. Nor is it known exactly how Esther told Peabody that she could not, after all, marry him—whether she wrote to him herself or asked someone else to tell him. At any rate, after her return to America in the fall of 1838, she again met Alexander Lardner and realized that her engagement to George Peabody had been a mistake.

She married Lardner, moved with him to Philadelphia where he was employed in the Bank of the United States. This marriage was a happy one, but Lardner died at the age of forty, leaving two children. Esther Elizabeth Lardner outlived her husband by sixty-five years and died in 1905. There is no record that Peabody ever saw her again, though it would have been easy to do so on his visits to Philadelphia in later years.

Esther was so young and inexperienced at the time of her engagement to Peabody that she could hardly have understood how unhappy he was. Nor could a woman as young as Esther have realized that, apart from his emotional disappointment, George Peabody must have experienced hurt pride. For Esther, the thought of him was more embarrassing than painful.

After he had learned that she would not marry him, he wrote to a mutual friend, Mrs. W. Hyde in New York, asking her to persuade Esther to keep some of his gifts to her. Mrs. Hyde, obviously not a happy go-between, answered Peabody's letter:

Miss Hoppin feels your kindness in wishing her to retain the muff and fur, at the same time propriety will not allow her to accept of your kind proposal. Custom has made it imperative that after an engagement is broken all presents shall be returned even to the value of a pin.

Peabody urged Mrs. Hyde to keep for herself the muff and the fur. "No-one," she wrote, "can regret more than myself the circumstances which makes the muff & fur mine. I shall keep them and value them highly for the giver's sake and accept my best thanks not only for this munificent present but for others and the parcel of silk today." Mrs. Hyde's conclusion of this letter makes it quite apparent that she had little understanding of Peabody's self-control and reticence concerning his private affairs: "I hope," she wrote without much tact, "on my return you will visit us whenever you feel inclined for a quiet cry."

What was particularly unpleasant for Peabody was the necessity of informing his friends about his broken engagement. His old friend William Bend wrote Peabody a most sympathetic letter when he heard the news. Bend must have known how deeply Peabody had been affected by this disappointment. Bend wrote on February 18, 1839,

I have this morning received your favour of 26th ulto and with my wife grieve sincerely and deeply over its melancholy intelligence. Having myself experienced a misfortune, somewhat similar to that which has befallen you, and remember most distinctly now, though twenty years have since elapsed, the agony which I endured, I feel the more called on and the more adequate to sympathize with you, than I otherwise should do. Then in the true spirit of friendship do I offer to you my most heartfelt condolence. I share in the anguish of your feelings, at the blighting of hopes so fondly cherished. . . . The pangs of despised love, though poignant must be resisted. The balmy effects of time, and the natural elasticity and recuperative energy of the human character, will afford you great relief and I hope to see you here in the Summer quite yourself again.

George Peabody did not answer this letter nor did he refer again to his broken engagement, but when he was an old man he mentioned a "disappointment" to a friend who had congratulated him on his amazing philanthropy.

"After my disappointment long ago," Peabody said, "I decided to devote myself to my fellow-beings, and I am carrying out that decision to my best ability."

The implication that George Peabody never really got over his disappointment about his broken engagement reflects a sentiment of faithfulness then very popular. Whatever Peabody's feelings about Esther, he never again expressed any intention of marrying. This does not, however, necessarily imply that he remained a lonely bachelor throughout his life. In fact, there were persistent rumors that lasted until long after his death that he maintained for years a secluded but dignified and permanent establishment in Brighton and that there was a daughter of this liaison, whose two sons rose to eminence in their professions of science and law.

It would be naive, and indicate a complete lack of understanding of the Victorian age, to wonder why Peabody did not marry the lady in Brighton, if there was such a lady. Class and background established a rigid code at the time, and a gentleman did not, as a rule, marry his mistress no matter how fond he may have been of her.

The rumors about Peabody's establishment in Brighton, rumors for which there is no definite proof, were strengthened by a document written in 1940 by John Pierpont Morgan Jr.

This Morgan, whose grandfather—as will be recorded later in this biography—was George Peabody's principal partner, had heard stories about Peabody's private life in Brighton from Perman, a clerk in the employ of John Pierpont Morgan Sr. No biography of George Peabody would be complete without quoting in full John Pierpont Morgan Jr.'s statement of 1940, though it should be borne in mind that this memorandum was a private paper which was largely reminiscent and in no way documented. At the time of writing, three years before his death in 1943, John Pierpont Morgan Jr. was seventy-six years old and his memory may not have been entirely accurate.

Mr. George Peabody, personally, was a strange man. He was a bachelor but he had a mistress who lived, I believe, at Brighton, whose wants he supplied quite generously (again on Perman's information). His method was by withdrawing certain of his own personal securities in the office, which he would have Perman to deliver to him, and for which he would initial the Securities Book. Sometimes it would be as much as £2,000 at a time, and in his Will when he died he left the woman nothing because he had so adequately provided for her during her life.

She had a daughter (who was Mr. Peabody's daughter) who married and had two sons. From time to time both Mr. J. S. Morgan and my Father had applications from the daughter asking for help, all of her dowry having been lost by her husband, who was not a very satisfactory person. Sometime after I became a partner in 1898 one of her sons wrote to the firm asking whether he could secure a certain amount of help, owing to his connection with Mr. Peabody. By my Father's direction I sent Perman to see him and when Perman returned he said "He is a very impressive young man. He is studying to be a barrister and his brother is studying to be something in a university, and both of them have the old man's nose to a dot."

This story passed on by Perman to John Pierpont Morgan Jr., and by him recorded so many years later, is not proved to be true by any but circumstantial evidence, but it is interesting nonetheless—a story so typical of the nineteenth century.

The Fight against Repudiation

IN view of Peabody's dedication to his business, it is not surprising that Esther Elizabeth Hoppin, a young woman who naturally enjoyed having a good time, was, even during their brief engagement, not pleased when she had to be satisfied with his very part-time companionship. There were many days when he had no leisure to see her, and she must soon have realized that, for him, personal relationships, even his relationship with her, were never quite as important as his feeling of responsibility toward his affairs and his clients. Business absorbed him, and in December 1838 he opened a London office at 31 Moorgate, in the heart of the City district. Perhaps he did not realize at the time that henceforth, for the rest of his life, London was to be his permanent home.

As one of the three Maryland commissioners appointed by the State Legislature to market the State's eight million dollar bond issue abroad, Peabody was having a difficult time. These bonds, issued to finance the Chesapeake and Ohio Canal and the Baltimore and Ohio Railway, were certainly not easy to sell, for the Panic of 1837 had resulted in a depression which persisted until 1845. It was known for some years to potential buyers of the Maryland bond issue in Europe that various states of the Union were already contemplating the repudiation of their bonded indebtedness, and between 1840 and 1845 nine states did indeed stop payment of interest. Maryland was one of these states. From 1837, the year of his appointment as one of the Commissioners, Peabody had tried to dispose of the Maryland bonds, but he and John Buchanan and Thomas Emory, the other commissioners, had little success in England, or in Holland or France. Everywhere European financiers were wary of American securities.

Discouraged, Emory and Buchanan returned to America, but Peabody remained in London and persisted in his efforts. In October 1838, Emory wrote to Peabody urging him to return to Maryland, and in Annapolis to encourage legislative proceedings which would help the loan. Peabody, however, was still hopeful of success in Europe. He wrote to Emory,

The heavy money operations which I have undertaken for the Chesapeake & Ohio Canal Company render it impracticable for me to leave London at present even for a week, and their business must necessarily prevent my leaving the Country for a long time to come. American stocks are becoming more difficult to sell because there are so many on the market. It will take several years for the Companies to dispose of the 8 millions in Europe unless they submit to a very low price.

Peabody understood that the Maryland bonds would have to be sold at a low price or not at all, and he was being urged by the Chesapeake and Ohio Canal Company to sell at any price. He finally succeeded in persuading Baring Brothers, one of the wealthiest and most famous banking houses in Europe, to buy the Maryland bonds.

Peabody was relieved to have concluded this business, but he was not satisfied with the low price he had been obliged to accept. He was also greatly concerned when he heard from William Bend and other friends in Baltimore that the Chesapeake and Ohio Canal Company was mismanaging its affairs and was, in fact, jeopardizing State funds. It was a very worrisome time, and Peabody wrote to the president of the Chesapeake and Ohio Canal Company explaining why he could obtain only a low price for the bonds. He emphasized in this letter the "unprecedented state of the money market and the almost total discredit of all American securities in Europe."

By the end of 1841 Peabody's uneasiness about the sale of Maryland bonds seemed justified. His friend William Bend wrote to him from New York: "You see by the papers how low state stocks have got. Your transactions in them have done you no good, I fear." By this time several of the states had repudiated payments on their bonds, and Maryland, as Bend said, "*can't* pay"—that is, she was not financially able to do so.

A scapegoat was needed, several in fact, for the mismanagement of the Chesapeake and Ohio Canal Company, and Peabody was one of them. It was generally understood by wiser Marylanders, as Peabody's fellow commissioner Emory comforted him, that Peabody had been subjected to unfair pressure by Francis Thomas, president of the Chesapeake and Ohio Canal Company, in the bond sale. Nevertheless, Peabody was attacked by a number of people. He was even blamed for selling the Maryland bonds so cheaply, and, more than that, by some he was quite unjustly accused of making private capital out of his dealings in these bonds.

One of the strange phenomena in the business world is the stubborn persistence of unpleasant rumors, whether they are based on facts or not, about the transactions of financial or commercial firms or of individuals. As late as 1936, about a century after these Maryland bond transactions, in a book entitled *A History of Great American Fortunes*, Gustavus Myers cites George Peabody's bond sales for the Chesapeake and Ohio Canal Company as objectionable and dishonest, and Myers's allegations reflect the malicious gossip to which Peabody and his friends were subjected at the time.

In 1839 the Chesapeake and Ohio Canal Company found occasion to complain bitterly of Peabody's methods as its financial representative in London. The stock of this Company was secured by bonds in Europe at ruinous discounts, and with large sums of money belonging to the Company in his possession, he refused to honor its bills. By this process he made large profits. His excuse was the critical condition of the European money markets. The directors of the company formally approved his action, probably to let him out gracefully, but were glad to accept his resignation [from his post as Maryland Commissioner].

Actually, there was no foundation for these accusations. Myers wrote without any basis of fact. He did not have access to George Peabody's papers or confidential letters. In these very detailed accounts there is no trace of the large profits he was said by Myers to have derived from the bond transactions. On the contrary, not wishing to add to Maryland's burden, Peabody of his own free will relinquished the $60,000 commission which was legally due him on the Baring deal. Later, after Maryland in 1847 resumed full payment on her bonds, Governor Thomas G. Pratt at the annual meeting of the Legislature on December 27, 1847, praised Peabody's work in London in the warmest terms. Pratt officially stated on this occasion that the other two Maryland Commissioners had accepted compensation, but that Peabody had "relinquished his claim to compensation, feeling himself sufficiently remunerated for his services by the restored credit of his State."

The reason for the persistent antagonism shown by some of Peabody's business rivals at the time was really quite simple: when they themselves no longer believed in the Maryland bonds, and favored repudiation, Peabody remained convinced that eventually Maryland and the other states would be able and willing to meet their obligations; that interest on these American investments would then no longer be cut off. Peabody acted upon this conviction, and during the period of repudiation, when American securities were looked down upon with suspicion all over Europe, he himself became a speculator on a large scale in the securities issued by American states. He had absolute faith in the ultimate value of these securities and in the business integrity of his countrymen.

Later, when, as he had predicted they would, the value of these securities rose, Peabody reaped a very substantial harvest, and between 1837 and 1843, when these securities could be bought very cheaply because they were not in demand, he laid the basis for his considerable fortune. It is not surprising therefore that some of his less farsighted rivals in Europe and America were jealous of his success; if they had been equally astute, they, too, might have become very rich men. In their irritation at their own mistaken judgment, they preferred to raise allegations against George Peabody, rather than admit that they themselves had been shortsighted and lacking in faith in the basic economic stability of the United States.

"My feelings," Peabody wrote during the period of repudiation to Joseph Speed, a lawyer friend in Baltimore, "are altogether American; and I trust the time is not far distant, when our country and her people will once more regain their former high character for honor and integrity which Repudiation has so unfortunately tarnished."

During repudiation Peabody never ceased to make a great effort to persuade European investors that, in the long run, American investments were sound. He exchanged letters about the subject with Speed and arranged for these letters to be published in English and American newspapers. Peabody pointed out again and again in this published correspondence that Maryland's financial stress was only temporary—that she would eventually pay the interest on her bonds and when she did so, she would make all payments of interest retroactive.

Peabody was respected in England because he was one of those Americans who were obviously trying to persuade the Maryland Legislature to pay her debts. The London *Morning Post*, for example, spoke of him as an eminent American merchant in London brave enough to tell his countrymen the truth. And by the time repudiation was over, Peabody was firmly established as a financier whose advice was sought and taken seriously in financial circles everywhere in England and on the Continent.

Peabody's growing reputation as a financier, and the decline of the affairs in Baltimore of Peabody, Riggs, and Company after 1837, caused Peabody to decide to give up the drygoods business and to become a full-time merchant and investment banker. In Peabody's opinion, the firm of Peabody, Riggs, and Company was less efficient than it had been in its early days. "Old houses," he wrote to William Bend, "after a series of years of success, get indolent and do not make great exertions to obtain business."

As early as April 1839, Peabody informed his partners of his intention to withdraw from the company when the current partnership had expired. In 1842, Samuel Riggs, too, left the firm, declaring that he would leave the business and live simply in the country "on milk and bread." For a few years before Riggs's retirement, Peabody had continued his association with the firm as a financial advisor, but in 1843 he finally withdrew his capital from Peabody, Riggs, and Company, thus publicly severing his connection with the firm after thirty years. Thereafter he devoted his energies entirely to the new firm of George Peabody and Company, which soon moved from Moorgate to larger premises in Warnford Court. George Peabody had all the attributes necessary for a merchant banker: he was a shrewd judge of men, he had great integrity, and he was trusted in the business world. He was familiar with many branches of commerce, had a specialized knowledge of trade in the United States, and he had long years of experience of world markets. He also had an amazing flair, an instinctive understanding of when and to whom and for how long it was wise to extend his credit. The Baltimore merchant had become a man to reckon with in international finance. Peabody was forty-eight years old. He had come a long way from Danvers, Massachusetts.

Life and Work in London

FROM the point of view of the telephone-minded, electric typewriter, and tape recorder mid-twentieth century, the voluminous correspondence of many Victorians seems almost incredible. It is amazing, apart from his other activities, how many letters, all, of course, written by hand, George Peabody had time to write. His relentless application to business after the founding of George Peabody and Company in London would have worn out most men. Yet for some years of this strenuous life he felt physically as well as he had when he was younger. In 1846, in an affectionate letter to his first employer, Captain Sylvester Proctor in Danvers, Peabody wrote, "My health is good and notwithstanding the great vicissitudes in commercial affairs since 1836 I am happy to say I have not retrograded in fortune."

Peabody did not mention in this letter that, despite the strain of business, he now somehow managed to maintain social relations in London, to keep in close contact by letter with friends in America, to entertain visiting Americans, and, as he grew older, to find increasing pleasure in going to the opera or attending purely social functions.

Books did not interest him or give him pleasure. He apparently bought only the newspapers, but these he read most carefully. Literature meant nothing to him, nor did art. He once confessed as much to James Read Lambdin, who painted his portrait in Baltimore in 1857. "You may be surprised when I tell you," he said to Lambdin, "that, although I have lived for twenty years [in Regent Street] within pistol shot of the Royal Academy and National Gallery in London, I have never been within their walls."

He had no occasion to find out whether an occasional voyage and change of scene would have refreshed him, because he had no leisure to travel even in England, and for years he remained continuously in London. It was impossible for him to contemplate a trip to the United States yet, much as he longed to go home. Some business or other always claimed his attention and made his presence in London imperative. In 1846, for example, during the famine in Ireland, Peabody, in collaboration with the firm of Wetmore and Cryder, financed shipments of grains, flour, and Indian corn to Ireland, but owing to shipping losses and the price fluctuations of Indian corn, Peabody was forced to withdraw suddenly from this trade, and had he not been in London to arrange matters, his losses would have been considerable. Then, in 1847, the bankruptcy of Coates, Hillard, and Company meant financial losses to Peabody—apart from a broken friendship. Ezra Jenks Coates, a Bostonian living in London, who had been a friend of Peabody, had been insolvent for years, but had managed to withhold this unpleasant fact from Peabody, who did not like to feel that his judgment of any man had been wrong. At any rate, Peabody had to be in London in order to straighten out his own involvement with Coates's firm.

Political developments, too, often made it seem wiser for him to stay close to his counting house at Warnford Court. Relations between Great Britain and the United States were strained for a few years over the Oregon question, and some politicians were making warlike noises. Peabody, who was personally and financially deeply concerned with Anglo-American relations, was worried about this tension between the two countries. Finally, in June 1846, a compromise settlement was made on the forty-ninth parallel and the treaty was signed by James Buchanan, then Secretary of State, and Richard Pakenham, the British envoy.

Two years later political tension of quite a different nature was a cause of anxiety for businessmen and politicians all over Europe. In 1848 and 1849 a revolutionary movement swept through Europe, and no one could tell to what extent these upheavals, disturbing many Continental countries, would ultimately affect world trade and finance. Peabody therefore concentrated his attention more diligently than ever on his affairs. His friend William Bend in Baltimore had heard with regret, so he wrote, that Peabody "lacked rest, ate the bread of watchfulness, and worked till nine o'clock at night."

Despite these long hours in his office, he always had time for American visitors in England, his own friends, or friends of his friends from New York or Baltimore. He was also in close touch with members of the American Legation in London. Until 1846, Gansevoort Melville, a brother of Herman Melville, had been Secretary of the Legation, and Peabody met Herman Melville when he was in London in November 1849 to arrange for the British publication of his early books, *Typee: a Peep at Polynesian Life* and *Omoo, A Narrative of Adventures in the South Seas.*

Herman Melville, who met Peabody at the home of Joshua Bates, an

American living near London, was much impressed by the financier. He mentioned the dinner party at Bates's house in his *Journal of a Visit to London and the Continent.* Melville's description of George Peabody as an elderly man brings one up with a start: when one is familiar with the scope of his many activities and with his vitality, one tends to forget that he might indeed have seemed elderly to Melville, a man of thirty.

"On my right," Melville described the dinner party at Bates's house, "was Mr. Peabody, an American for many years resident in London, a merchant, & a very fine old fellow of fifty or thereabouts." (Actually, at the time, Peabody was fifty-four years old.)

There was a Baron opposite me and a most lovely young girl, a daughter of Captain Chamier the sea novelist. Half the company were foreigners. The dinner was superb—the table was circular—the service very rich. . . . Everybody was free, easy & in good humor—all talkative & well-bred. . . . Mr. Bates seemed to be quite a jolly old blade.

Herman Melville had planned to accept Bates's invitation to spend the night at his home, but then, as the young writer remembered,

Peabody invited me to accompany him to town in his carriage. I went with him, along with Davis, the Secretary of the [American] Legation. . . . Mr. Peabody was well acquainted with Gansevoort when he was here. . . . He told me that Gansevoort rather shunned society when here. He spoke of him with such feeling.

It was very much in character when Peabody drove back to London and then pleased the young author by expressing a friendly interest in Melville's brother. Peabody was known to members of the American colony and to his English friends for his generous hospitality. He had become quite a man of the world. He now entertained English friends and visiting Americans at dinner at the Star and Garter Hotel in Richmond or in Willis's Rooms. He sent bouquets to the ladies and offered friends his box at the opera. He was also consistently thoughtful of others. He welcomed requests that he attend to commissions for his friends in America; whenever they wanted anything done or arranged in London he obviously enjoyed helping them.

Some of these errands were of a confidential nature. For his old friend Richard Bell, now with the Bank of America in New York, he assumed a special responsibility. Bell had an illegitimate son in England who was looked after by George Peabody. It is not recorded how long this informal guardianship lasted, or how often or where Peabody saw the boy, but early in 1845 Bell had informed Peabody that he hoped to buy a cottage in New Jersey and that he intended "to bring out the parties [from London] in August per Quebec or Victoria."

When "the parties" reached New York, Bell, who was devoted to his son, married the boy's mother and passed the boy off as his stepson, but the marriage was not a happy one. Henceforth, Bell, whose wife was from a background very different from his own, lived in seclusion and avoided his old friends and acquaintances. Rumor had it that Bell's wife was socially "beneath him"; she would not therefore have been acceptable to his old friends or their wives. It was a miserable situation and a lesson to any Victorian man who might have contemplated marrying his mistress—even for the sake of any children of such a union.

As was to be expected, Peabody was entirely discreet about Bell's marriage. Not even his and Bell's mutual friend, William Bend, who wrote asking Peabody about Bell's wife, was able to get any information from Peabody. He was equally uncommunicative about the growing number of his private charities to personal acquaintances in need. His gifts to public bodies, however, inevitably became known.

He was already seriously considering what he could do for the South Parish of Danvers, his boyhood home. He was kept closely in touch with Danvers news in letters from his two sisters Judith and Sophronia and his brother Jeremiah, the only three apart from himself still living of Thomas and Judith Dodge's original family of eight children.

Peabody learned in 1843 that a serious fire in Danvers had destroyed many buildings in the town including the South Congregational Church where his family had always worshipped. Peabody had at once sent $250 toward the rebuilding of the church. Three years later he sent money to the Proctors in Danvers, asking Mrs. Proctor to distribute it among the poor of the parish. He also asked her to send him a list "of the present male residents of South Danvers who had arrived at the age of 70 years" so that he could send gifts to these old townsmen.

Some years later, in 1850, when Captain Sylvester Proctor himself, then over eighty, was in financial difficulties, George Peabody instructed his sister Judith to pay the Proctors's debts, place the old couple in a comfortable home with a family with whom they could be happy, and to give old Captain Proctor pocket money and a regular sum for all of his needs. Peabody wrote to Judith explaining why it meant so much to him to know that the Proctors were enjoying a carefree old age:

Although 40 years have elapsed, I have not forgotten that both himself &

Wife were kind and indulgent to me and endeavoured by example and instruction to imbue my mind with Religious and Moral principles which, however, had little or no influence at the time, but in after life . . . they have often occurred to my mind and I . . .have the satisfaction to think that at least a partial compliance with those good lessons in my intercourse with my fellow man has in some measure led to my almost unexampled success in life.

This financial aid to old friends such as the Proctors indicated that, unlike the benefactions of many rich men, Peabody's charities were never impersonal or given without special thought for the cause or the individual whom he had decided to help.

Peabody's growing interest in philanthropy and his obvious intention to give away more and more of his money did not entirely please all of his former associates. The emotional reaction of his old friends William Bend and Richard Bell toward his outstanding success, a success which made these charities possible, was ambivalent. On the one hand, they were naturally proud of his prominence in the financial world; yet they were occasionally jealous of him because his career had so markedly outstripped their own. They had plodded along while he had forged ahead. His interests were so much wider than theirs that they felt that he had changed toward them and that this change had caused a loss of intimacy toward them. They tended to look back on their carefree youth, while Peabody, even as an elderly man, always looked ahead.

"When the fit prompts," Bell once wrote to Peabody nostalgically, "I should be very glad to have a private letter from you upon all sorts of matters and things connected with bygone times in our hot youth. What calm sober greyheaded old Gentn. we are now. . . . But *your* hairs are I believe not grey!"

On another occasion, Richard Bell wrote almost disparagingly about Peabody's charities. "I wish you would spend some long Evening in Warnford Court writing to an old friend in place of Counting over your gains and planning foundations for Schools . . . when you are gone. . . ."

William Bend's lack of understanding for Peabody's charities is reflected in a letter which barely concealed his envy:

[You] do not leave your business five days in five years! . . . To what purpose, for whose good? If like me you had, instead of wanting a family, wanted an independent fortune, I could understand the case. But I suppose you will imitate the noble example of Mr. Smithson, and benefit posterity by the endowment of some charitable benevolent or literary institution, from your industry, skill and character. . . .

One of the reasons Bell and Bend thought Peabody had changed was his increasing social as well as financial prestige in London. They never understood that he never for a moment "lost the common touch"—as Bell and Bend would have expressed it—even when he became a member of the City of London Club, and later of the Athenaeum, whose members included the most famous and distinguished men in England.

Richard Bell wrote to Peabody with apparent jealous hostility: "I have heard of Boxes at the Opera filled with Ladies and a certain portly Gentleman of the same name as yourself playing the Gallant there in Princely Style."

If Peabody was hurt by such remarks by Richard Bell and William Bend, he never showed it in his letters to them. Perhaps he regretted the loss of his old intimacy with these men, but he had learned not to be disturbed by things he could not change. He accepted the inevitable; he relied on his own judgment; he did and said whatever he thought right.

His independence of thought was illustrated by the help he was willing, in 1850, to give to Lajos Kossuth, the great Hungarian writer and journalist who inspired Hungarian patriots in their fight for a Hungarian Parliament and who bitterly opposed feudal burdens laid upon Hungarians by the Austro-Hungarian monarchy. In the late eighteen-thirties, Kossuth, who was a compelling public speaker and had attracted a large following, had been imprisoned by the Austrian Government. There was, however, so much agitation for his release that Metternich finally gave way and Kossuth was allowed to leave prison. He continued his attacks on the Hapsburgs and was the acknowledged leader of the Hungarian Revolution in 1849. When the Revolution was crushed, he fled to Turkey but was caught and again imprisoned by the Austrians.

In England and other Western European countries, especially in countries where the Hapsburgs were not popular, men of good will were making efforts to help Kossuth escape. In England, the group actively concerned with his liberation was led by William Cobden, the Liberal Member of Parliament.

Money, precisely £200, was needed by Cobden's supporters for their share of the funds required to organize Kossuth's escape by sea and overland routes. Peabody received an appeal for help when the fund was still £80 short. Unless he had been known to be open-minded and generous, Cobden would not have approached him, for though Kossuth was, above all, a Hungarian patriot, he was also a revolutionary who was actively opposing the status quo of the Hapsburg monarchy. And almost all merchant bankers were, of course, supporters of the status quo; upheavals of any kind were never to the advantage of banks and international business.

No one knows what went on in Peabody's mind before he finally agreed to contribute money to the Kossuth Fund. True, he at first made a condition: he would subscribe to the fund only if Cobden's group of Kossuth supporters were quite certain that their plan to free Kossuth would succeed. Cobden, however, could not give Peabody this assurance, for no one could be sure that the complicated arrangements to liberate Kossuth would not fail. Peabody must again have thought deeply: should he or should he not become involved in the plot to liberate a man considered in Vienna to be a most dangerous revolutionary. In the end he made his decision and he sent £50. Later, in 1851 and 1852, when Kossuth was freed, he made a triumphal tour in the United States, and Peabody's assistance to the Hungarian was fully justified.

Kossuth's escape was not the only unusual affair with which Peabody was involved in the early eighteen-fifties. Though he remained almost obsessively concerned with his banking business and still worked indefatigably, his mind was increasingly occupied with matters that had nothing to do with his countinghouse in Warnford Court.

One of the events which stirred his imagination was the tragic fate of Rear Admiral Sir John Franklin, the famous explorer whose disappearance in the Arctic made headline news in England for many years. Though Franklin served with distinction in many seas with the British Navy—he had fought at Copenhagen and in the battle of Trafalgar—his dominant interest had always been his search for the Northwest Passage, and in 1845 he had been appointed to command a large British Naval expedition which set sail to find this passage to the Pacific Ocean. The wooden ships were fitted out in the most modern manner; each was, in fact, equipped with a small auxiliary engine. But the expedition ended in tragic disaster. After being sighted for the last time by a whaler in July of 1845 in Melville Bay, Franklin and his ships were not heard from again and seemed to have vanished without trace in the white wastes of the Arctic.

For years Franklin's widow and the British Navy continued to think that there might yet be news of the expedition, but by 1848 it was generally believed that the ships were lost, though hope persisted that Franklin himself or some members of his crews might have survived. Between 1848 and 1854 at least fifteen expeditions, British and American, were dispatched to the Arctic to try to find out what had happened to Franklin. Finally articles belonging to Franklin's ships and skeletons of members of his crew were found along the west and south coasts of King William's Land. These relics told a tale of terrible disaster.

Lady Jane Franklin had been indefatigable in her efforts to urge the British Navy to organize rescue expeditions. She made efforts to raise funds necessary for these expeditions. She even wrote to President Zachary Taylor asking for American support. She begged him "to join heart and mind in the enterprise of snatching the lost navigators from a dreary grave."

Lady Franklin's appeal found a lively response in the United States. Henry Grinnell, head of a mercantile firm in New York, was eager to help. Grinnell, interested in whaling in northern waters, had learned a great deal about the Arctic, and the search for Franklin stimulated his imagination as well as his sympathy. Besides, he had close ties with England, and as a gesture of international good will he offered to equip two ships. He asked Congress to man these vessels with American Navy personnel. When Congress agreed, Dr. Elisha Kent Kane, a naval surgeon and a great pioneer in American Arctic exploration, volunteered to join the expedition initiated by Grinnell.

This first American expedition sent out in search of Franklin was organized in 1850 and spent sixteen months in the Arctic vainly searching for Franklin's ships. A second expedition was planned for 1852. This time Congress had been approached by Senator Hamilton Fish of New York, and again naval personnel were assigned to the venture. This second expedition had a dual purpose. Apart from trying to find Franklin, this second American expedition was to do scientific and geographical research. British naval ships, too, though chiefly looking for Franklin, were naturally furthering scientific knowledge on these expeditions. The Franklin rescue operations thus became one of the earliest co-operative efforts of England and the United States to further international technical co-operation.

It is not surprising, therefore, that Peabody became actively involved. For apart from his human sympathy with Lady Franklin and the concern everyone felt for Franklin's fate, Peabody was always enthusiastic about any undertaking which encouraged joint Anglo-American efforts.

Peabody heard that Dr. Kane was in need of more instruments and equipment for the second expedition than Congress had thus far provided. Peabody wrote at once to Grinnell that he was willing to transfer $10,000 to Dr. Kane's account whenever this would be useful. "I hope," Peabody had written, "that Congress will nobly respond to what appears to be the feeling of the nation; but aware of the uncertainty of votes on appropriation of money for such objects . . . I . . . subscribe for the purpose . . . ten thousand dollars."

Other Americans, too, sent donations for Kane's equipment, but Peabody's was the largest contribution. Kane never forgot what Peabody, by this gift, had done for his work and for American Arctic exploration generally. As a token of appreciation for Peabody's help, Kane named Peabody Bay, off Greenland, for him. In his report about the expedition to the Secretary of the Navy, Kane wrote, "The large Bay which separates it [Washington Land] from the coast of Greenland and the Glacier I have described bears on my chart the name of our liberal countryman and contributor to the expense of the expedition, Mr. George Peabody."

The Great Exhibition and Anglo-American Trade

GEORGE PEABODY's philanthropies, which benefited his own as well as succeeding generations, were made when he was well over fifty, at a period in life when many men who have accumulated great wealth think about retirement and more leisure. Outwardly, Peabody had not changed very much, and his health, despite such hard concentrated work over a number of years, was still unimpaired. He seemed to be as vigorous as he had been in his youth.

When he was fifty-seven, a contemporary wrote that "he was a large-framed man, six feet in height, slightly stooping at the shoulders, of easy address, retiring in manner, rather reticent of speech, neat in apparel and dignified in bearing—he appeared rather the English gentleman of leisure than an American merchant."

Peabody is today chiefly remembered as a philanthropist, and his remarkable achievements in connection with Anglo-American trade and Anglo-American relations are often forgotten. His active contribution toward greater trade relations between England and the United States began at the time of Prince Albert's famous Crystal Palace Exhibition of 1851, an exhibition which was the first modern world's fair.

At first there was opposition in the House of Commons and among prominent Englishmen to Prince Albert's conception of this Great Exhibition. Finally, however, his ideas and the designs for the Crystal Palace by Joseph Paxton were accepted. The Crystal Palace was a huge edifice built of glass and supported by barrell-type transepts. Until the Palace was destroyed by fire in the nineteen-thirties, it was one of London's famous landmarks.

When the plans for the Great Exhibition were first discussed, Peabody was shocked to learn that the governments of all other participating countries were subsidizing their exhibitors, but that the United States Government alone was not providing funds. Congress, when officially invited to ask American manufacturers to show their products at the Exhibition, had appointed administrative commissioners but made no financial appropriation. The commissioners who came to London to supervise the American exhibits were unpaid, voluntary officials. The Government had done nothing by the time they arrived in England except to authorize the use of a naval frigate, the *St. Lawrence*, as transport for American goods to be shown at the Exhibition.

A space of 40,000 square feet had been allotted in the huge Crystal Palace to American exhibitors, but no arrangements had been made to decorate this American pavilion and to display the goods to advantage. Americans in London were disappointed and resented the government's lack of interest.

"It is a national disgrace," wrote the London correspondent of the New York *Evening Post*, "that American wares, which are good, are so barely displayed, so vulgarly spread out over so large a space."

Some Englishmen, especially journalists, who were privileged to have a preview of the Exhibition before it was officially opened on May 1, 1851, were unpleasantly gleeful about the meager and unattractive American exhibits.

Punch noted unkindly,

We could not help . . . being struck by the glaring contrast between large pretension and little performance . . . of the large space claimed by . . . America. . . . What was our astonishment . . . to find that their contributions to the world's industry consists . . . of a few wine-glasses, a square or two of soap, and a pair of salt cellars! For a calculating people, our friends the Americans are thus far terribly out in their calculations.

The American Minister, Abbott Lawrence, was perturbed by the situation, for the Legation had no funds which could be assigned to the American displays. Then in March, two months before the Exhibition was opened, Peabody offered the Legation a loan of £3,000, about $15,000, to be spent on the American exhibits. This timely loan—to the credit of Congress it should be said that Peabody was later repaid—made it possible for the American pavilion to be suitably prepared and decorated. With the help of this financial contribution by Peabody, Alfred C. Hobbs's unpickable lock, Samuel Colt's revolvers, Hiram Powers's statue of a Greek slave, Cyrus McCormick's reaper, and Richard Hoe's printing press were laid out so that they could impress visitors to the Exhibition. Peabody's loan had made this possible.

Many years later, the New York *Times* recorded Peabody's generosity and farsightedness with gratitude: "The whole affair," the *Times* wrote in 1869 after George Peabody's death,

looked like a disgraceful failure. At this juncture Mr. Geo. Peabody, of whom not one exhibitor in twenty had ever heard, and who was personally unknown to every member of the commission, offered through a polite note addressed to Mr. Lawrence, to advance £3,000. . . . This loan afterwards paid by Congress, relieved the Commission of its difficulties, and enabled our countrymen to achieve their first success in industrial competition with the artisans and manufacturers of Europe.

After the Exhibition was opened, and until it was closed in October, six million people paid an entrance fee to visit the Crystal Palace. The Exhibition was a great financial success, and the famous Victoria and Albert Museum in London was later built on the proceeds.

The American pavilion was very popular. Peabody, of course, had a season ticket to the Exhibition but had little free time to go there often. On May 23 he wrote to a friend in Washington that the Exhibition was "becoming more interesting everyday," but that he himself was so busy that he had "passed but one hour in it since the first day it opened."

This was typical of Peabody. He had made the attractive American display possible, but now that this had been done he left details to others and did not think it necessary to visit the American pavilion. He himself was already concerned with new ideas which required his attention.

The project which now interested Peabody was stimulated by the large number of American businessmen and other tourists who had come to London to see the Great Exhibition. He hoped to foster closer social relations as well as business co-operation between Englishmen and Americans. He understood that this would bring about better relations between the two countries. This was not an easy task, as the rivalry between the two countries had in fact been heightened rather than lessened by the exhibition.

Americans, often talking volubly and very sure of themselves, were seen everywhere: at the opera, in places of amusement of a less highbrow nature, in hotels, restaurants, and at race tracks. Peabody himself, trying to keep in touch with many visitors in London, had a heavy schedule: he made social calls and satisfied requests for tickets for the House of Commons or the botanical gardens. He also kept many dinner engagements with new friends or clients of his merchant bank.

Many of these Americans in London were, not surprisingly, annoyed by the attitude of some Englishmen. Witty digs in the London papers, such as the one quoted from *Punch*, annoyed American tourists. Some Englishmen, on the other hand, unaccustomed to direct methods of sales and advertising, thought Americans vulgar and boastful.

One instance of this brashness—as the English saw it—involved the well-known American locksmith Alfred C. Hobbs. He walked into a Piccadilly locksmith's shop and pointed to a sign offering £200 reward to anyone opening the firm's lock. He then successfully picked the lock, demonstrating how ineffectual it was, and demanded the reward. He repeated this performance in another locksmith's shop where he was equally unpopular, especially since by his action he had ridiculed London locksmiths in general and had, at the same time, advertised his superior product.

In this atmosphere, Peabody realized, it would certainly not be easy to create a spirit of greater trust between American and English businessmen. Besides, they were still separated by political differences. The War of 1812 was only thirty-seven years in the past and, as every generation has learned, the memories of wars die very slowly. And there were, in 1851, a large number of Englishmen who had never forgiven the American colonies for their defection, though this had happened seventy-five years before. This English resentment toward citizens of their former colonies and toward the United States as a whole was now, in the eighteen-fifties, often directed against the long dispute about the northern boundaries of the State of Maine. The final settlement of this dispute in 1842 still rankled in the minds of many Englishmen.

Despite this difficult background, Peabody decided to act boldly. He proposed to give a huge dinner and ball to which he would invite English and American friends. And more daring still, he planned to hold this elaborate social function on the Fourth of July, a date which, for the English, was a symbol of their defeat and the final emancipation of the American colonies. Tactful Americans in London usually avoided public gatherings on Independence Day for fear of giving offense.

Before making final arrangements for this Fourth of July banquet, Peabody asked some of his friends for their opinion about the proposed function, and, as a matter of courtesy, he also sought the advice of Abbott Lawrence, the American Minister.

Lawrence, with delicate diplomacy, asked leaders of London society whether they would attend such a festive occasion on the Fourth of July. He knew that if they were invited and declined to come, the publicity given their refusal in the press would do greater harm to Anglo-American relations than no dinner at all. For in the eighteen-fifties, Society with a capital S was extremely influential in England, and no one in politics could afford to offend fashionable hostesses. The ruling class was then extremely powerful; English society was not yet democratic.

The American Minister was not encouraged when he discussed Peabody's plan for a dinner with prominent people. He was wary, as diplomats so often are, and on June 24, less than two weeks before the Fourth, he sent Peabody a "confidential" letter urging him to give up his idea of an international gathering on Independence Day.

Lady Palmerston was here. She has seen the leading ladies of the town and quoted one as saying the *fashionables* are tired of balls. I am quite satisfied that the fashionables and aristocracy of London do not wish to attend this Ball. Lady Palmerston says she will attend. I do not under those circumstances desire to *tax* my friends to meet Mrs. Lawrence and myself—Your party then I think must be confined to the Americans—and those connected with America, and such of the British people as happen to be situated as to enjoy uniting with us.

Before receiving this letter, Peabody had been making up his own mind about the proposed banquet. He was grateful for the trouble Lawrence had taken, but he did not agree with him. Peabody was certain that the presence of an outstanding public figure would insure the success of his party. It is not known how or through whom Peabody approached the most famous living Englishman and invited him to his dinner; but to the astonishment of Lawrence, the Duke of Wellington accepted Peabody's invitation. Wellington, then eighty-four years old, had called Peabody's proposal for a joint Anglo-American gathering a "good idea," and when it was known that he was coming, members of London society were eager for invitations.

Peabody planned his dinner and ball with the utmost care. He never overlooked details in any of his projects, whether they were far-reaching financial deals or social affairs such as these Independence Day celebrations.

He engaged Willis's Rooms (often called Almack's by London clubmen) for the evening, and chose a famous professional master of ceremonies, a Mr. Mitchell of Bond Street, to supervise the arrangements—the food, service, decorations of the rooms, music, entertainments, and all the rest. Mr. Mitchell entered into the spirit of the affair. American flags and the Union Jack were skilfully hung together against the walls, flowers were placed on the tables in the spacious one hundred-by-forty-foot ballroom. At one end, portraits of young Queen Victoria and of George Washington were draped in the national colors of both countries. The ballroom was lit by five hundred wax candles in cut-glass chandeliers.

More than a thousand guests came to Willis's Rooms on that Friday evening, July 4th, 1851, eight hundred of whom were entertained for dinner before the ball began. The guests reflected Peabody's idea of Anglo-American amity. Among the distinguished people who attended the celebration were the Lord Mayor and Lady Mayoress of London; Thomas Hankey, then Junior Governor of the Bank of England; Miss Burdett-Coutts, the greatest woman philanthropist of the nineteenth century; Joseph Paxton, the architect of the Crystal Palace; Minister Abbott Lawrence, his wife and staff; Governor Neill S. Brown of Tennessee, at the time United States Minister to Russia; and a large number of prominent American businessmen who lived in London or who had come to see the Great Exhibition.

At functions of this kind in the middle of the nineteenth century, guests were afforded little opportunity for casual conversation. They were kept busy every minute being entertained. There was the dinner—really a word understating the elaborate banquet—followed by a concert featuring performers from Her Majesty's Theatre famous in their day, and then the ball began.

At 11 p.m., with careful precision, the arrival of the victor of Waterloo was announced. The band struck up "See the Conquering Hero Comes." Everyone rose as Peabody approached the Iron Duke. The two men shook hands, and, amid the applause of the gathering, they walked slowly across the vast hall toward Minister Lawrence and his party from the Legation. Peabody presented the Minister to Wellington who, though so old, still found pleasure in a gay evening of this kind. He was obviously enjoying himself, and it was reported that "His Grace left at a late hour."

Peabody's Independence Day dinner was one of the social events of the season and emboldened Peabody, the next year, to give a dinner on June 17, the anniversary of the Battle of Bunker Hill.

The Fourth of July dinner of 1851 was considered a memorable occasion. London newspapers acknowledged how much Peabody, "this eminent American merchant," had done for Anglo-American relations, and the *Ladies Newspaper* included a large woodcut illustration of Peabody introducing the Duke of Wellington to Abbott Lawrence. Correspondents of American newspapers in England were equally impressed, and through their reports Peabody began to be more widely known in the United States. A Philadelphia correspondent, in describing the Independence Day ball, referred to Peabody as "a bachelor belonging to one of the most aristocratic London clubs, reputed to be worth between five and seven million dollars, yet plain in his manner and living."

Abbott Lawrence, who had at first expressed so little enthusiasm for Peabody's proposed Fourth of July gathering, was glad to admit that his judgment had been wrong.

"I should be unjust to myself and to our country as its representative at this Court," Lawrence wrote to Peabody after the ball, "if I were not to offer my acknowledgments and heartfelt thanks for myself and our country for the more than regal entertainment you gave to me and mine, and to our countrymen generally here in London in commemoration of one of the most important events in the political history of the world."

Then, after a somewhat rambling historical discourse about the far-reaching results of the Declaration of Independence, Lawrence continued his letter to Peabody: "I am quite certain that the effects of mingling together of British and American people on the Fourth of July will not be limited to the two countries. There is not a despotic government in Europe that will not pause and reflect upon this extraordinary meeting of which you have been the author and finisher."

The success of his banquet had given Peabody a taste for sociability, and, to the surprise of many of his acquaintances, this reticent, almost shy man now began to enjoy large dinner parties and elaborate, even sumptuous social gatherings. He had suddenly discovered his own talents as a host, and his extraordinary memory, so useful in business, now helped him in his social relations as well. He never forgot a name or the particular likes or dislikes of his guests who always felt at ease when he entertained them. Peabody also delighted in receiving friends in his offices in Warnford Court and inviting them to his private apartments in the Club Chambers in Regent Street.

By the end of the summer, many of Peabody's old and new American friends who had come to London for the Exhibition were preparing to leave England. "London will soon become dull," Peabody wrote to his friend William Wilson Corcoran in Washington. "Already the Americans are leaving for Scotland and the Continent etc."

Before they went, Peabody, determined to see as much of them as possible, gave a large dinner party for these Americans at the Star and Garter Inn in Richmond and another at the Brunswick Hotel, Blackwall, overlooking the Thames, a few miles from St. Paul's Cathedral. More than sixty guests had been invited to each of these functions. Peabody derived an almost childlike pleasure in the success of his dinners which again were widely reported in American newspapers. For he had invited American correspondents to attend. He did not shun this publicity and was a firm believer in public relations. "If I deserved half the compliments paid me in the American papers," Peabody, obviously delighted, wrote to a friend in Washington, "I ought to be a very happy man. All I claim is good motives."

Some of the American participants in the Great Exhibition had remained longer in London, and in the fall, before they finally left for the United States, these visitors invited Peabody to be their guest of honor at a farewell dinner. He courteously declined this invitation; the reasons he gave for not accepting seem vague and irrelevant.

He wrote to Charles F. Stanbury, the spokesman for the Americans, thanking him and his friends for their invitation, but saying that they had "overestimated his services at the time of the Exhibition." Despite fifteen years in London, he wrote, he had many friends all over the United States. His long absence, he added, had erased from his mind all sectional and party lines; it was his interest to further the welfare of the country as a whole.

This letter could not have implied any disapproval of Stanbury and his associates because a few weeks later, on October 27, 1851, Peabody entertained them at a farewell dinner. Perhaps he felt more comfortable as a host than as a guest.

This dinner, which was attended by one hundred and fifty English and American businessmen, was given at the London Coffee House on Ludgate Hill, the same Coffee House in which Benjamin Franklin and his friend Strahan had met to discuss the affairs of the Colonies over a mutton chop. Again Peabody had arranged to have the flags of Great Britain and the United States hung together, peacefully entwined, and the somewhat fulsome "hands across the sea" speeches extolled the growing friendship between the American and British business communities.

The guests of honor at the dinner were Abbott Lawrence and Sir Henry Bulwer-Lytton, British Minister to Washington, who was at home on leave. The two ministers set the official seal of approval on the proceedings. Both diplomats urged their listeners to ignore small differences between the two countries and "make as public as possible . . . points of union."

The addresses delivered at this October 1851 dinner were later compiled into book form by Peabody's friend Henry Stevens, an American bibliophile, who had been employed in 1845 to collect Americana for the British Museum. He acted as agent in England for a number of American libraries and became one of Peabody's most able advisors in connection with the book collections he made for the educational charities which he founded or supported.

Since Peabody's day, speeches such as those given at his Anglo-American gatherings have become commonplace. In these speeches, the same phrases and clichés are repeated so often that they have become monotonous. It should be remembered, however, that in the eighteen-fifties such declarations of unity between the two countries were a new departure, and very important. It was George Peabody who had initiated these personal and productive contacts between Englishmen and Americans, and the speeches they made at his dinners were a vital factor in bringing them closer together. The farsighted New York *Times* had understood that George Peabody's dinners were "timed just right."

For years there have been built up antagonism and recrimination. Suddenly, a respected American, long resident in London, with a host of American and English friends, brings them together. The thing works and what is more surprising elicits applause and appreciation from both the American and the English press.

The First Peabody Institute and Growing Fame

GEORGE PEABODY never allowed his social activities to distract him from his work, but the encouragement of good Anglo-American relations grew to be one of the purposes of his life. Yet he remained first and foremost an investment banker, whose reputation for integrity as well as for shrewdness was steadily increasing his business and his personal fortune. His firm was soon in almost sole control of the London sale of American securities.

He once admitted to a friend, John Cryder, that it never suited his disposition to proceed too cautiously or to "circumscribe his transactions to a small figure." On the contrary, when he saw an opportunity for a successful operation, he felt compelled to "embark on it even should he remotely hazard the loss of a few thousand."

He backed up his investments with his astute judgment of securities and of the financial situation generally. This meant continuous concentration on international markets. Up to 1851, he had not left his London office for two consecutive days. He was at No. 6 Warnford Court ten hours a day, and often during evenings and on Sundays as well, and for six years he had not been a hundred miles away from the capital.

"I consider you," a Baltimore friend teased him in a letter, "like a Horse in a mill condemned to your perpetual round, tho' if that gives you more pleasure than any other life would give, hold on upon it."

Actually, as the years passed, he increasingly felt the strain, and his busy life did not always give him satisfaction. He was now often unwell from overwork. "I am almost tired of making money," he wrote to a friend, "without having time to spend it."

In this letter he did not mention that for a long time he had been seriously considering the worthwhile causes on which he would spend his money—quite apart from his discreet almost secretive personal generosity to individuals in need.

In October 1851, he had seen a notice in a Baltimore newspaper appeal-

ing for funds for the Maryland Institute for the Promotion of the Mechanic Arts, and he had at once sent a donation of $1,000 for a chemical
school and laboratory.

Early in the following year, he remembered the Maryland Historical
Society with a most imaginative gift. He commissioned his friend Henry
Stevens to extract items concerning Maryland history from English manuscripts filed away in the Public Record Office and elsewhere in London
and from the Bodleian Library in Oxford. The result of Stevens's researches
were presented to the Maryland Historical Society in seven bound volumes containing references to the colonial history of Maryland from 1633
to 1711.

Peabody's gifts to the institutions in Baltimore were a reflection of his
persistent concern for the city with which he had been so closely connected. He had not visited the United States for sixteen years, but as he
grew older his memories of Baltimore and of Danvers, where he spent his
childhood, were more and more vivid and real to him. It has never been
fully explained why he never insisted on taking time to go home at least
for a few months. Probably the explanation is quite simple; he was literally
so involved with the day-to-day affairs of George Peabody and Company
that he felt he could not be away. He was for years tied down to his office
desk by knots of his own making.

In the spring of 1852, an occasion arose that caused him to remember
Danvers in a very concrete manner. In June of that year, Danvers was
celebrating its one-hundredth anniversary as an independent township; in
1752 Danvers had been separated from Salem. Peabody, already Danvers's
most celebrated son, was invited to attend the centenary festivities and to
prepare a toast for the great occasion. As he could not be present in person,
he sent to the organizers of the celebrations a letter as well as a sealed
envelope which was to be opened and read to the citizens of Danvers on
the great day. John W. Proctor, Peabody's old school friend, the brother
of Sylvester Proctor Jr. and the son of old Captain Sylvester Proctor, was
asked to present Peabody's letter and the contents of the sealed envelope
to the town.

The Danvers Centennial Celebration was noisy and gay. The Salem
Brass Band supplied lusty music, and the spirited march through the town
by 1,500 Danvers schoolchildren dressed up in their Sunday clothes was
a happy beginning of the festivities. Later, a procession of adults paraded
through the town carrying flags and banners. They were accompanied by

uniformed members of the Light Infantry Company and the Danvers Fire Brigade.

A public dinner was held under a large tent in the afternoon, and speeches were made by the Governor of Massachusetts and other civic dignitaries. Then John W. Proctor rose to read Peabody's letter which contained the usual congratulations to Danvers on the town's hundredth anniversary, recollections of Peabody's childhood there, and his expressions of gratitude for the principles he had learned in the Danvers school he had attended for the few short years of his education.

Certainly there was nothing special or original in this letter. It might have been written to citizens of his home town by any successful man. Then Proctor opened the sealed envelope which had been included in the letter, and suddenly men and women who heard the contents realized that Peabody, despite the platitudes contained in the letter, was a most unusual man.

He first presented the town with a motto, a few words which embodied an American ideal, an ideal which henceforth was to guide Peabody himself in his benefactions. The words were quite simple, yet implied so much. They were "Education—a debt due from present to future generations."

After these words, in the communication in the sealed envelope, Peabody had added a memorandum which laid the foundation for the first Peabody Institute and showed that he himself was already resolved, in a most practical manner, to live up to the motto he had sent to Danvers:

In acknowledgment of the payment of that debt by the generation which preceded me in my native town of Danvers, and to aid in its prompt future discharge, I give to the inhabitants of that town the sum of TWENTY THOUSAND DOLLARS, for the promotion of knowledge and morality among them.

Peabody went on to say that he had been contemplating such a gift for some years and, after careful consideration, he added certain conditions: he asked the legal voters of the town to meet, to accept formally the gift, then to elect twelve trustees who were to establish a Lyceum for lectures which were to be free to everyone. Of his gift, $7,000 was to be spent on the erection of a new building for the Lyceum and $10,000 was to be invested as a permanent fund to support the Lyceum.

He left all other decisions regarding the Lyceum to the citizens of Danvers through their elected trustees, but he most seriously advised them never to use this new institution for political ends or as a center of heated religious arguments. The Lyceum was to be an institution where Danvers people could acquire knowledge. In his own words, he urged them "to exclude sectarian theology and political discussion."

In writing to the citizens of Danvers about his gift, Peabody had allowed himself a moment of sentiment: "If Captain Sylvester Proctor [his first employer] shall be still living then and there is no objection, I shall request that he be selected to lay the corner stone of the Lyceum building."

Soon after the centennial celebrations, the trustees met, selected a site for the Lyceum, and decided to call it the Peabody Institute. They found, however, that the $7,000 which Peabody had allotted to the site and building was not enough. He was tactfully informed of this fact by an old friend, Robert Shillaber Daniels, and he at once agreed to give a further $10,000 to Danvers citizens. Danvers was also remembered by Peabody in the following year when he promised to give $200 annually during his lifetime for prizes to be awarded to outstanding high school students of the town.

The cornerstone of the Danvers Institute, the first of the Peabody Institutes, which would include a lecture hall seating 800 people, was laid on August 20, 1853, by Abbott Lawrence (Proctor being indisposed), now retired from his post as American Minister in London. One of the speakers at this cornerstone ceremony was Rufus Choate, already prominent as a lawyer and congressman. Other well-known men were present at the ceremony, which was attended by more than two thousand people. Eastern newspapers gave prominence to the planned Danvers Institute, and Danvers was suddenly a much discussed little town. Peabody, too, became known to a great many Americans who had never heard of him before. As his friend William Wilson Corcoran said, he was now becoming "a national man."

Details of the Danvers ceremony were sent to Peabody in London, and he was pleased to learn that his two nephews, Othniel Charles Marsh and George Peabody Russell, had come from Phillips Academy in Andover to hear the speeches about their distinguished uncle. Soon George Peabody Russell would be a student at Harvard, while Othniel Charles Marsh went to Yale.

More and more Americans visiting London were now eager to meet Peabody, this brilliant financier who was also such a philanthropist. Traveling businessmen and bankers called at his office, and the lucky ones were invited to the dinners he was giving regularly. With some of these visitors, Cornelius Vanderbilt, for example, Peabody had financial dealings, and he was also most helpful in a personal way to Vanderbilt and others while they were in Europe. Manufacturers, too, came to see him. Charles Good-year, for example, in London where he hoped to market his new vulcanized rubber, sent Peabody samples of his invention.

Many journalists began to call at Peabody's office, and his relationship with them made it apparent that he was increasingly aware of the importance of good relations with the press. His business and his philanthropy were furthered by friendly notices in the newspapers.

Among the journalists he met in 1852 was Thurlow Weed, the editor of the Albany *Evening Journal* and a prominent politician in New York State. Some years later, in 1861, Peabody and Weed were to meet again when Abraham Lincoln sent Weed to London as one of his personal emissaries during the Civil War. Then, when Peabody was contemplating a gift to London's poor, he asked Weed's advice about this venture. Peabody had great confidence in Weed and suggested that he might undertake the direction of his future educational gifts to institutions in the United States. Weed, however, declined and suggested Robert Charles Winthrop of Massachusetts for this work.

Another journalist whom Peabody met in London at this time was Horace Greeley, the founder of the New York *Tribune*. Peabody acted as Greeley's private banker; he paid the American sculptor Hiram Powers, who was then in Europe, the money owed him by Greeley. Greeley, in common with other travelers who met Peabody, was impressed by his reliability, and when Mrs. Greeley went on a trip to Sweden by herself, Greeley wrote to Peabody:

"I believe she is carefully provided with friends and funds but if an unforeseen calamity should overtake her, I beg you to act the good Samaritan and believe me to be . . . grateful." It is not recorded just why, if Mrs. Greeley were to be in trouble in Sweden, Peabody was asked to help her, except that he seemed a fatherly type who, so Greeley felt, would know what to do in an emergency.

Not all of Peabody's American friends were as easy to help as the Greeleys. There were times when he was called upon to solve really tricky problems. Colonel John Charles Frémont, soldier, politician, explorer, and a former Governor of California, was one of the difficult visitors to London. He had come to raise funds for his Mariposa mining lands in California. It seems that when he was acting governor of California, at the outbreak of the Mexican War, he had borrowed (and not paid back) money to meet his expenses as governor.

His creditors had somehow caught up with him in London, and one evening, it was April 7, 1852, as he and his wife Jesse were stepping into a carriage, he was arrested and taken to jail. Frémont at once sent a hurried message to Peabody, who went to the prison, paid the bail demanded, and arranged for Frémont's release the next day. One might ask why Peabody was asked for help and not the American Legation. Probably the reason was that, despite his somewhat ponderous manner, he always acted quickly in emergencies.

Occasionally Peabody was called upon to cope with one of the eccentrics found among each season's tourists in London. The odd personality who appeared in 1853 was Miss Delia Salter Bacon, the first American exponent of the theory that Shakespeare was not the author of his works but that the plays had been written by Francis Bacon, Sir Walter Raleigh, and Edmund Spenser. She was convinced, and told everyone of her conviction at great length, that the proof of her theory was to be found in Shakespeare's grave in Stratford and that Bacon's letters contained a cipher which would clear up the whole affair.

Miss Bacon came to London with a letter of introduction to Peabody. He not only felt obliged to listen patiently to her for long stretches at a time; he had to secure a loan for her from Charles Butler in New York, find her lodgings, get her an interview with Thomas Carlyle, and generally see that she was well looked after in London. One does not feel somehow that Miss Bacon was one of the overseas visitors who was an outstanding success at his dinner parties, for not everyone among the other guests was interested in Shakespeare or Miss Bacon's conversation.

One of Peabody's most successful entertainments at this time was given on October 12, 1852. This large farewell dinner to Abbott Lawrence and his wife, who were leaving England, served also to introduce to London society Lawrence's successor, Joseph Reed Ingersoll of Pennsylvania. Ingersoll was accompanied by his niece, Miss Wilcocks, who often acted as his hostess while he was Minister to the Court of St. James's.

Miss Wilcocks was one of those Victorian ladies who flit across the pages of contemporary gossip columns and letters without a Christian name. Whatever her name, she was apparently romantically interested in George Peabody. He took her to the opera, and they were frequently seen together at various social functions. Though Peabody was now fifty-seven years old, he was still considered a most eligible bachelor and there were rumors in London and New York about his attachment to Miss Wilcocks. The London reporter of the New York *Tribune* was interested in this gossip.

"Mr. Ingersoll," the reporter wrote, "gave his second soiree recently. Miss Wilcocks does the honors with much grace, and is greatly admired here. The world gives out that she and Mr. Peabody are to form an alliance, but time will show. . . ."

Whispered comments about Peabody and Miss Wilcocks were further stimulated by the outspoken jealousy of another young lady, Elise Tiffany of Baltimore. Elise Tiffany, who had met Peabody while visiting London, went so far as to tell her brother she had no messages (from Paris where they were staying) for Mr. Peabody "whilst Miss Wilcocks was there."

Peabody was not seriously interested in either girl. He had no matrimonial intentions whatsoever. "I have now arrived at an age that throws aside all thoughts of marriage," he wrote to his friend Corcoran, "though I think Miss Wilcocks a very fine woman."

When George Tiffany, Elise's brother, on his return to London, rather tactlessly told Peabody what his sister had said, Peabody must have been astonished to be the object of rivalry between two young ladies. He was less surprised to realize that his outstanding and increasing attainments as a banker and his emergence into a place of prominence in London society created envy among men who were not as successful. He had matured into a man of the world, and he undoubtedly understood that eminence in any field of endeavor embittered some lesser men whose efforts to attain outstanding achievements had been frustrated.

One of these men was one Benjamin Moran, Secretary at the American Legation, who was infuriated by Peabody's popularity with succeeding American ministers. Moran, who had never been invited to Peabody's dinners, obviously found it unbearable when Minister Lawrence or Minister Ingersoll asked Peabody's advice.

This Moran, who kept a secret diary during the two decades he worked at the American Legation in London, was a frustrated character who would have interested modern psychologists. He had begun life as a modest printer in Philadelphia with the firm of John Grigg. When Lippincott bought Grigg's firm, Moran, whose father had been English, took his savings and went to London, where he became a free-lance writer. He was inordinately ambitious, socially and professionally, and he hoped to become a great author and a shining light in society. His one book, *The Footpath and Highway, or Wanderings of an American in Great Britain in 1851 and 1852*, was not widely read, nor was his marriage to an English woman, who was never in good health, a success. To earn his living, Moran did secretarial jobs for the American Minister in London. Later he was appointed to the permanent post as an assistant secretary at the Legation, but he was never accepted socially by members of the Legation. He was discontented and embittered by his failure and hated the world at large. In an account by Henry Adams, whose father Charles Francis Adams was the American Minister in London during the Civil War, Moran is described as "a sort of dependable work horse to fill in for any duty that might come up from the changing personnel."

In later years, Peabody was one of Moran's chief *bêtes noires*; he often attacked him in his diary. Peabody, of course, did not know about Moran's secret diary, but the man's animosity was often a nuisance at the Embassy, and occasionally Peabody had to complain about his unco-operative attitude. Moran's resentment was expressed frequently.

He once wrote in his diary,

It seems old Peabody and his friends in the city have made several attacks on me of late, charging that I have used my position here to advance my own interests. This man is one of the most malicious I ever knew, & his attacks on my character are all prompted by envy. He is heartless, and has never given a farthing in charity that he did not expect three fold return. All his benevolence is based on future personal gain.

On another occasion, Moran wrote that Peabody "generally bags the *new* American Minister for his own purpose and shows him up around the town, if he can, as his puppet to a set of fourth-rate English aristocrats and American tuft-hunters who eat his dinners and laugh at him for his pains."

One does not feel that men such as the Duke of Wellington or Cornelius Vanderbilt, who had enjoyed Peabody's hospitality, would have appreciated remarks of this kind in Moran's secret diary. Nor would the people of Danvers or other citizens who were so greatly benefiting from Peabody's philanthropies have been pleased by the sarcastic and ill-informed attacks against him in a few newspapers. The editor of the *Weekly Day Book* in New York, for example, had ventured to ask, "Who is this god of the American dollar? What has he done but make a fortune in America and spend it abroad? He gives large dinners to English aristocrats and a few Americans who publish his name in the newspapers."

Peabody, of course, took no notice of remarks of this kind, but he could not afford to ignore suggestions in the press and elsewhere that he was in poor health. For though he was soon to take partners into his firm, he still headed a one-man business which would have been harmed had his correspondents and clients thought him too ill to attend to their affairs efficiently. In July 1853, when there were reports concerning his indisposition, Peabody took the trouble to deny them. He wrote to the firm of Duncan, Sherman in New York requesting them to give publicity to his denial of such reports.

"We are asked to say," the New York *Times* stated, "that Duncan, Sherman and Company have received a letter written by George Peabody himself saying he is not in ill-health. Ogden Haggarty came over on the *Arctic* and states he left Mr. Peabody in perfect health."

Actually, this statement was not entirely true. For some time before it was issued, Peabody had not been well. Constant strain and continuous application to his business had finally left their mark. He suffered badly from gout and rheumatism and was often subject to intestinal complaints. For years his friends had urged him to take a full partner into the firm. In January 1852, he decided to appoint at least a junior partner, Charles Cubitt Gooch, who had been the trusted confidential clerk in George Peabody and Company since 1843.

Peabody, however, continued to keep control of all moneys, bills, and securities in the business so that he was almost as overworked as he had been. Finally, he himself realized that, as he grew older, he must indeed find a suitable equal partner to share the responsibility for the company. The man George Peabody finally chose was Junius Spencer Morgan, who became a partner in George Peabody and Company in the summer of 1854.

The Morgan Partnership

GEORGE PEABODY had devoted much time and thought to the selection of a financier who would be a suitable equal partner. The stability of Peabody and Company, the security of his clients, of his own wealth and thus of the future of his philanthropies, depended upon this choice. Several considerations were to him essential in a partner: the man had to have absolute integrity; he needed daring on occasion—must not be a "two penny man"—and yet be careful and shrewd at all times. And, important to Peabody, the new partner *must* be an American.

Peabody was determined that his firm should always remain an American enterprise. "It has been," he once wrote, "and is now, a favourite object with me so to arrange all by business, that my house will be purely American, that its continuance for many years will not depend on my life, and that my American friends will feel that, in every respect, the house is worthy of their entire confidence."

His offices, too, were to be arranged in an American manner, and since founding George Peabody and Company in London, he had, to use his own words, consistently determined "in the constitution of the firm's members and the character of its business to give it an American atmosphere." In the reception room of his offices in Old Broad Street, current American newspapers were laid out on the table. American clients and visitors were made to feel welcome. Thus Peabody's offices became, as he once remarked, "a center for his American friends visiting England."

The character of men whom Peabody weighed up, but in the end did not choose as his partner, reflected the standards he set for the associate he was seeking. William Shepard Wetmore, Peabody decided, was too engrossed in personal problems: his new marriage followed by the mental illness of his wife sometimes caused him to neglect his business. John Cryder, so Peabody believed, tended to be overcautious. Curtis Miranda Lampson, a Vermonter who had originally made a fortune in the fur trade, was a possibility. Lampson, an old friend of Peabody's, had lived in London since 1830. He had married an English girl, was a senior partner of the merchandising firm of C. M. Lampson and Company in the City, and had become a naturalized British subject in 1849. He later was made a baronet for his outstanding work as a director of the Atlantic Telegraph Company. Had Lampson not been a British subject—and also, according to Peabody, too enthusiastic about the long, work-free English weekend—Peabody might have considered asking him to join George Peabody and Company. But, attached though Peabody always was to Lampson, he would not do as a partner, as he was no longer an American.

In May 1853, Peabody finally met the man who seemed to have everything he desired in a partner. This man was Junius Spencer Morgan, a partner of J. M. Beebe, a respected drygoods mercantile firm in Boston. Morgan and his family, including his eighteen-year-old son John Pierpont, were traveling in England that spring, and Peabody was impressed by Junius Spencer Morgan from the very beginning of their acquaintance. Morgan, born in 1813, was then forty, eighteen years younger than Peabody.

Morgan, also a man from Massachusetts, had begun his career at the age of sixteen as a bank clerk. At twenty-one he had been a partner in the New York banking firm of Ketchum, Morgan, and Company. After that he had been associated as a junior partner in the drygoods business of Howe, Mather, and Company, and finally in 1851 he had joined the firm of J. M. Beebe, with whom Peabody had dealings. Beebe had given Morgan a letter of introduction to Peabody, who had already heard about Morgan. And what he had heard had satisfied Peabody, for Morgan had severed his business connections with Ketchum when he discovered that Ketchum was an unscrupulous speculator. This was the kind of integrity Peabody expected in a partner.

On May 18, 1853, Morgan and his wife were invited to attend a large dinner which Peabody was giving for 150 English and American guests at the Star and Garter in Richmond in honor of Joseph Reed Ingersoll, the new American Minister in London. Again Peabody was pleased by Morgan, this time by the younger man's obvious ability to mix charmingly with many kinds of people. He obviously understood the importance of public relations in business. He had at his command, as the Victorians and probably Peabody himself would have expressed it, all the felicities in dealing with people. Morgan, for his part, was undoubtedly impressed by the great respect shown Peabody everywhere in London.

Shortly after this dinner, Peabody had a long talk with Morgan and discussed with him a possible partnership. Morgan was interested and promised to think seriously about Peabody's suggestion. He returned to the United States with his family and visited a number of American firms with which Peabody and Company did business. Meanwhile, Peabody and Morgan exchanged letters regularly. Peabody was obviously determined to bring about this partnership. He was eager to have the matter settled as soon as possible, for he was not feeling at all well in that summer of 1853 and was beginning to realize painfully that, at fifty-eight, he was approaching the day when he could no longer manage the firm by himself. Besides, he wanted to be free soon to visit the United States.

By the following summer, in 1854, Morgan had made up his mind to join George Peabody and Company. Larger premises were found and the firm moved to 22 Old Broad Street. A formal announcement of Morgan's entry into the firm was printed and circulated to Peabody's correspondents. The notice emphasized that this partnership was to be permanent.

"Our arrangements with Mr. Morgan have been made," the announcement declared, "with a view to establish our House permanently; and, if our Prior [George Peabody] is removed by death before the expiration of the time contemplated by this arrangement, a large portion of his capital" will be used for the firm.

The business of the house, as before, was to consist of sales and purchases of stock, foreign exchange, banking, and credits. George Peabody and Company—the name of the firm was not changed—was also to continue the execution of orders for railroad iron, the purchase and sale of produce, together with general mercantile transactions.

For Junius Spencer Morgan and his son John Pierpont (the family called him Pierpont), the partnership was to be equally fruitful. This association with Peabody was their stepping stone to commercial greatness, to wealth and to power. Peabody, on the other hand, was freed from some of his overtaxing responsibilities for the detailed problems in the office.

When the pressure of work was too great even for the partners, young Pierpont sometimes came to Old Broad Street to be of assistance. Besides, Peabody welcomed young pupil-bankers to his offices. The year before, to mention one of these lads, his distant cousin Joseph Peabody had worked in the London office.

Now, in the summer of 1856, when Peabody was getting ready to go to America, Pierpont spent some weeks in the office. He was then a student at the University of Göttingen in Germany and was spending his vacation in London with his father. To the youth, the tall, stout figure of his father's partner seemed dignified and unapproachable. Young Pierpont was "arranging Mr. Peabody's letters" and his files "which had accumulated for over twenty years." Nevertheless, Pierpont obviously liked the older man, whom he described to a cousin in New York as "a very agreeable gentleman and very full of wit, but a regular old bachelor."

Peabody was pleased with his partner who relieved him of routine work. And now, with the new partnership going well, he had enough leisure to plan seriously some of the smaller gifts and philanthropies he had been contemplating for some years. The idea of a Washington Monument, to be erected in the capital, greatly appealed to him, and he asked Corcoran to add his name to the subscribers' list for the sum of $1,000.

A far more important gift, too, was already in his mind. When James Watson Webb, a New York journalist and later American Minister to Brazil, and Reverdy Johnson, a prominent Baltimorean, were in London in 1854, Peabody discussed with them his hopes of creating an educational institution in Baltimore and asked their advice about the selection of such an institution. When Johnson later that year returned to Baltimore, he discussed Peabody's proposed project with John Pendleton Kennedy, who was later to become one of the chief promoters of the Peabody Institute in Baltimore.

"I will endeavor," Kennedy noted in his diary after his talks with Reverdy Johnson, "to plan something on a munificent scale which may serve to educate a large number of students in the most useful arts & sciences."

Peabody looked forward to the foundation of the Baltimore Institute and other educational establishments bearing his name. It was only human that he hoped, in the future, to be remembered in connection with these philanthropies. He decided to have his portrait painted; this first portrait was to be presented to the Danvers Institute.

In his choice of an artist, as in most of his decisions, he showed a preference for Americans, and the man selected was George P. A. Healy, who was working in Paris and was soon to be well known as an American painter. Peabody paid Healy $1,000 for the portrait and helped him in other ways as well. Healy came to London where Peabody sat for the portrait in April 1854. Later, when the artist returned to the United States, he took with him letters of introduction from Peabody to many influential men. "Everything," Healy wrote gratefully to Peabody, "has prospered with me since the success of your picture."

Peabody was gratefully aware that it was the reliable presence of Morgan in the office in Old Broad Street which gave him more leisure. He was now able to travel occasionally to the warm south, to southern France or to Italy, and he also went salmon fishing in Scotland.

Soon after the partnership with Morgan began, Peabody took the time to sit for his portrait, to make plans for the future, and, in due course, to go to the United States for a protracted visit. For despite so many successful and rewarding years in England, home for Peabody was always America—Baltimore in particular. He never felt really rooted in England—always, oddly enough, considering himself an outsider.

The Sickles Affair

IN 1854 Peabody faced an unpleasant incident that was widely discussed. This was the so-called Sickles affair which began at the Independence Day dinner given by Peabody that year at the Star and Garter Hotel for about one-hundred and forty English and American guests. The guest of honor was James Buchanan, later President of the United States, who had just succeeded Ingersoll at the American Legation in London. Sickles, then a secretary of the American Legation, was a printer and lawyer from New York.

As usual in banquets given in foreign countries, Americans observed the courtesy of drinking the first toast to the head of state of the host country. In this case, therefore, the first toast after the banquet was drunk to Queen Victoria, and the second to President Pierce of the United States.

Daniel Edgar Sickles, obviously not familiar with diplomatic usage, despite his post at the American Legation, was enraged by this apparent insult to the American President. He remained seated during the toast to the Queen, and after that he ostentatiously stormed out of the gaily decorated diningroom at the Star and Garter. Sickles's tactless action received wide publicity in English and American newspapers. Experienced men of the world, English and American, objected to his rudeness to the Queen; but some people agreed with him that the United States had been slighted. This controversy threatened for a short time to undermine much of Peabody's patient efforts to bring about better relations between citizens of the two countries. At a distance of more than a century, this affair does indeed seem a storm in a teacup; at the time it was taken quite seriously.

Before the dinner, Peabody had been on pleasant terms with Sickles. Before his arrival in London in March 1854, Sickles had written to ask Peabody to reserve rooms for his wife and himself and their baby in a good hotel. Peabody had been glad to do so. A few weeks afterwards he and Sickles had discussed the annual Fourth of July banquet and Sickles had suggested that the dinner should be a subscription banquet which he,

Sickles, wanted to organize. Peabody did not accept this suggestion. He insisted on paying for the banquet himself so that everyone attending would be his guest, but as a concession to Sickles he allowed him to plan some of the details of the entertainment, to send out the invitations, and to help make up the list of guests.

Peabody did not often misjudge people, but he had obviously not realized before the dinner that Sickles was one of those belligerent, narrowminded patriots who have a nationalistic chip on their shoulders and who always seem to be waiting for insults to their country. In connection with Sickles's behavior at the dinner, his subsequent career should be mentioned, for soon his ungovernable temper became obvious to everyone. In 1859, while believing that he had a chance to become President of the United States, he shot and killed a man, Philip Barton Key, because of scandalous rumors involving Mrs. Sickles. He was tried for murder but was acquitted on the ground that he was of unsound mind at the time of the shooting. His mind, not surprisingly, did not become more stable during and after the Civil War, when tragically, he lost a leg at the Battle of Gettysburg, where he had fought with conspicuous bravery.

It is difficult to understand why Sickles was appointed to the London Legation, for as early as 1854 his lack of self-control was well known in Washington. Besides, as Peabody learned from a New York business friend during the Sickles affair, he had been indicted by the New York grand jury for fraud. The indictment was still standing, and evidence to convict him had come to Peabody's attention shortly after the dinner.

Sickles's bigoted patriotism was inexcusable, but one must remember that it had been stimulated by the climate of American opinion in 1854 at the time that he walked out of Peabody's dinner. American arms had triumphed in the Mexican Wars; Texas, Oregon, and the Mexican Cession fell easily to the United States. The State Department's delight about these successes was reflected in somewhat unwise and certainly undiplomatic advice to American representatives abroad. Shortly before the Sickles controversy, Secretary of State Marcy had issued a "Dress Circular" instructing members of American legations to appear at official functions at foreign courts in plain dress, and not in diplomatic uniform as was then the custom accepted by diplomats.

Sickles's America-only-and-first impulses were obviously aroused at Peabody's Independence Day dinner by the diplomatic uniforms of so many guests. His biographer Edgcumb Pinchon says that on this occasion

Sickles was "dumb, stiff and red-gorged" with fury. He resented the presence of any Englishmen—still to him the enemies—at an Independence Day celebration. He seriously thought and said that this should be an occasion to recall, and to read aloud, the entire Declaration of Independence. His dislike of Peabody's English guests verged on hatred.

Peabody's point of view, of course, was diametrically opposed. He firmly believed that the present and future co-operation between the two countries was absolutely essential. To this end, since 1850, he had invested a great deal of energy and thought sponsoring Fourth of July dinners which would develop and strengthen friendship between the United States and England.

Sickles was by no means satisfied with his dramatic exit from the dinner at the Star and Garter. He wanted to go farther, and now began a vicious newspaper campaign against Peabody. In an article in the Boston *Post*, first published anonymously and later acknowledged to be his, he accused Peabody of many sins: of having proposed the toast to the Queen in a servile manner; of toadying to the English; of being lukewarm when he drank President Pierce's health; of being unpatriotic and pro-English.

As a result of this letter and other garbled accounts of the dinner, Peabody had numerous unpleasant letters from newspaper readers and others who accepted Sickles's venomous account of what happened. Some of his correspondents went so far as to accuse him of being no longer fit to call himself an American citizen.

For Peabody, Anglo-American relations seemed at stake. He was seriously worried, and he took the trouble to deny Sickles's allegations in the Boston *Post* and other newspapers. He also arranged for many of the prominent Americans present at the dinner to send signed statements to the press refuting Sickles's accusations. Some of his friends, who knew that Peabody's position was unassailable, could not understand why he took the Sickles affair so much to heart.

"We are astounded," one friend wrote to him from New York in November 1854, "that you lower yourself by a correspondence with the most contemptible of all Americans, Sickles, who was indicted by a New York Grand Jury for fraud, which indictment stands to this day."

Though Peabody was well aware of Sickles's unsavory reputation in New York and elsewhere in the United States, he never once took advantage of this knowledge nor alluded to it in his correspondence and public utterances about the affair. He concentrated on the matter in hand—his passionate wish to continue peaceful Anglo-American relations; besides, his unwavering integrity would never have permitted him to bring in outside issues to discredit Sickles.

Peabody was disappointed in Buchanan. Letters from the future president to Sickles, who had left London after the affair, made it clear that Buchanan thoroughly disapproved of the man and did not want him to return to the Legation. But Buchanan never officially acknowledged that Peabody was right in the controversy and Sickles wrong. Two years later, after the Sickles affair had blown over and Buchanan had realized his political ambitions and become president, Peabody never liked him. When Peabody visited Washington in 1857 there was a marked coldness between the two men. Buchanan's friends made an effort, when Peabody's American visit was a triumphal tour and he was made much of everywhere, to reconcile the two. But Peabody, as he wrote to a friend, "refused any interferences to bring us together without a direct explanation from him [Buchanan]." Peabody's partner, Junius Spencer Morgan, always an upholder of the importance and dignity of their firm, thoroughly approved of Peabody's attitude toward Buchanan. "It is for *you to receive* him," he wrote to Peabody, "if either is to be received, but any reconciliations now would look like truckling to a man because he happens to be in power!"

The attitude of Peabody's old friend Abbott Lawrence, the former American Minister in London, compensated Peabody for Buchanan's lack of active support at the time of the Sickles Affair. Lawrence wrote to Peabody,

> I know you to be incapable of compromising your honor or that of your country. The attack made upon you [by Sickles] I deem unworthy of any man who professes to be a gentleman. Your misfortune was in having persons about you who were not worthy to be at your table. I had hard work to get rid of some men in England who hung about me, but cost what it would, I would not permit a certain class of adventurer to approach me.

Peabody never said whether he regretted the energy the Sickles affair had cost him. At any rate, in the years that followed, he never allowed this unpleasant incident to interfere with the lavishness of his Independence Day and other banquets. The Fourth of July dinners in 1855 and 1856 were as successful as ever, despite the fact that this was during the Crimean War when American public opinion, though not exactly pro-Russian, was certainly anti-British.

The British Army needed recruits, and John Crampton, who had succeeded Buchanan as American Minister in London, was indiscreet enough to try to enlist American volunteers for the British Army. Not surprisingly, Crampton was recalled to Washington by Secretary of State Marcy. This created an awkward situation, especially as Henry Bulwer-Lytton, former British Minister in Washington, was to have proposed the main toast at the Independence Day dinner of 1856, and now regretfully had to decline to do so since he was a friend of Crampton, who had been relieved of his post. Peabody was able to accept gracefully Bulwer-Lytton's regrets, and the dinner was a success. He had again demonstrated that, no matter how delicate the situation, he was in a position strong enough to bridge all difficulties and to maintain social intercourse between the two nations. The Sickles affair was soon forgotten.

Visit to the United States

IN the spring of 1856 Peabody was ready for his visit to the United States. He booked a passage on the *Atlantic*, sailing on September 3. He did not dread this crossing as he had the five seasick and miserable journeys he had from 1827 to 1837, though there were still very rough passages and occasional disasters at sea. In the winter of 1854 the *Arctic*, a Collins Line vessel, was sunk, and many passengers were lost. This misfortune had affected Peabody personally, for he had sent on this ill-fated vessel $35,000 in Virginia bonds. Afterwards he waited for years for Virginia to redeem the lost bonds, and finally, in July 1869, he presented the value of the bonds with accrued interest to General Robert E. Lee as a gift for Washington College.

Despite the loss of the *Arctic*, most people no longer considered journeys between England and America hazardous undertakings. Transatlantic travel was becoming quicker and more comfortable, and Cunard steamers and the ships of the American Collins Line competed with each other for the passenger business. In fact, the Collins ship *Pacific* had already broken all records and had made the crossing in nine days and twenty hours.

Peabody had every reason to look forward to the rest and relative quiet of an ocean voyage; during the summer he was overwhelmed with the work involved in getting ready to leave London. His stay in America was not to be a casual visit. He once said during his American tour that he felt like Rip van Winkle, but nothing was farther from the truth. In fact, in America he was not merely an observer of the American scene, an ineffectual *revenant*; he intended to study the emerging power of America and use what he learned to benefit his business, his family, and the philanthropic institutions with which he was concerned.

He had been away from home for two decades; now he was excited at the great progress of the United States. After all, the country was only eighty years old and already had a population of twenty-seven million. Railroads were being built in every direction. Commercial centers widely separated a few years before were easily linked by rail.

Peabody had a set design for his activities in the United States during this visit. He anticipated being reunited with his family, including the nieces and nephews he had never met; he hoped to travel extensively to see at first hand the industrial and commercial growth which had occurred during his absence of twenty years; and he planned to widen the scope of his philanthropic activities. He resolved to strengthen the Peabody Institute in South Danvers and to organize another in North Danvers (in 1855 the Danvers township had been divided). One of his gifts to education was already very much in his mind. This was to be a large institute in Baltimore, and it was his intention while in the States to lay the groundwork for this institute. During the year he spent in the United States, Peabody did in fact give away more than half a million dollars.

The perfection of these plans required Peabody's systematic application to detail before he left London. Young John Pierpont Morgan, as has been said, was instructed to sort out the bundles of letters Peabody wished to re-read in preparation for his discussions in America. He wanted to have a clear understanding of every individual with whom he would confer, whether this person was a friend, a relative, or merely a business acquaintance. He also meticulously went over the statements and accounts of the Danvers Institute and his other charities. He was as conscientious about this homework, this getting ready for interviews, as he had been as a young and less experienced man.

While still in London, Peabody also gave much thought to the relatives he would see in America. He considered himself most definitely, and rightly so, the head of his family. To his kinfolk this tall, stout, elderly man, with the benevolent but extremely firm and decisive manner, must have seemed a stern patriarch. In some ways he appeared to them to be ageless: older, yet, in his will power and energy, younger than his sixty-one years.

His sister Judith Russell, a regular correspondent, had been his chief source of information about the family. She herself had frequently needed her brother George's financial help; her husband Jeremiah Russell, an unsuccessful lawyer, was often in debt. Judith lived in Georgetown, Massachusetts, a village of about a thousand inhabitants, twenty-eight miles northeast of Boston. George Peabody and his brothers and sisters were attached to Georgetown, formerly Rowley, because their mother had been born there.

Before leaving England, Peabody asked Judith for a list of all the members of the family and a statement of what each one of them was doing.

Judith herself had only one child, George Peabody Russell, who was soon going to Harvard. Peabody's other surviving sister, Mrs. Sophronia Little, who lived in Portland, Maine, had four sons. Jeremiah, Peabody's only surviving brother, had remained in Zanesville, Ohio; he had five sons and three daughters. Since the death of Peabody's unfortunate brother David, his second wife, Phebe, had joined the family in Zanesville, where she lived with her young daughter Julia Adelaide. Julia was to become Peabody's great favorite while he was in America.

He anticipated with particular pleasure seeing Othniel, the son of his beloved sister Mary, who had died so long ago. In 1856, Othniel had almost finished his studies at Phillips Academy in Andover. Othniel's older sister, Mrs. Mary Waters, had died, and her small son of ten, Robert Henry Waters, boarded with a family in New Haven.

During his long absence from America, George Peabody had paid for the education of his nephews, but in return he expected them to work hard. He never gave them money beyond the expenses for their schooling. Their good education, he insisted, would and should enable them, by their own initiative, to get on in the world. He admonished all of his nephews, that if any of them disgraced himself or Peabody or became engaged or married before he was financially able to support a wife, he would withdraw his financial help and strike the name from his will.

As these nephews were industrious, Peabody was consistently generous, but he was careful with money and he expected to receive annually, or more often, accurate accounts from Judith, who distributed the funds he gave the family. The 1855 accounts of Othniel Marsh at Phillips Academy, accounts totaling $327.00, included every item, no matter how small, of the boy's expenditure: washing, for example, $9.47; postage, $2.70; newspaper, $2.00.

Peabody not only read the accounts Judith sent him, he mastered them, practically knew them by heart; for he loved detail almost as much as he loved grand designs. And his memory for detail, as for people, was phenomenal: he rarely forgot a date, the record of an expenditure, or any such trivial item, and the sight of a face not seen for decades at once brought the right name to his mind. Later, when he reached America, people were surprised when he remembered them after years of separation. In South Danvers, where he arrived in October 1856—just to cite one of many examples—when he was met by a large welcoming committee, one old man stepped forward and said, "You don't remember me, Mr. Peabody." Quick as a flash came Peabody's answer: "Yes, indeed I do, Prescott Spaulding." This

Mr. Spaulding was the man who, more than forty years before, in 1812, had given the then young Peabody some goods on consignment.

Peabody's memory and alertness were particularly striking, for if one did not know him well, or at a first meeting, he appeared to be a slow, almost bumbling elderly gentleman who tended to be fussy and overconcerned with little things. Certainly young John Pierpont Morgan, while helping him sort out his papers before he went to the States, was not yet aware of how remarkable old Peabody was.

"If you could have seen," Pierpont wrote to his cousin James Goodwin in Hartford, Connecticut, before Peabody left for America, "the quantity of nic-nacs which he [Mr. Peabody] carried with him to America, and which were stored away in his trunk with the greatest precision, you would most certainly have thought he was going to Central Africa to some unexplored regions, rather than to America."

Probably John Pierpont Morgan (and everyone else in the office in Old Broad Street) was relieved when, on September 3, the *Atlantic* finally sailed for New York with George Peabody aboard. The ship docked in New York on September 15.

From the day of Peabody's arrival in New York until his return to England a year later, his visit resembled a triumphal tour. He was familiar to hundreds of businessmen, many of whom he had entertained while they were in London; with others he had done business by correspondence. A large number of younger people, in Danvers, Baltimore, and elsewhere, had already benefited from his educational endowments, and his international prominence as an investment banker who had inherited nothing and had made his own way to the top caused him to be an object of interest and curiosity.

He was a living legend of the poor boy who has made good, a legend that captured the imagination of the American public at a time of expanding opportunities for those who worked hard. It was a period of history when the self-made man was the national ideal. Most boys hoped one day to be President of the United States or a great financial success.

Peabody was also well known for his other achievements, quite apart from his financial eminence. He had helped to win the fight against the repudiation of state debts; his international dinners in London had raised him to the status of an unofficial diplomat; his aid to American exhibitors at the World's Fair in 1851 had won him the gratitude of manufacturers; and the Peabody Institute in South Danvers had enhanced his reputation as a philanthropist.

If ticker tapes had been in use that September day in 1856 when Peabody landed in New York, he might well have had a ticker-tape welcome to the city. Even James Gordon Bennett's *Herald*, later hostile in its articles about Peabody, was, on his arrival, still fairminded and not unfriendly.

Letters from American friends which had reached Peabody in London reflected a desire to give him an elaborate reception. He had replied that he preferred to return to his native shores without any formal or organized welcome; nevertheless, there were many industrialists, bankers, and others at the dock to meet him. He was informed that a hundred New Yorkers, including Washington Irving, William B. Astor, E. Cunard, and August Belmont, hoped to give a banquet in his honor. Peabody declined courteously; instead he remained quietly for a few days at the St. Nicholas Hotel.

He had said "no" to this invitation on the grounds that the busy American tour he planned would not leave him free for public dinners, especially since he intended to devote much of his time to his family. He had another reason for declining the New Yorkers' invitation: he wanted no banquet or other demonstration in his honor to detract from the great welcoming celebration which, as Judith had informed him, the town of South Danvers was planning for October 9.

Besides, though this was a subject Peabody mentioned to very few people, he realized that too much sociability as well as the hard travel he was planning would affect his health. He could no longer rush at life as he had done when younger. In fact, he was frequently unwell throughout the American tour. In November in New York he was confined to bed for two weeks; in Georgia he had a swollen face and suffered excruciating pain; his gout was often troublesome, and during the cold winter of 1856–57 he was troubled by boils and other ailments.

When he arrived in New York in September 1856, the weather was mild; he felt relatively well, and he set out with anticipation for the moving reunion with Judith and his nephews. He always gathered vitality for the great occasions, and his own enthusiasm stimulated others and often caused them to be at their best.

The excitement he must have experienced at the thought of seeing Judith again and the towns he had known as a youth did not cause Peabody to hurry to her home in Georgetown or to alter the schedule he had fixed for his trip to New England. After leaving New York he stopped first in Newport, Rhode Island, to see his old friend William Shepard Wetmore. Then followed a brief stay in Providence, and after that, at last, Judith welcomed her brother in Georgetown. At her house he met Othniel

Charles Marsh, Judith's son George Peabody Russell, and his other relatives. The young men were in awe of him. He was kind and very gracious to them, but he could not resist giving them a little lecture and telling them what he expected of them.

The reunion with Judith was a complete success. The old affection and trust had survived the years of separation. In fact, devoted as she was to her home and friends in Georgetown, she would have been willing to leave them and, had he wished, join Peabody in South Danvers. "George," she wrote to him during his travels, "if you want me to move to South Danvers and make a home for you among people who love you, I will do so."

While he was in Georgetown, Judith did everything possible to make him happy and comfortable. If her backward-looking sentiments occasionally irritated him, he never said so. One suspects that the sentimentality he himself sometimes expressed in his letters was merely a reflection of the flowery language popular in the nineteenth century. For even when no longer young, Peabody consistently looked forward. To him the past was the past and often best forgotten.

There is no reason to suppose that now, as he grew older, he seriously regretted not having married or recalled with any distress his broken engagement to Esther Hoppin. Judith said that he once referred to Esther as "the young lady whom he would have married had he been silly enough." Nevertheless, while he was in the States, Judith tried occasionally to comfort him for this disappointment which had happened so long ago. She assured him in words, as well as by her actions, of her deep devotion, and she told him that "one affection, at least, deeper, stronger, *steadier* than that of a wife" was his "through all his wanderings."

One cannot imagine the reserved George Peabody listening without embarrassment to such remarks even from Judith, for through the years he had become less and less inclined to discuss his personal affairs with anyone. Naturally, Judith had never heard any false or true rumors about a lady in Brighton or anywhere else. As far as she and the world were concerned, Peabody was a confirmed bachelor.

To Judith's friends, he appeared as a kind of conquering hero. They came to her house to see him, and other citizens of Georgetown, too, crowded around wherever Peabody went; everyone wanted to shake him by the hand. Nearby Newburyport—later he gave the town $10,000 for a library—hoped to receive him suitably, but instead of encouraging an official reception, he went over to the town casually by the 9 A.M. train one morning to see the Essex County Fair which was then in progress. How marvelous it was, when he remembered the long walks of his footsore youth, to find trains connecting these small New England towns.

The date fixed for Peabody's great civic welcome in Danvers was October 9, 1856. The town—renamed Peabody in 1868—had experienced a tremendous expansion since his boyhood. Then there had been 3,000 inhabitants; now there were more than 10,000. Since his youth the town had built seven churches; there had been two when he was a boy. In the early years of the century only two small schools, with an annual expenditure of $2,000, gave children a meager education. In 1856 the town had spent $10,000 on fifteen schools.

On the day of Peabody's civic reception he drove to Danvers from Georgetown with his sisters and nephews in an elegant carriage. He had acquired in England a sense of pageantry and decorum. The warm fall day showed off the town's preparations to advantage. For months, various committees had been at work to make the reception of their famous son a memorable occasion.

Flags were flying from every possible pole, roof, and balcony, and a welcoming arch had been erected at the entrance to Maple Street where Peabody's carriage stopped for the addresses by distinguished citizens of Danvers and other towns. Bands of uniformed firemen and cadets, school children waving American flags and Union Jacks, prominent citizens from as far away as Boston, marched in a procession of five thousand that followed Peabody's carriage. It was later estimated that twenty to thirty thousand people from Danvers and the neighboring area lined the route. In the evening, a large banquet was given in a tent and, except for the guests of honor, 1,500 citizens paid $1.50 each for tickets of admission to this dinner.

The speeches given during the day from a raised platform in front of the Peabody Institute by Governor Henry J. Gardner of Massachusetts and others praised Peabody at great length. He was obviously much moved as he responded to this acclaim. Later, there were cheers when he announced a gift of $10,000 for a branch library in North Danvers and promised to add $1,200 each year during his life.

In his speech he emphasized to "his young friends" in the audience the importance of education.

"To be truly great," he said, "it is not necessary to gain wealth or importance. Every boy may become a great man in whatever sphere Providence places him. Truth and integrity unsullied by unworthy acts, constitutes greatness."

Peabody's address and those of the others could in those days before microphones be heard by only few people, but no celebration would have been considered complete without long speeches. Alice L. Putnam, a seventeen-year-old high school girl from Salem, who had come to Danvers in an omnibus for the festivities, was deeply impressed.

"We could not hear the reception address . . . but witnessed the pantomine of gesture and read the accounts in the papers," she wrote afterward in a letter to a friend.

Though Alice and her friends did not know what Peabody was saying, they were pleased to have seen the great man.

He is, Alice wrote, "a fine looking man, quite tall and stout; he looked warm and dusty from his long ride [from Georgetown], but had a fine countenance." It was apparent to young Alice and to others in the crowd that Peabody was greatly moved. He "appeared very much affected," she concluded her letter, "and his hand trembled very much."

Danvers' welcome to Peabody was news and was reported in American and foreign papers. When young John Pierpont Morgan, then in Göttingen, read about it, he wrote to his cousin:

"Mr. Peabody's reception in Danvers must indeed have been a glorious affair. I should have liked immensely to have been present to have seen it. The report has been copied in several of the European journals, and very well spoken of. I trust Mr. P. did not have an attack of gout after the sumptuous dinner!"

Some American newspapers were not enthusiastic about the Danvers festivities. James Gordon Bennett was annoyed to learn that, on this occasion, some children had waved Union Jacks as well as the Stars and Stripes. Bennett's *Herald* recorded with irony that "the Financier was almost smothered with Flags, Beautiful Women, Bouquets, Lovely Babies and Banners." In his comment Bennett also mentioned that the Danvers celebration had cost the *Herald* between $200 and $300 in telegraph bills! "But," Bennett added condescendingly, "we are under some obligation to Mr. Peabody, and we think the money well laid out." Perhaps Bennett begrudged any outlay not connected with current political events, for 1856 was, after all, an election year.

Peabody himself did not worry about Bennett; he was fully occupied with his tight travel schedule. In mid-October he went first to Albany, N.Y., and to Buffalo, where he stopped briefly to call upon his old acquaintance Millard Fillmore, by then the defeated candidate for the presidency. Then Peabody traveled north to Toronto and Montreal, and in

November he returned to New York before going to Zanesville, Ohio, to see the members of his family there, and to Cleveland to visit Bishop Charles Pettit McIlvaine, the President of Kenyon College in Gambier, Ohio. Peabody, who had already met the Bishop several times in London, was always interested in Kenyon and ten years later he gave the college $25,000 to found a chair of mathematics and engineering.

In Zanesville, where he visited his brother Jeremiah and his family, he met—as has been mentioned—one relative toward whom he experienced a genuine and quite unexpected warmth of emotion. This was pretty nineteen-year-old Julia Adelaide Peabody, the daughter of his late brother David—the cause of so much anxiety while he lived—and his second wife Phebe. Peabody invited Julia to join him on his return journey East; she was with him when he visited Philadelphia, and he later sent her to a good school. Judith approved and, thinking of the past as usual, she wrote to her brother: "I trust that Julia will yet be a solace to your declining years, and by her affection wipe away the remembrance of the wrongs you have received from her father."

To Peabody, his niece Julia was a person in her own right and not merely David's daughter, and his capacity to experience this personal attachment for her surely made him feel younger and less locked up within himself. His fatherly association with this niece had filled him with deep satisfaction and given him something in 1856 which his business successes could not rival.

In the last weeks of 1856 and the first eight months of 1857—Peabody returned to England in August—he traveled and saw people continuously, except for days or occasionally weeks when he was confined to a hotel room with the gout which now frequently attacked his knee and made walking difficult. Despite this painful disability his travel itinerary was so strenuous that it would have staggered many younger and more robust men. The as yet half finished railway system in the Middle West made journeys distinctly uncomfortable, though as compared with transport in Peabody's youth, traveling seemed luxurious. It was wonderful to realize that Cincinnati was no longer the "Far West" and that the railway connecting that city with St. Louis "was almost completed." And when no "cars" were available there were always, for his journey to New Orleans for example, the paddle steamers on the great American river highways.

In November 1856, when Peabody returned to New York from Ohio, the severe cold was very bad for his gout. Nevertheless, after a brief rest at the Hotel St. Nicholas, he roused himself to go to Portland, Maine, for a visit with his sister Sophronia. After that he spent Thanksgiving Day in Georgetown with Judith and her family; then he went to Boston and New York before setting forth on a longer tour of the South and West.

His itinerary was impressive. A partial list of the cities included reflects his eagerness really to familiarize himself with America: he traveled to Philadelphia, Pittsburgh, and Harrisburg; to Baltimore and Washington; to Charleston, South Carolina; to Mobile, Alabama; to Natchez, Mississippi; then north to Cairo, Illinois; to St. Louis; to Terre Haute and Indianapolis.

Everywhere Peabody was received by city mayors, by presidents of chambers of commerce, by businessmen, and by men and women concerned with education. Often on arrival in a town Peabody was asked to be the guest of honor at a public dinner; these invitations were sincere expressions of admiration and respect.

"We welcome George Peabody," one was typically worded, "for his character as a man, merchant, and American for his courtesies to Americans abroad, for sustaining our commercial interests, and we invite him to a public dinner."

Peabody graciously replied to these invitations but he rarely accepted them. He preferred private and informal gatherings which were a more fruitful source of economic information about the city visited. On some of his trips he transacted business on the spot. In the spring, to mention one such instance, he and Curtis Miranda Lampson, then in America, went to Oswego, New York, where in Luther Wright's bank they discussed in a practical manner how to finance the completion of the railroad line from Syracuse to Oswego.

While he was traveling, letters were forwarded to Peabody. He kept in close touch with Junius Spencer Morgan who sent regular reports about the business in London by every vessel leaving England for the United States. Morgan, already interested in Cyrus W. Field's Atlantic Telegraph Company, of which Lampson was an active shareholder, had proposed Peabody as a director. Morgan also urged Peabody, while in America, to use his influence in Washington to obtain government support for the new steel process then being introduced in industry.

Peabody's correspondence during his travels was extensive. He had the habit of giving his undivided attention to every letter he was writing, to every interview, to every business meeting. While he was performing any task he concentrated on it alone, but what was in his mind early in 1857 was the great institute in Baltimore which for many years he had hoped to endow. His visit to Baltimore on January 26 was therefore of great importance to him; he cherished this Baltimore Institute, as well as the one in South Danvers, as long as he lived.

Peabody Institute of Baltimore

THE Peabody Institute of Baltimore was a cultural achievement large in its time. Though advised by others, George Peabody had outlined its general purpose and manner of operation; his vision gave it permanent form and substance, and without his financial backing the institute could not have been founded.

Later, Peabody's institute was, indirectly, to become the root of other great benefactions to Baltimore. From the institute was to come the Enoch Pratt Free Public Library, the finest in the state and one of the best in the whole country. And from Peabody's educational idea for Baltimore was also to emerge the first graduate university in the United States, the Johns Hopkins University, its medical school, and its hospital.

Peabody's original institute in Baltimore was a co-operative venture. Several farsighted and socially minded men joined with George Peabody in fashioning its form: John Pendleton Kennedy, William Edward Mayhew, Charles James Madison Eaton, Enoch Pratt among them. The problems and disagreements experienced by these trustees are reflected in the fact that almost ten years elapsed from the date of Peabody's founding letter, February 12, 1857, until the institute was finally opened to the public. Difficulties were faced by the men concerned with the institute soon after their plans were made. During the financial panic in the fall of 1857, the institute project was temporarily halted, for the trustees were confronting their own serious business troubles. Then there were times during the Civil War when the trustees of the institute were divided into hostile camps, and it seemed as though they would never again agree about anything.

Peabody's own faith in the ultimate success of the institute never wavered. Throughout his life he had a very special attachment to Baltimore and confidence in Baltimore people. For, from 1815, when he was only twenty, to 1837, when he was a mature man of forty-two, Baltimore had been his home and the center of his expanding mercantile business.

In Baltimore, he learned to understand himself and to appreciate his own abilities; the city had been the springboard of his success.

He had, by letter and in talks with men from Baltimore whom he had entertained in London, kept in close touch with the city, and for some years he had been aware that Baltimore's cultural and educational development had not kept pace with her remarkable commercial and economic growth. Since 1851 he had been seriously considering what could be done to remedy this situation.

In 1851 in London he had first discussed his plans with Charles James Madison Eaton, then president of the Baltimore Library Company. In 1854 he had talked to Reverdy Johnson, another Baltimorean visiting London, and in December of that year he had written to William Edward Mayhew, asking him to consult with John Pendleton Kennedy and other Baltimore friends about founding an institute in Baltimore. For two years there was no response. One has the impression that these Baltimore men were a bit slow, and when Kennedy, who kept a diary, was in London in 1856 Peabody said to him quite frankly, "I suppose you Baltimore people do not care to have an institution established among you, as I have heard nothing of the suggestion made through Mr. Mayhew some years ago."

Kennedy, trained as a lawyer, was more alert than were Johnson, Mayhew, or Eaton. He did not tend to pause between making up his mind and taking action. Kennedy was an unusual man in every way. Besides, he was a very old friend of Peabody. They had been comrades in a volunteer regiment during the War of 1812 and had then lived for a time in the same boarding house in Baltimore.

In the years that followed, Kennedy was not only a successful lawyer; he had also been a member of Congress from 1838 to 1848, and he had been Secretary of the Navy under President Fillmore from 1852 to 1853. In his spare time he wrote fiction and biography; his *Memoirs of the Life of William Wirt*, published in 1849, had established him as a Southern author of note.

Above all, Kennedy had vision. As a member of Congress he had made it possible for Samuel F. B. Morse to demonstrate his telegraph, and as Secretary of the Navy he had approved sending Commodore Matthew Calbraith Perry to the Far East to open up trade with Japan. Obviously Kennedy was just the man culturally equipped, and full of initiative, to help Peabody realize his plans for the Baltimore Institute.

Kennedy had long been conscious that the collection of books owned by the Library Company of Baltimore, founded in 1790 and not expanded since, was quite inadequate, and he and Eaton, president of the company, hoped that a merger of the library with the Maryland Historical Society would be possible. Beyond that, Kennedy had more far-reaching hopes for Baltimore. In his journal he had outlined lectures he wished to give in which he could point out how the city's cultural life could be improved. In one of these lectures he had suggested "sundry matters" in relation to Baltimore's institutions. These sundry matters included a plan for "a free Public Library, a Museum and a School of Art, and provision in the way of Lectures."

Kennedy therefore heard with deep satisfaction about Peabody's desire to found an institute in Baltimore. Heretofore the money needed for Kennedy's grand scheme had been lacking; now it was clear that Peabody would be responsible for the financial needs of the proposed institute. Kennedy, Mayhew, and Eaton outlined a plan and were ready to present it to Peabody when he came to Baltimore in late January and early February 1857.

Two elaborate receptions were given in Peabody's honor when he reached Baltimore. One on January 30 was given by the Maryland Historical Society and one a few days later, on February 2, given by the Institute for the Promotion of the Mechanic Arts. On both occasions there were many speeches that took up much time, but Peabody had an opportunity at these functions to meet old friends. After the reception at the Institute for the Promotion of the Mechanic Arts, Peabody conferred in private session with Kennedy, Eaton, and Mayhew. During these discussions the hopes for the founding of the Baltimore Institute took shape and became a reality. Peabody arranged to have Duncan, Sherman, and Company credit the trustees of the new institute with $300,000. At the same time he gave $1,200 annually for gold medals to "female high school graduates" in Baltimore, for he was ahead of his time in his support of the education of women.

It was time to draft the founding letter which would officially announce Peabody's gift of an institute to Baltimore, a letter which could be sent to the newspapers for publication. On February 9, 1857, Kennedy, Mayhew, and Eaton called on Peabody in his hotel. He was in bed with a swelling of the knee. For the biographer, quite without conscious reason, there are moments in the life of George Peabody which stand out vividly, as though held in a Victorian painting, and these final discussions in the Baltimore hotel room present such a picture: Peabody in bed, his bad knee resting on a cushion, his smooth, well-shaven face controlled but bearing the marks of pain, and around him his three friends, bending forward eagerly contemplating the final draft of the letter which represented their joint effort for the education of the ordinary people of Baltimore.

Important details still had to be decided, and the twenty-five trustees for the institute were to be selected from the 150 names submitted by Peabody to his friends. The draft of the founding letter, written by Kennedy, was submitted to Peabody, who approved it. He mentioned, however, as Kennedy later noted in his journal, that an important point had been omitted from this draft of the founding letter.

This point was "an injunction against the Institute's ever being used for the nurture of Sectarian theology or political dissension." On the contrary, as Peabody had said to Kennedy, the institute was always "to show itself, in every emergency, the firm defender of our 'Glorious Union.'"

In view of the later disharmony among the trustees during the Civil War, this last phrase had somewhat ironical connotation. But when the founding letter was published on February 12, 1857, Peabody and his friends did not foresee these difficulties. The founding letter set out in clear terms and great detail the provisions and purposes of the Peabody Institute of Baltimore.

The institute provided for a library, courses of lectures, an academy of music, a gallery of art, and prizes to encourage private and public school pupils. All departments, so it was first planned, were to be administered by the Maryland Historical Society under a governing body of twenty-five trustees. The institute was legally incorporated the next year, in 1858.

As the institute developed, this close connection with the Maryland Historical Society was to prove a stumbling block. Whether Peabody's new institute or the older society was to be dominant and how the lines of organization were to be drawn were questions which plagued the organizers for years. This problem was finally solved by Peabody himself in a practical manner: he gave $20,000 to the publication fund of the Maryland Historical Society. Henceforth, the Peabody Institute operated separately from the Historical Society, and each organization went its separate way.

Other growing pains of the institute developed during the selection of the site and the use of the building. Kennedy admitted in his journal that he, Eaton, and the other trustees had "been wrangling" about the site.

"Some of them," he recorded, "would make it [the institute building] a kind of literary and gossiping club house." Kennedy, on the other hand,

and luckily his view prevailed in the end, "wanted a large lot and arrangement for an Institution that would be national as well as local."

Kennedy urged the trustees to buy ground for the institute in the suburbs of Baltimore, where land was cheaper, but, finally on this point Eaton had his wish, and the trustees decided to purchase the Howard lot, at Charles Street and Mount Vernon Place, the present location of the Peabody Institute. Eaton wrote many letters to Peabody after he returned to London telling him about these differences; Kennedy, on the other hand, confined his annoyance to outbursts in his private journal.

Peabody was not surprised by the problems confronting the institute. Experience had taught him that one cannot have twenty-five trustees without arguments. He never forgot the human factor in any undertaking. But he was disappointed when, as has been said, it took almost ten years to complete the institute and open its doors to the public.

Two years after the publication of the founding letter in 1857 he realized that more than his original gift of $300,000 would be needed, and his endowment was increased to $500,000. In 1866 he raised it to $1,000,000, and finally in 1869, just before his death, his gift was increased to $1,400,000.

When Peabody returned to England, his agents, Henry Stevens and Horatio Gates Somerby, kept him in close touch with the needs of the institutes in Baltimore and in South Danvers. They had permanent instructions to notify him when interesting books or whole libraries were for sale. From an old institute being broken up in Islington, London, for example, he had his agent purchase fifty-four volumes of the London *Times*, volumes which covered the years 1834–60. This rare item was sent to the Baltimore Institute. In January 1864 he purchased in England two thousand volumes which were shipped to the South Danvers Institute.

There were few parallels to Peabody's gift to Baltimore. James Smithson, an Englishman, had endowed a scientific institution in Washington which was the basis of the Smithsonian Institution. Stephen Girard had founded a school for boys in Philadelphia, which developed into Girard College. Joshua Bates had endowed the Boston Public Library. The Peabody Institute of Baltimore, based largely on John Pendleton Kennedy's plan, was perhaps grander in its original design than any previous benefaction in America.

Looking back, in view of this great achievement, it may seem strange that Peabody did not remain in Baltimore until February 12, 1857, the day the founding letter was printed in the newspapers. He seemed to shun publicity, and by the time the letter was published he had left for Washington. He did not return to Baltimore until some months later. This visit to Baltimore occurred in the course of his long Southern tour, which preceded his departure for England from New York on the *Persia*.

The Panic and Recovery

In August 1857, when George Peabody returned to England from the United States, the financial panic of that year, a panic which had been threatened for some months, overwhelmed many banks and commercial firms in New York. Hundreds of business concerns in the United States and Europe were suddenly ruined, and the very foundations of George Peabody and Company in London were shaken.

The panic was caused by American speculation in western lands, by the growing demand for capital on the part of the new railroads, and by the rash overbuying of many goods in eastern cities. Money was dangerously scarce, business slumped, and many firms found it virtually impossible to collect outstanding debts.

A good wheat harvest in the United States, with wheat selling at high prices, might possibly have relieved the situation, but American wheat was not in demand in Europe. The harvests in Europe had been abundant, and, besides, Russian wheat was selling at lower prices than the American product.

In the United States, country bankers withdrew their accounts from New York banks to pay for produce moving from the interior of the country to the Atlantic coast. New York banks were therefore forced to reduce their loans, with the result that some railroad securities fell sharply. And, as so often happens in periods of financial stress, some unscrupulous administrators of various railroads, banks, and insurance companies pushed the vicious business cycle along and the situation deteriorated further.

To make matters worse, in August and September 1857 four packet ships bringing California gold to New York were late to arrive, while one of these vessels, with $1,600,000 in gold bullion aboard, sank during the journey. Then, on September 25 the Bank of Pennsylvania failed, and within four days the other banks in the state had closed. Finally, suspension became general throughout the country.

By mid-October, not surprisingly, the panic was felt in England; banks failed in Glasgow, Liverpool, and London. In other cities many commercial firms saw their work of a lifetime swept away. Much British capital was invested in bonds, and the serious situation of some railroads made it impossible for them to meet the annual obligations of their bonds. Thus British as well as American banks everywhere were affected by the slump in American securities.

Peabody described the "unparalleled gloom" which prevailed in London in a letter to his niece Julia, who was now his confidante:

What will happen, Heaven only knows. Lack of confidence . . . is universal here and in the United States. I hope my house will weather the storm. I *think* it will do so even though so many in debt to me cannot pay. If I fail I will bear it like a man. In my conscience I know I never deceived or injured another human being. . . . Nearly all the American houses in Europe have suspended operations and nothing but great strength can save them. It is the loss of *credit* of my house I fear.

The firm of George Peabody and Company was, as he had written to Julia, in serious trouble. The house of Baring held bills on the firm to the amount of £150,000 (then equivalent to $750,000) and was pressing for remittance. Peabody, on the other hand, had extended vast credit to at least one Boston house—Lawrence, Stone, and Company—which now could not pay its debts to him. So Peabody, unable to collect the capital owed to him, was in no position to meet Baring's demands.

It was clear that unless Peabody could secure a substantial loan, his firm would fail, and an equally distressing possibility for him was that the failure of George Peabody and Company would cause other firms involved in his financial house to fail. He had, however, been able through the years to safeguard much of his own private fortune.

"In any circumstances," he wrote to Julia during the panic, "only a small part of my private fortune will be lost. I will have enough for all my required purposes."

This in no way meant that Peabody was less concerned in saving his firm from calamity. There was only one institution from which the large amount of capital he needed might possibly be borrowed, and that was the Bank of England itself. Peabody's boldness and courage had increased with the years, and he applied at the Bank of England for a loan of £800,000 (equivalent to four million dollars).

For a week Peabody carried on delicate negotiations with officials of the Bank, and it was during this eventful week, which was to decide the future of George Peabody and Company, that some of his jealous commercial rivals tried to force him out of business. A confidential proposition was quietly relayed to his partner, Junius Spencer Morgan. Certain individuals, Morgan was told, would guarantee a loan to Peabody on condition that the firm of George Peabody and Company would cease doing business in London at the close of 1858! It is recorded that when Morgan brought this preposterous message to Peabody, "he was in a rage, like a wounded lion, and told Mr. Morgan to reply that *he dared them to cause his failure."*

By the middle of November, the Governors of the Bank of England had made up their minds to grant George Peabody and Company the loan Peabody wanted—four million dollars. His securities were sound, his firm had always been reliable and of great repute, and the guarantors for this loan were unimpeachable. Besides, Peabody's satisfactory transactions with the Bank in 1837, when he had come to the aid of the Brown Brothers' firm in Liverpool, were on record in the Bank of England's files.

Peabody had confounded his business rivals. Benjamin Moran, who was keeping up his secret diary warfare against Peabody, was furious. He had been spreading tales to Peabody's clients about the impending doom of the firm, and he now wrote angrily, "This [Bank of England loan] it appears, has been secured and once more the great American money swaggerer is able to hold up his head."

Peabody's success in obtaining this very large loan indicated not only the Bank of England's confidence in him but reflected as well the faith in his firm felt by many English clients. As a rule, the charter of the Bank did not permit the lending of money on any but English securities, and in Peabody's case, since the majority of his securities were American, at least some English guarantors were required. Therefore, some of his English connections had to be approached. Respect for the firm was enhanced when these English associates and several other commercial firms in London guaranteed £90,000 of the loan granted by the Bank of England.

The news that George Peabody and Company had received a loan from the Bank of England created a sensation in financial circles in New York and elsewhere in the United States. People in America were impressed by the significant fact that this assistance had been given so promptly. But news traveled slowly, and at first only garbled reports of the transaction were current. American newspaper clippings reached Peabody by every packet arriving from New York. John Pierpont Morgan, now sharing rooms in

New York with Peabody's young cousin, Joseph Peabody, sent Peabody the New York *Herald*, and from Charles Eaton in Baltimore he received the New York *Times*.

Some of these newspaper reports were fantastic. The New York *Times*, for example, stated that Peabody's acceptances—the bills for which he was liable—at the time of the loan amounted to £6,000,000 (then equivalent to $30,000,000). At Eaton's suggestion, to correct misstatements of this kind, Peabody himself wrote a courteous letter to the editor of the *Times*. This letter was published on February 9, 1858.

"With a few exceptions," Peabody stated,

the American press has extended me more sympathy than blame for my course in the panic. Your respectable journal's account in late December, 1857, of my house's acceptances of six million sterling is inaccurate. Here are the facts:

About November 20th, my house considered it prudent to borrow funds to protect our own credit and save many of our American correspondents unable to meet engagements. The bills my house was liable for at the time of the loan were £2,300,000, not £6,000,000. I applied for a loan of £800,000 from the Bank of England on good securities but have only taken £300,000 to this date. Of the £2,300,000 bills liable, my house paid more than £1,500,000 at the time of the loan. The strength of our correspondence is such that our losses will be but trifling. In justice to American credit and to my house these facts are at your disposal.

When Peabody's firm was "free from all danger," he wrote to his niece Julia explaining in simple terms what had happened. He wanted her to understand. The many gifts and attentions he sent her and his correspondence with her were, during the financial crisis, an important outlet for his private feelings. It was perhaps easier for him to maintain affectionate personal relations at a distance of 3,000 miles than face to face with another human being.

He was growing old gracefully—he was now sixty-three. He no longer dyed his hair, and when Julia, in an upsurge of Victorian sentimentality, asked him for a lock of his hair, he was glad to respond to her wish. She was delighted and mentioned the incident in a letter to her mother.

When I last wrote to Uncle, I told him that "Somebody once promised me a piece of his Hair, which I had never received," & in this [enclosed] note was a little folded paper labelled "Somebody's Hair." There is a little lock just as soft, and fine & white as it can be. I am going to have it put in a locket & wear it on my chain. He sent me also a Telegram [in code] which had travelled 2,700 miles of the Atlantic Cable. Of course I could not read it, but those who are initiated can.

The mention of a telegram to Julia shows that, with the panic behind him, Peabody was again concerned with current financial ventures such as the Atlantic Telegraph Company. George Peabody and Company had invested heavily in this company's stock and Peabody naturally followed with interest the reports of the laying of the cable in 1858. This great project did not succeed without difficulties, and when the cable was temporarily broken the following year, Peabody and his partner Morgan experienced periods of anxiety.

On the whole, however, business was running smoothly again, and Peabody resumed his social activities, receiving and helping a number of visiting Americans. He was particularly pleased to welcome to London his old friend John Pendleton Kennedy from Baltimore, who told him about the progress of the institute. The site had finally been chosen; the trustees, on March 9, 1858, had secured a charter of incorporation; and the construction of the building was to begin that year.

These developments seemed quite satisfactory, and the visit with Kennedy and other friends was a source of satisfaction. But in that summer after the panic Peabody experienced a personal disappointment. The London Fourth of July banquets, which he had enjoyed organizing and justifiably considered his own creation, were taken out of his hands by an American club called the "American Association in London," which was formed early in the year.

The membership of this club consisted chiefly of "new" Americans, businessmen who had settled in England recently and who resented the dominant position in commerce and banking, as well as in society, of the older, established Americans such as George Peabody, Joshua Bates, or Russell Sturgis. The younger men considered them autocratic, narrow minded, and obstructive.

The older Americans, very much Victorian gentlemen themselves, fitted unobtrusively into English social life and business, while the newer arrivals, more self-assertive and often critical of England, had not learned how to approach tactfully their English associates. Peabody also objected to the avowed intention of the new association to embark on public "charitable purposes." He and his friends had always believed that charity to individuals in distress should be kept private and confidential.

As was to be expected, Benjamin Moran, who personally disliked not only Peabody but most of the older generation of Americans, was one of the founders of the American Association. He himself kept in the background, for, as a secretary of the Legation, he could not too markedly favor the "new" Americans at the cost of the long-established and highly respected older members of the American community.

Moran chose Dr. J. Weldon Fell, an American physician practicing in London, to be the leading spirit of the new association. Dr. Fell, an old friend of Moran's, had attended Mrs. Moran until her death, and was, at the time, well known in London for his cancer cure experiments at the Middlesex Hospital.

Moran, Dr. Fell, and the other members of the association appreciated that their club would not have a good start without the official blessing of Peabody and his influential friends.

"Peabody the Great," as Moran sneeringly wrote in his diary when the club was founded, "was elected President and that is enough to damn the thing eternally."

Soon, however, Peabody, Bates, and Sturgis decided they would have nothing more to do with the association. They were convinced that the type of members the club was attracting would harm American prestige in London. They therefore veered away from the association, much to the annoyance of Moran and his associates.

Moran noted in his diary,

Old Peabody goes with Bates, and others of their stamp, against it [the American Association], as I expected. They are a mean souled set, who dislike all of decided character who will not follow them, and consequently oppose this, as they know it will put them in the background. Both Bates and Peabody are selfish and heartless men. They have led people heretofore & hate this scheme because it will destroy their rule.

Without the support of Peabody and other prominent Americans, the new association limped along and its members arranged a Fourth of July banquet. These plans did not, however, proceed smoothly, and the club members quarreled among themselves. Moran was indignant when he heard that his former friend Dr. Fell "had the impudence to wish to preside at the Fourth of July dinner. . . . He is an ignoramus and would disgrace us irretrievably."

Neither Fell nor Moran would give way. The Fourth of July party, so important to the new association, seemed doomed and the members took this failure very seriously. Finally, three members of the association's committee, in order to save the situation, approached Peabody and asked him whether he would agree "even at this late date" to preside at their Independence Day celebrations. The brashness of these "new" Americans was well illustrated by their assumption that they could deprive Peabody of "his" Fourth of July dinners, and yet ask him at the last minute to officiate at theirs.

His letter declining the invitation was written in his usual dignified manner.

I received your communication and your resolution inviting me to take the chair on the approaching celebration of American Independence. I'm gratified to learn that no hostility to me personally or the course of my previous Fourth of July dinners prompted the measure you adopted.

Taking into consideration the circumstances of your arrangements and the late period of your explanation, I respectfully decline.

Despite Peabody's refusal to attend, this first Fourth of July dinner organized by the American Association in 1858 went off quite well. General Robert Blair Campbell presided. There were many speeches which George Mifflin Dallas, then American Minister to the Court of St. James's, thought tedious and too long.

George Peabody took little notice of the antagonism shown toward himself and his friends by the members of the new American Association. He felt, when he thought about it at all, that their association could not in the long run be a great success without the support of more experienced men such as Bates, Sturgis, and himself.

He was right, for in a few years' time, as even Benjamin Moran admitted in his diary, the association, "at a meeting in March, 1860, was almost determined to dissolve."

Moran wrote,

The fact cannot be denied that we have failed. So far as I am able to account for this, the cause is simple. Our distinguished minister here and his hopeful son give the organization no approval, & Mr. Bates, Sturgis and others follow suit. These people shrug their shoulder when the Club is mentioned & cry it down: and as they disapprove, our countrymen follow their humane example and the Asso'n has thus obtained a bad name for no earthly cause beyond the fact that it did not originate with these poor fools. And then I regret to say, that the casual American visitor to London won't join us.

While the association was struggling for recognition in the summer of 1858, Peabody continued to entertain his friends as usual. On July 9, to mention one of his parties, he organized a banquet at the Crystal Palace to which he had invited fifty guests. A week later he arranged one of several dinners he gave that summer at the Star and Garter Hotel in Richmond. The efforts of the American Association had not succeeded in undermining his position as a host; his banquets continued to be among the most sought-after social functions in London. At a distance of more than a hundred years, and in view of Peabody's lasting influence as a philanthropist, this fact may seem of little importance, but to the former poor boy from Danvers his social success meant a great deal.

He was gratified to read in the New York *Times* a report from the London correspondent about one of his dinners:

If by circumstances Mr. Peabody was deprived of bringing his countrymen together on the Fourth of July, he has since made amends by two successful banquets, one at the Crystal Palace . . . and the other last night to a larger circle. . . . About thirty Britishers and sixty Americans enjoyed the grand dinner. John P. Kennedy of Baltimore was there and toasted the "City of London." Mr. Henry Raymond, Editor of the New York *Times*, toasted the Press. The guest of honor for whom the banquet was given was John Y. Mason, the United States Minister to France.

Peabody, puritanically upright in small as well as in important matters, would have been deeply shocked had he ever known that Benjamin Moran was continuously trying to spy on his private affairs. On one occasion, for example, three evenings after one of Peabody's dinners at the Star and Garter, Moran and an American friend happened to dine there. Moran was told by one of the waiters that they were in the room in which "the great American banker" usually gave his dinners. Moran questioned the waiter and later carefully made notes of the man's answers in his diary. He noted how many people had attended the dinner, what it had cost, and who had been the prominent guests. (In the middle of the twentieth century, Benjamin Moran would have made a good reporter for one of our less reputable newspapers.)

By the late summer of 1858 George Peabody had little time or inclination for social activities. His gout had become acute, and such energy as he could muster was needed in the office, for Junius Spencer Morgan had left for his annual visit to the United States, a visit always extremely useful to George Peabody and Company. Apart from attending to business, Morgan was very good about looking up Peabody's relatives in America and bringing him news of them when he returned to London. During that summer of 1858, for example, Morgan traveled as far "west" as Zanesville, Ohio, to pay a special visit to Peabody's beloved niece Julia and her mother.

Peabody, in London, was really ill. For days at a time his gout was so bad that he had to use crutches. His attacks often came upon him at night with an intense burning, wrenching pain in the ball of his great toe or some small joint, and the pain was often accompanied by fever. The prescribed treatment at the time was a careful diet and exercise in the fresh air.

Finally, early that fall, he decided to go to Vichy, France, to take the mineral water cure under the care of a medical specialist. By October his condition had improved sufficiently for him to return to London, though his hands and legs were still troublesome. A letter to William Wilson Corcoran reflected his state of mind. His letters to Corcoran were always very frank, even about his ailments. They were close friends, and both of them very much on their own. Corcoran's wife had died many years before. He had lost two of his children in infancy, and his life was centered on his daughter Louise Morris Corcoran, now twenty-one, whom Peabody affectionately called Loula or Louly. Loula had recently married a man from Louisiana, George Eustis, a lawyer and Congressman.

Peabody wrote to Corcoran,

I have been a great sufferer by rheumatic gout in my knees and arms, as also my right hand, for several months. I have been here [in Vichy] for three weeks for the benefit of the waters, and may remain a fortnight longer. I am now quite well, except my right hand, which is painful when I write, and I fear you will hardly be able to make out what I have written.

Though writing was difficult, Peabody enjoyed a regular correspondence with his family in America. Judith continued to send him news as well as accounts of the money he sent to her for herself and other relatives. Her allowance of $1,500 a year, and her annual expenditures for all Peabody's relatives, totaling $5,149.43 (as usual, pennies were carefully noted), were conscientiously listed in detail:

Othniel Charles Marsh	$715.00
Charles B. Peabody	$273.00
Judith, Ellen, and Arthur Peabody	$600.00
Robert Singleton Peabody	$481.78
George Peabody Russell	$679.95
Sophronia Peabody	$100.00
Mrs. Phebe Peabody	$400.00
Mrs. Tempy Jewett	$100.00
R. L. Daniels	$294.07
Mrs. Gogswell	$5.00
Benjamin C. Perkins	$200.00
Judith's allowance	$1,500.00

While he was ill, Peabody seemed to think with increasing affection about his family in America. His severe bout of illness in 1858 left its mark on him physically as well as psychologically. For the first time his mind turned with anticipation toward his retirement, and he wrote to Julia that when his partnership with Morgan expired in 1864, he contemplated leaving the business and returning to the United States, where he hoped to lead a quiet life of leisure.

In a letter to a young man, William Heath of Boston, who applied for a position with George Peabody and Company in London, Peabody mentioned his future retirement:

The influence of the panic year upon my feelings have been such as to greatly modify my ambitious views and I have fully determined not only to keep snug during the term of my present copartnership, but if my life is spared to its end, to then leave business entirely and shall most likely pass any remaining years that may be allotted me by Providence in my native land.

When he wrote this tired letter Peabody was obviously unaware that some of his greatest philanthropies were still to come, and that, despite increasing ill health, he would be busier than ever before in the years which remained to him.

Origin of the Peabody Homes of London

IN 1859 Peabody reached that unhappy state in the career of many busy men when he was forced to realize that he could no longer be as active as he had been. His energy had to be conserved, and this was easier to do away from his office where urgent problems confronted him daily.

He formed the habit of going to Harrogate for an occasional cure or spending weeks at a time in Brighton where he could relax. Occasionally he traveled farther afield, preferably to the Highlands of Scotland. Frequently he went abroad, to Aix-la-Chapelle or to other resorts which he hoped would benefit his health.

When he returned to London after any journey, he always attended to business as usual. He never neglected his office routine. In his private life he was less active, and he suffered one real deprivation: because of ill health he was now often obliged to forego social engagements with American and English friends, meetings which had meant so much to him when he was younger.

"At our age," he wrote to his old friend Corcoran, "we require change of air and scene, and to throw off our minds everything, in our power, tending to create annoyance or anxiety. I have been acting on this principle for a year or two past, and I now find my health greatly improved."

"But," he added with obvious regret, "while in town during the last season, I was deprived of my usual pleasure of entertaining, or, except occasionally, even calling upon my American friends."

Peabody soon learned that it was not easy to "throw off his mind" matters of annoyance or events which caused him anxiety. He was annoyed, for example, as the building of the Baltimore Institute progressed, when Charles Eaton sent him details about the disagreements among members of the committee, disagreements which were often smoothed over by the time Eaton's letters reached him. Nor was Peabody interested in the Maryland Historical Society's various proposals regarding the role the society wished to play or not to play in the affairs of the new institute. These somewhat acrimonious debates went on for years until, seven years later, the Historical Society finally withdrew.

In the meantime, Peabody had become bored with news of the society's quarrels. Finally he drafted a firm letter to Eaton, which, however, for the sake of peace, he did not send. This letter, which has been preserved, reflected Peabody's vexation; he emphasized that he was "a great lover of harmony." "I trust," he added, "that harmony will be preserved. . . . If there should be dissensions, do not write me anything about them. . . ."

Peabody was more angry than irritated by gossip published in the New York *Herald* in late 1859, asserting that there were serious differences between him and his partner Junius Spencer Morgan.

"There is a rumour," the *Herald* had stated, "that the firm of George Peabody and Company, is to be dissolved or remodelled." The *Herald* also published the ludicrous opinion that Peabody had great influence on the policy of the London *Times*. "This newspaper," the *Herald* wrote, "has been declining in influence because Mr. Sampson who writes the money articles has an American wife, and is intimate to the point of control with George Peabody."

These remarks about Peabody's influence on the London *Times* were so silly that they could not be taken seriously by anyone, for had they been true, as a friend wrote to Peabody, he would have been more powerful than Lord Palmerston.

The insinuations that Peabody and Morgan had quarreled were more serious, and though they were patently untrue, Peabody felt he must publicly refute them. His denial took the form of letters to the Baltimore *American* and to the New York *Times*.

In these letters Peabody categorically denied the rumors spread by the *Herald* and stated, among other things, that "Mr. Morgan joined his firm on October 1, 1854, and since that period our business has been most satisfactory to all parties interested, and a difference of opinion on the subject of its management has never occurred between Mr. Morgan and myself."

Actually Peabody's relations with Junius Spencer Morgan and with his son John Pierpont had never been closer. By 1859, the year of the *Herald*'s attacks, young John Pierpont, who was still sharing rooms with Peabody's young cousin Joseph in New York, was a private representative of Peabody and Company in that city. And when, a year later, John Pierpont founded his own firm, the business of this new company at first consisted chiefly in collecting outstanding accounts for George Peabody and Company and in making investments in the United States for the company in London.

George Peabody never understood why James Gordon Bennett, the editor of the New York *Herald*, attacked him. Peabody's young cousin, Joseph Peabody, attributed these offensive articles to Bennett's desire to incite controversy. He published startling gossip—whether factual or not—about prominent men; interest in his newspaper was thus created and as a result more papers were sold. In the middle of the twentieth century, these tactics are more common than they were a century ago, but probably Joseph Peabody's judgment of Bennett's policy was correct.

Peabody's prompt response to Bennett's article indicates the extent to which, despite his troublesome gout, he continued to look after his business. Yet, increasingly, he thought about his future retirement and his return to the United States. In 1859 he believed he might be able to settle his affairs and go home in a few years, and Judith, worried about his health, was urging him to spend his last years quietly with her.

The prospect of leaving England caused him to think with very special affection of London, where he has prospered for so many years. In recognition of what London had meant to him, he decided to give her citizens some gift which would be a lasting memento of his gratitude.

Two years before, Peabody had expressed this intention to John Pendleton Kennedy, and now, in 1859, he discussed his plan with his close friends Curtis Miranda Lampson and Bishop Charles Pettit McIlvaine, who was then in London on a visit. Later the Bishop returned to England as one of President Lincoln's unofficial emissaries whose purpose was to promote the Union cause in Great Britain.

Peabody mentioned one possible endowment for London to Lampson and another to the Bishop. He talked to Lampson about an elaborate scheme of drinking fountains which would benefit the people of London. Water would be centrally purified, then piped to a network of fountains to be erected in various parts of the city, so that passing Londoners could drink and refresh themselves. This idea of drinking fountains was finally abandoned, for Peabody agreed with Lampson that "something more immediately beneficial to the suffering and helpless poor might do more good."

Peabody's early talks with Bishop McIlvaine were concerned with the Ragged Schools, the foundation of which was originally inspired by Lord Shaftesbury. The Ragged Schools, maintained by the Ragged School Union for the children of the very poor, offered religious (Church of England) instruction, and some teaching of reading and writing.

Lord Shaftesbury, the great social reformer, then a man of sixty, was at the height of his powers. For almost twenty years he had been promoting various enlightened bills in the House of Commons. He worked unflaggingly for better medical care of the mentally ill, for limiting the working hours of women and young children to ten hours a day, for the regulation of conditions in workshops. He had supported Peel's repeal of the Corn Laws, and he had joined the Ragged School Union as early as 1843. He was, when Bishop McIlvaine made contact with him, particularly concerned with the terrible condition in which most industrial workers in London and other large cities were forced to live. Shaftesbury had used his influence for the benefit of the Common Lodging House Act and the Labouring Classes Lodging Houses Act, which were passed by Parliament in 1851.

The Ragged Schools, with which Lord Shaftesbury, despite his other interests, was always deeply concerned, presented many difficulties to the sponsors. Unless they had a missionary spirit, trained teachers did not accept positions in these institutions, and the government was apathetic toward the education of slum children. Poor citizens themselves were often antagonistic to the schools, for there was widespread child labor in England, and many parents preferred to send their young children out to work at a very early age to earn a few pennies rather than have them learn to read and write.

Peabody was aware of these problems when he discussed with Bishop McIlvaine the possibility of giving financial aid to the Ragged Schools, of establishing some kind of training for the teachers, of building new schools and thus creating an educational system that would benefit poor but bright and ambitious boys and girls.

McIlvaine wrote to Shaftesbury informing him that an as yet anonymous American philanthropist was considering a gift to the Ragged Schools. Shaftesbury replied that his first "hasty" reactions were negative, though whoever the American might be, "he thanked God for so good and generous a man." McIlvaine then called on Lord Shaftesbury and after a talk with him, explained to Peabody why Shaftesbury was not enthusiastic about a gift to the Ragged School Union.

"He does not think, at first view," the Bishop wrote to Peabody, "that the scheme would meet with favor. It would, by most persons, be pronounced unnecessary."

Shaftesbury's response reflected public opinion which then prevailed in England and which had not yet accepted the fact that a decent education was necessary for children, no matter how humble or poor their family background. Even Lord Shaftesbury, though he was one of the most farsighted reformers of the day, held the view, as he wrote to Bishop

McIlvaine, that "the education given by the Ragged Schools was sufficient for all practical purposes for those who were eventually to emigrate or to take up some service or other of an honest description."

Another point was brought forward by Lord Shaftesbury: he was convinced that the expansion of the Ragged School Union, a development which would result from Peabody's gift, would make the organization of the union too unwieldy. Shaftesbury felt that with expansion "the duties of supervision of the work would be beyond the duties of an ordinary committee."

Possibly Shaftesbury declined Peabody's offer of financial assistance to the Ragged Schools simply because, as he was not a young man and disliked change, he could not envisage a cumbersome reorganization of the Ragged School Union. On the other hand, deeply concerned with the shocking condition of London slums as he was, he may already have hoped to divert the gift of the American philanthropist to his scheme for improving housing conditions. He and other social reformers in England were trying to replace gradually the slums in London with model dwellings in the form of flats for the "deserving poor."

Reformers had been agitating for better housing in the large cities of England for thirty years. The Industrial Revolution and the coming of the railways had attracted people to London and greatly increased the population of the capital. Besides, the construction of the railways had made it necessary to demolish large sections of working-class housing.

The first private group formed to improve housing conditions, the Metropolitan Association for Improving the Dwellings of the Industrial Classes, had received a royal charter in 1842. And Miss Angela Georgina Burdett-Coutts, a great English philanthropist of the nineteenth century and a friend of Charles Dickens, had been concerned with housing reform since the eighteen forties.

One of the organizations interested in improved housing before Peabody became involved in the work was the Society for Improving the Conditions of the Labouring Classes, and during the Great Exhibition of 1851 the Prince Consort had asked an architect, Henry Roberts, to design blocks of model dwellings. Sir Sidney Hedley Waterlow, a pioneer in the building of model housing in England, was the first man to prove that a good housing project could pay its way commercially as well as be a great philanthropic enterprise. At his own expense he had erected a block of model dwellings in Mark Street, Finsbury, a district close to the inner City of London.

In other words, at the time that Peabody was contemplating his gift to London, housing reform was in the air, and Charles Dickens, Charles Kingsley, and John Ruskin were among the distinguished literary figures whose writing stirred the apathy of nineteenth-century England and roused concern for better living conditions of the laboring classes in London. Apart from painting a realistic picture of conditions in his novels, Dickens encouraged philanthropists to do something to alleviate the misery of the poor. "They will never save their children from the dreadful and unnatural mortality now prevalent," he wrote to Miss Burdett-Coutts, "or save themselves from untimely sickness and death, until they have cheap pure water in unlimited quantity, wholesome air, efficient drainage, and such alterations in building acts as shall preserve open space in the closest regions."

Late in January 1859, Bishop McIlvaine and Shaftesbury had a long and final meeting to discuss Peabody's proposed gift. In this conversation the Bishop told Shaftesbury about Peabody and emphasized Peabody's genuine desire to do something of lasting benefit for the people of London. Shaftesbury, understanding the magnitude of the donation contemplated by the American, described the distressing housing conditions of the working classes and stressed the urgent need for reform.

McIlvaine sent Peabody a report of his conference with Shaftesbury. The Bishop's report made it clear that he had been deeply moved by Shaftesbury's account of the slums of London. Peabody, too, was impressed by Shaftesbury's plea for housing reform. The idea of model dwellings had captured his imagination as well as his humanitarian impulse to help Londoners. The suggestion of providing drinking fountains or of assisting the Ragged Schools was no longer under discussion. Peabody and McIlvaine never forgot Shaftesbury's description of the slums.

"The dwelling," Shaftesbury had told the Bishop, "of all ages and both sexes, crowded in the same room, brothers and sisters in the same beds, the crimes, the fevers, the dreadful air, the prostration of all energy, the impossibility of doing the people any good till they can *dwell* better,"—none of these dreadful conditions could be improved, Shaftesbury had said, until better dwellings were somehow provided. Some of the men and women living in these degrading conditions had work and wages, Shaftesbury added, and they could have paid for better lodgings, but the lodgings available were too far away from their place of employment, so they were obliged to continue living in the slums.

After McIlvaine left England for America in March, Peabody's mind was made up; his gift to London would be a number of model dwellings. Education continued to be his greatest concern and interest, but he was aware that no children or adults anywhere could possibly be receptive to education while they lived in such slums. For only clean, self-respecting living conditions would combat filth, disease, the evils of unhealthy proximity in cramped quarters, and the apathetic stupor of these slum dwellers. Good housing, so Peabody had been convinced by Shaftesbury, was the first step toward social improvement of every kind, including education. Without respectable, clean homes even intelligent boys and girls would remain stupid and illiterate all their lives.

These were Peabody's convictions when in 1859 his gift to London, later known as the Peabody Donation Fund, was conceived. After announcing his earlier gift to the Baltimore Institute, Peabody had said to his sister Judith, "I shall have an immense amount more [of money] to give away. I do not know what I shall do with it."

He had now found another great purpose for his philanthropy, but before his scheme for London materialized, the Civil War in the United States, which had painful repercussions in England, intervened. Peabody's plans, including his hopes for his own retirement, were delayed, and it was not until March 1862 that the official founding letter for the model dwellings in London was published or the trustees of the fund were appointed.

The Beginning of the Civil War

1860 and 1861 were unhappy years for all the Americans in London, including George Peabody. Before the Civil War they had had many differences, but they were fundamentally united by the bonds of a common nationality, bonds which were especially strong in a country against which their grandfathers had fought for liberty. Though they were an extremely diversified group, representing different business or professional interests and coming from geographically separated sections of the United States, their feelings of a common national heritage had been strong and they had habitually turned to each other in times of trouble.

With the outbreak of the Civil War the American colony was sharply divided by the loyalty of some to the Union and others to the Confederacy. Our own generation witnessed a similar dilemma confronting "Free" Gaullist French and followers of Pétain and Vichy France.

By May 1860, when Abraham Lincoln was nominated on the third ballot by the Republican National Convention in Chicago the disharmony in the American community in London was already obvious. The "no extension of slavery" clause in the party platform was, of course, bitterly resented by Southerners everywhere.

Yet for some months, until the fall of that year, life in London seemed to continue as usual. As usual the Fourth of July banquet was organized by Moran and his friends; as usual he complained in his diary that George Peabody, Joshua Bates, and Russell Sturgis did not attend; and, as usual, many of the men who were present complained about the cost of the banquet (which was no longer given at Peabody's expense). For the cost of a ticket was one pound ($5.25), an enormous price more than a hundred years ago.

Though Peabody now had no time to bother about the Fourth of July dinner, he too in the first part of the year followed the usual pattern of his life made necessary because of his gout. He left an increasing number of day-to-day business decisions to his partner and was away from the capital frequently. From the end of May to the end of September he was in London only two weeks. The rest of the summer he spent in Brighton or Harrogate, and he stayed two whole months in the Highlands of Scotland, at Dunkeld, a village in Perthshire. He was aware that to preserve his health, such as it was, "he must make business subservient to health."

In Scotland he devoted much thought to family problems and wrote many letters to his relatives, especially to his niece Julia. He had the leisure to be almost a full-time patriarch, at least by correspondence. A straightforward reprimand was sent to his young cousin Joseph Peabody in New York, who had been negligent about writing to him. Joseph was also scolded for the poor quality of some nuts and apples which he had shipped to Peabody at his request in 1859, more than a year before. For George Peabody never forgot anything. Civil War might be threatening, but the nuts and apples sent by Joseph were still remembered.

His sister Judith was equally severe and, in that summer of 1860, her annoyance was centered on her nephew Othniel Charles Marsh, the budding scientist, because his education had cost twice as much during the preceding year as that of her own son George Peabody Russell, just graduated from Harvard, and one third more than that of Robert Singleton Peabody.

Judith was irritated, not only by Othniel's alleged extravagance, but by his apparent inability, or unwillingness, to keep accurate accounts. She wrote to George Peabody that Othniel Charles "was a good scholar, a smart energetic man, but in pecuniary matters he is decidedly Marshey." (This was a frank and unkind reference to Othniel's unfortunate father, Charles Marsh.)

It should be mentioned in this connection that Othniel Charles was no longer a boy but a man of twenty-nine. He had earned an excellent science degree at Yale and hoped, with the help of his uncle, to do graduate work at Yale's Sheffield Scientific School and prepare himself for a professorship of natural sciences at Yale. This would require a considerable sum of money—$500 a year or more—and his Aunt Judith did not encourage him to think that Uncle George would be glad to come to his assistance.

"I consider an irregular and careless way of keeping accounts as dishonesty," Judith had written to Othniel. "If I were to send the whole matter to your uncle . . . I should not wonder if it relieved you from further hard study!"

In another letter Judith presented to Othniel an image of an unapproachable and unsympathetic George Peabody. He is, she admonished

Othniel, "eagle-eyed, and if he thought you were laying up, at his expense, anything for your future benefit, and not expressly needed in your present studies, it would be greatly to your pecuniary disadvantage."

Othniel had apparently asked his Aunt Judith for money to buy mineral samples and scientific books, but Judith rejected this suggestion.

"Minerals," she wrote, "and books on that subject, are to you just what a law library is to George [her son, George Peabody Russell] and Singleton [Robert Singleton Peabody] and I am certain it would not do for *them* to get them. They are tools to work with—*after* the business is learned."

His aunt's reluctance to support his request did not prevent Othniel from writing directly to his uncle, and George Peabody received this letter while he was in the Highlands. He had his family records with him and studied them to see how much money he had so far given his nephew Othniel. The sums were most carefully noted, and every penny was, as usual, included in Peabody's accounts.

> In 1857 $726.84
>   1858 $700.95
>   1859 $774.90
>   1860 $920.03

Judith had been right when she said that George Peabody was "eagle-eyed" and extremely careful about the expenditure of dollars and cents, but she did not share his farsighted interest in Othniel's career nor understand the pride he took in the young man's success as an undergraduate at Yale. Besides, Othniel was his sister Mary's son, and though she had been dead for twenty-six years, she was one of the memories on which he dwelt with affection.

Peabody willingly agreed to finance Othniel Charles Marsh's graduate work and wrote to tell him of his intention. It must, however, have been hard for a man approaching thirty to have the money dispatched to his Aunt Judith who would then pass it on to him as though he were a child. But Peabody, consistently tactful, did not wish to make Judith unhappy.

He wrote to Othniel on September 28, praising his achievements at Yale. He said that he considered his nephew "worthy of his trust," but "requested that the young man would at all times treat his Aunt Russell with the utmost confidence with regard to expenses as she would, as usual, pay them as authorized by him [George Peabody] and consequently feel the responsibility of attending them."

When Peabody returned to London in October, a month before the

Birthplace of George Peabody, 205 Washington Street, Peabody (formerly Danvers), Massachusetts, and now the site of George Peabody House Civic Center.

Oil portrait of the young George Peabody. *Courtesy Archives of the Peabody Institute of the Johns Hopkins University. (Original in the Maryland Historical Society).*

Portrait of Elizabeth Knox (Mrs. George Carson), to whom George Peabody twice offered his hand. *Courtesy Archives of the Peabody Institute of the Johns Hopkins University.*

The Peabody Institute of Baltimore, at the corner of Charles and Monument Streets, c. 1866. *Courtesy the Peabody Institute of the Johns Hopkins University.*

Interior of the George Peabody Library of the Johns Hopkins University. *Courtesy Archives of the Peabody Institute of the Johns Hopkins University.*

The Peabody Homes of London in 1866. As of 1994, 26,000 people lived in the Peabody Homes of London.

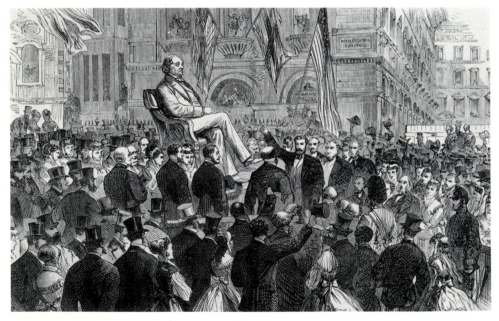

Dedication of the Peabody statue on London's Threadneedle Street in 1869.

Windsor Castle.

March 28. 1866.

The Queen hears that Mr. Peabody intends shortly to return to America & she would be sorry that he should leave England without being assured by herself how

Letter from Queen Victoria to George Peabody, March 28, 1866. *Courtesy Archives of Peabody College of Vanderbilt University. (For full text, see pages 148–49.)*

Autographed photograph of George Peabody about two years before
his death. *Courtesy Archives of the Peabody Institute of the Johns Hopkins
University.*

Engraved portrait of the original trustees of the Peabody Education Fund. *Left to right:* George Washington Riggs, George Peabody Russell, George N. Eaton, William Maxwell Evarts, William Alexander Graham, Edward A. Bradford, Charles Macalester John Henry Clifford, David G. Farragut, George Peabody, Hamilton Fish, Ulysses S. Grant, William Aiken, Robert Charles Winthrop, Charles Pettit McIlvaine, William Cabell Rives, Samuel Wetmore.

George Peabody's funeral at Westminster Abbey, London.

George Peabody's funeral at Harmony Grove Cemetery, Salem, Massachusetts.

presidential elections, tension was growing among his fellow countrymen in England. After Lincoln's election in November as the sixteeth President, events leading up to war followed quickly. On December 20, 1860, South Carolina seceded from the Union, and by the first of February, 1861, six other Southern states had followed: Georgia, Alabama, Florida, Mississippi, Louisiana, and Texas, and the Confederacy came into being. Then, only about six weeks after Lincoln's inauguration on March 4, Fort Sumter in Charleston harbor was fired upon on April 12, and the Civil War had begun.

In England the American Civil War was widely discussed, usually with passionate partisanship for one side or the other. The British upper classes on the whole—though there were notable exceptions—defended the South, which was considered to represent the cause of American gentlemen. Gladstone, at the time leader of the Opposition in Parliament, went so far as to accuse Palmerston, the Prime Minister, "of desiring the severance [of the Southern States] as a diminution of a dangerous power, but prudently holding his tongue."

The mass of the people, on the other hand, especially the laboring classes, favored the Union, to which hundreds of thousands of their countrymen had emigrated in search of freedom. The North seemed to them a bulwark of democracy and a haven for free labor. This point of view was also firmly supported by John Bright, the reformer, and Richard Cobden, the "Apostle of Free Trade."

Some English people who supported the Confederacy were pure romantics. They had Southern friends or had visited the South, where they had experienced the famous Southern hospitality. Thackeray, the novelist, was such a person. In his *Education,* Henry Adams described Thackeray's reactions to the Civil War. "The last time Henry Adams saw Thackeray," Adams wrote,

before his sudden death at Christmas in 1863, [he] was entering the house of Sir Henry Holland for an evening reception. Thackeray was pulling on his coat downstairs, laughing because, in his usual blind way, he had stumbled in the wrong house and not found it out till he shook hands with old Sir Henry . . . who was not the host he expected. Then his tone changed as he spoke of his— and Adams's—friend, Mrs. Frank Hampton, of South Carolina, whom he had loved as Sally Baxter and painted as Ethel Newcome. Though he had never quite forgiven her marriage, his warmth of feeling revived when he heard that she had died of consumption at Columbia while her parents and sister were refused permission to pass through the lines to see her. In speaking of it, Thackeray's voice trembled and his eyes filled with tears. The coarse cruelty of Lincoln and his hirelings was notorious. He never doubted that the Federals made a business of harrowing the tenderest feelings of women—particularly of women—in order to punish their opponents. On quite insufficient evidence he burst into violent reproach. Had Adams carried in his pocket the proofs that the reproach was unjust, he would have gained nothing by showing them. At that moment Thackeray, and all London society with him needed the nervous relief of expressing emotion; for if Mr. Lincoln was not what they said he was—what were they?

Members of the American community in London were, as a rule, even more emotional about the war than Thackeray and other Englishmen. After all, America was their country. Now Americans from the North and the South who had been friends or associates in London for years avoided each other, they declared that they hated each other, and, not surprisingly, an atmosphere bordering on hysteria prevailed.

Peabody, who had, by temperament, an aversion to extremes of any kind, tried to keep aloof from the feverish partisanship expressed by the people about him, especially by his fellow Americans. He made an effort not to align himself with the abolitionists, though he privately accepted their humanitarian ideals, nor with the states'-rights group. As a result, he was often called a "traitor" by Northerners.

Personally he suffered greatly when hostilities began, and his mental conflict was very painful. As the war progressed, he supported the North, but he could never forget his many Southern friends nor fail to see their point of view. And besides, he had lived and worked for more than twenty years in Baltimore, a Southern city, a city where he had experienced his first great success and to which he was grateful.

The Civil War was particularly distressing for Peabody because, rightly or wrongly, he was convinced that the conflict could have been avoided. As a businessman of international standing, he had settled many difficult commercial and financial situations by negotiation, and he never understood why it had not been possible for politicians to find some compromise acceptable to both the North and the South.

Months before war began, Peabody was fully aware of how disastrous it would be for business. "The threat of war," he wrote in a letter to the Boston *Courier*,

has already lost the European market for United States securities. Concession and compromise alone would reinstate our credit abroad. . . . If not and war comes it will destroy the credit of North and South alike in Europe. Worse, our prestige and pride will disappear. Second rate powers may insult our flag with impunity and first rate powers wipe away the Monroe Doctrine. May Providence prevent this.

When war came, he was never free from a feeling of deep depression. "The War might have been, should have been prevented," he once said during the War in an interview to the London correspondent of the New York *Post*. And he added sadly, "But the Union is cheap even at this great sacrifice of blood and treasure."

As the War progressed, Peabody increasingly hated these terrible sacrifices, but, as he had said to the *Post* correspondent, he was concerned with the United States as a whole. He wrote to his Baltimore friend John Pendleton Kennedy, who had taken the Union side, a step of which Peabody thoroughly approved, that he hoped one day the Peabody Institute in Baltimore might yet be dedicated to the United States as a united country.

Peabody eagerly questioned Americans newly arrived in London who had news of the wartime situation at home. He wished to be well informed and not guided merely by prejudice as were so many of his compatriots in London.

In October 1861, President Lincoln sent three emissaries to Europe to counteract the influence of Confederate agents in England and the Continent. They were Peabody's old friends, Bishop Charles Pettit McIlvaine and Thurlow Weed, and Archbishop Hughes, the Roman Catholic prelate of New York.

Peabody was glad to be helpful to these men and to their mission. Through him, Weed met several influential Englishmen, including Sir James Emerson Tennent, Lord Clarence Paget, Major General Sir John Wilson, and several Members of Parliament. One of these, William W. Torrens, later a trustee of the Peabody Donation Fund, a prominent Member of the House of Commons, spoke up for the Union cause in the House and supported the North in the English press.

Whenever Peabody and Weed met alone, Peabody tended to ask searching questions about the war and its conduct, and in these talks he displayed an objectivity which was not, of course, always pleasing to Weed, a staunch Union supporter and Lincoln emissary. Weed always tried to explain to Peabody why the war had been inevitable.

Weed later recalled one particularly interesting conversation he had with Peabody in December 1861. Weed had first called on the United States Minister, Charles Francis Adams, who had succeeded George Mifflin Dallas in May of that year. Then, after leaving the Legation, Weed drove to 22 Old Broad Street to see George Peabody. There were, as usual, a number of visitors in Peabody's office, anxious English and American merchants who had come to discuss their problems with Peabody and to ask him how the war would affect banking and trade.

Peabody himself was calm and apparently unworried. He took Weed into his private office and they sat down to talk. Weed made careful notes of their exchange of views and of another discussion they had on the following day. These conversations, important to an understanding of Peabody's attitude toward the war, were concise and to the point, and reflect the frankness with which he discussed the situation with Weed:

Peabody: I am surprised and I regret that the United States has become unnecessarily involved in Civil War.

Weed: Yes, it was a great calamity, but it was forced upon the North.

Peabody: Could not the Federal Government have avoided it?

Weed: That opens the whole question. If I can, I would like to explain why the rebellion was both premeditated and inevitable.

Peabody: I would like to hear your views. It will require strong evidence to satisfy me that wise and good men could not have prevented this unnatural war.

After these questions and answers, as Weed recorded them, he talked for twenty minutes unemotionally explaining to an attentive Peabody the historical background of events which led up to South Carolina's secession and finally to the war itself. Peabody listened without interrupting. When he finally responded to Weed's careful summary of the issues involved, Peabody spoke with great deliberation, obviously intending his remarks to be accepted by Weed as his final opinion of the war:

I think now that the Northern side is more in the right than I had thought it was. For several months my talks have been with Americans who presented the question differently. The business years of my life, as you know, were spent in Georgetown, District of Columbia, and in Baltimore. My private sympathies while in England have been against the institution of slavery. But during these many years of excitement on that subject I regarded the extremists of both sides as equally mischievous. This view made me think that extreme men were alike enemies of the Union.

Then, dropping his habitual reserve for a moment, Peabody spoke with a rare display of feeling.

"Mr. Weed," he said, "my devotion to our Government and Union is so strong, that, painful as the thought of war with our brothers is, if I were at home, I should stand by the Government. Whatever I can do, here and now for the Union cause, I will cheerfully do."

Unfortunately, just at this time when Peabody had reluctantly admitted his support of the Union, he became personally involved in the *Trent* affair, which seriously threatened the peace between England and the Union. One of the men directly concerned with this affair was George Eustis, son-in-law of Peabody's old friend William Wilson Corcoran and husband of "Loula" Corcoran, of whom Peabody was so fond. Peabody's solicitous interest in Eustis during this affair caused a number of people to be convinced that he was pro-Confederate and a traitor to the Union cause.

The indirect cause of the *Trent* affair was the sending of Southern agents to Europe. At the outbreak of war, the Confederacy had sent three such emissaries: Pierre A. Rost, William L. Yancey, and A. Dudley Mann. A few months later these agents were followed by two special commissioners, James M. Mason of Virginia was sent to England; and John Slidell of Louisiana to France.

Mason's secretary was J. E. McFarland; Slidell's secretary was Loula Corcoran's husband, George Eustis. The Confederate agents and their parties managed to slip through the Union blockade and arrived in Havana, Cuba, where they boarded a British mailpacket, the *Trent*.

At noon on November 8, 1861, Captain Wilkes, commander of the Union sloop *San Jacinto*, stopped the *Trent*, commanded by Captain Williams, by firing a shot across her bow. Wilkes then sent Lieutenant Fairfax of the *San Jacinto*, a Virginian who was fighting for the Union, aboard the *Trent*. Fairfax's orders were to arrest Mason, Slidell, McFarland, and George Eustis, take them to the *San Jacinto* and then transport them back to America as prisoners of war.

Mason, who happened to be an old friend of Lieutenant Fairfax and was also related to him by marriage, was polite and silent. Slidell, on the other hand, whose wife and daughter were traveling with him, was very angry and excited when he and the other Confederate diplomats were ordered aboard the *San Jacinto*. When the vessel reached America, Mason, Slidell, and Eustis and McFarland were later held under arrest at Fort Warren in Massachusetts.

News of the arrest of passengers on the *Trent*, a British vessel, soon swept through the United States and England. Northern extremists rejoiced and made a hero of Captain Wilkes, who had acted entirely on his own initiative and without official orders from the Navy Department or the Union Government. More thoughtful people in the North, however, realized that this high-handed breach of neutral rights and the stopping of a British ship had been a serious error of judgment on the part of Captain Wilkes.

When Reuter's telegram announced the seizure of Mason and Slidell, people in England were enraged by Wilkes's action. The British Navy had been insulted and public opinion grew increasingly hostile, especially among English supporters of the Confederacy. There was a threat of war between the Union and England.

Thurlow Weed, with the help of William W. Torrens, the pro-Union Member of Parliament, secured an interview after the *Trent* affair with Lord John Russell, then British Foreign Minister in the second Palmerston administration.

Russell told Weed frankly that he considered the seizure of passengers on the *Trent* as unauthorized and illegal and a breach of the rights of Great Britain, a neutral country. He also delicately reminded Weed that in the past the British seizures of men from American ships on the ground that they were British subjects had finally caused the United States to resort to the War of 1812. Russell added that an armed conflict might be avoided by the release of Mason and Slidell.

Weed and Lord John Russell parted with diplomatically worded assurances of goodwill on both sides, and Mason and Slidell were in fact released early in the following year, 1862.

Russell's actively hostile attitude toward the Union and his efforts for intervention were not fully appreciated when he gave this interview to Weed. The details of Russell's intentions remained a diplomatic secret for more than two decades, though in July 1862 it had been apparent that he had done nothing to prevent the escape from British waters of the Confederate warship *Alabama*.

Before the release of the two Confederate agents taken prisoner during the *Trent* affair, wild rumors circulated in London. According to one story, told and retold in England, Captain Williams of the *Trent* stood in front of the Union men from the *San Jacinto* who were alleged to have been menacing Slidell's daughter with fixed bayonets. "Back, you damned cowardly poltroons," Captain Williams was reported to have said to the Union naval officers, including Lieutenant Fairfax.

In London, men in the streets and in clubs repeated to each other sensational reports about the *Trent* affair, and passengers on the *Trent* who had actually witnessed the incident were questioned wherever they went. On one occasion Peabody's name was brought into these discussions. Captain Williams of the *Trent* was asked at a dinner party what had actually occurred. Williams claimed that when Lieutenant Fairfax of the *San Jacinto* came aboard the *Trent* demanding to see the Confederate emissaries, and the men appeared on deck, Miss Slidell clung, weeping, to her father. After Fairfax had separated her from her father, so Captain Williams alleged, she slapped his face.

At this distance of time, it is difficult to understand why this alleged slapping of Fairfax's face was considered important, but it was obviously taken seriously, and Captain Williams's account of the incident was printed in the Liverpool *Daily Post*. Trying to be fair, however, the *Daily Post* also published a contradiction of Williams's version of the incident, and this contradiction, the paper added, was based on the authority of a Member of Parliament who, it was alleged, had *his* information "from George Peabody, the well-known banker and merchant."

Peabody was angered by these false allegations and by the stupid publicity. The fuss and bother, the hearsay gossip, seemed to go on and on. A Mr. Allen S. Hanckel, who claimed to have been a passenger on the *Trent*, wrote a sharp note to Peabody, blaming him for having betrayed a confidence about the events on the *Trent*, a confidence, so Hanckel alleged, that Peabody had obtained from Miss Slidell and her mother, who were then in London. In his letter, Hanckel rudely accused Peabody of having made a most extraordinary use of a young lady's unguarded conversation in her private drawing room. Hanckel claimed that Peabody had "called on Mrs. Slidell, and behaved ungentlemanly." All this was pure invention. Later Mr. Hanckel admitted as much, but then blamed Junius Spencer Morgan instead of Peabody for "having burst uninvited into Mrs. Slidell's room."

Peabody was irritated by the fabrications in Hanckel's communication, and he was made uneasy by the implied violence in the man's letters, for Hanckel had threatened to call at 22 Old Broad Street. So Peabody decided to end the matter. He wrote a letter, written in the third person, which was to be handed to Hanckel should he ever appear at the office of George Peabody and Company.

This letter stated that if Mr. Hanckel wished to see Mr. Peabody he could do so only before witnesses, and that he must "apologise to Mr. Peabody and his partner, Mr. Morgan, for the unwarrantable liberty he had taken with their names." In fact, Mr. Hanckel, probably off on another wild goose chase, never came to 22 Old Broad Street, and he was soon forgotten.

Peabody was impatient, not only with Hanckel and his kind, but with the wave of emotionalism engendered by the war in usually well-balanced men and women. He did not understand the psychology of war and the effects it had on so many people. He wrote with unconcealed annoyance to William Wilson Corcoran, "You cannot conceive of the nonsense there is among our strong-minded women and weak-minded men."

The nervous strain Peabody was experiencing was again reflected in his health. Besides, toward the end of 1861, an atmosphere of deep gloom settled down on England. On December 14 the Prince Consort had died of typhoid fever at Windsor Castle. London was draped in black. Men and women who could afford to do so wore black mourning clothes, and all social functions were canceled. It was indeed a depressing Christmas, especially as a thick fog had descended on the capital.

Early in 1862, not surprisingly, Peabody was confined to his room for ten days with a painful attack of gout in his feet and knees, and he was so weak and nervous that writing became increasingly difficult. This did not prevent his trying to keep up with his correspondence.

He learned with relief of the release of Loula's husband, George Eustis. "I have never for a moment," he wrote to her on January 11, 1862, "lost my confidence that such [Eustis's release] would be the case, for mad as I think my countrymen have acted in bringing about the dreadful war that now exists, I could not suppose that they would voluntarily place themselves in a position to be entirely *crushed* by England."

This was a very outspoken remark to the wife of a Confederate in time of war, but it was typical of George Peabody. For there was no doubt about it, as he grew older he suffered fools even less gladly than he had when he was younger, and as the war went on, he was increasingly given to plain speaking whenever his countrymen, Confederate or Union, had, in his opinion, made fools of themselves.

As a result, Peabody, in many circles, was not popular during the war. In fact, because of his continued loyalty to Southern friends, he was more and more often accused of being a traitor to the Union cause. If a man did not, as it were, continuously wave the Stars and Stripes, he was considered by ardent Union men to be disloyal. Peabody's detractors had obviously not been told how helpful he had been to Thurlow Weed and the other emissaries from Washington.

Before the war ended, there were many men who accused Peabody of being a Confederate sympathizer. Benjamin Moran, as was to be expected, supported this point of view; Moran also said that Peabody was two-faced. Moran wrote venomously that "Peabody's whole manner is that of a hypocrite, and he is carrying water on both shoulders, being determined to stand well on both sides, in any event."

Other, more sensible men, too, could not understand Peabody's apparently neutral attitude during the war. John Bigelow, United States Consul General in Paris, went so far as to write confidentially to Secretary of State William Henry Seward that Peabody exaggerated Federal reverses in order to cause financial panic, and so to reap a personal fortune.

There was never any truth whatsoever in this accusation, but the charge has persisted. Carl Sandburg, in his biography of Abraham Lincoln published in 1939, quoted an unverified statement published in the *Springfield Republican* after the Civil War (October 27, 1866), which claimed that Peabody's and Morgan's New York and London offices deliberately weakened the Union's financial position in order to make profits for their firm.

Oddly enough, these critics of Peabody and Morgan failed to point out that the firm could not possibly have made money on American securities during the Civil War, because the sale of such securities was no longer possible in 1861 and 1862. Even the threat of war, as Peabody had pointed out in his letter to the Boston *Courier*, had lost the European market for American securities, and the Civil War had caused more and more European investors to dispose of their American holdings instead of buying new ones. The flow of capital to the United States did not begin again until the Union victory was assured in 1864.

Peabody was also accused during the war and later of having made a fortune speculating in Confederate bonds. This was not true. Whatever his sentiments about Southern friends, Peabody's business acumen was as great as ever. He never mixed sentiment and business, and from the beginning of the war, when many influential Englishmen believed that "Jefferson Davis could create a nation," it was apparent to Peabody that the Confederacy was not viable from an economic point of view. Without the North and its industries, he was sure, the South could not win, and its bonds were therefore not a promising investment. Peabody did not invest in Confederate bonds even in the summer of 1862 at the time of the great Union disaster at Bull Run in August or during Lee's invasion of Maryland early in September.

Peabody did, however, acquire enough Confederate bonds to win a gamble—more a bet than a speculation—which netted him $60,000. When he was in New York after the War, in 1866 and 1867, he told friends about this gamble.

He described how, during the war, agents of the Confederate government called at his office asking him to negotiate a loan for the Confederacy in England. Peabody refused and told them severely that, in his opinion, "any American should be ashamed to have anything to do with an attempt to break up and destroy such a [Union] Government as they enjoyed."

When the Confederate emissaries left Peabody's office, they went to see the English bankers who, they hoped, would give financial aid to the South. The sympathy of many English capitalists at the time was with the Confederacy, and the agents succeeded in enlisting four or five London financiers willing to negotiate with the Confederacy a loan of $75,000,000, receiving as security bonds at fifty cents on the dollar.

Two of the English capitalists, however, acquaintances of George Peabody, decided to consult him before finally signing the papers and closing the deal. After they had explained their problem to him, they were somewhat startled when he asked them why they were willing to pay fifty cents on the dollar for Confederate bonds, when, by waiting a year, they would certainly be able to get them for twenty-five or thirty cents.

"You do not believe do you, Mr. Peabody," one of the Englishmen asked incredulously, "that these bonds can be bought a year hence for that price?"

"I certainly do," was Peabody's firm answer, "and to prove that I am sincere, I will stipulate to sell you a million dollars worth in one year from today at 25 cents on the dollar."

The Englishmen did not quite believe Peabody, but he had made them feel uncertain, and they did not, in the end, promote the proposed loan to the Confederacy.

"But to show that nevertheless they had no faith in what I had said about the future value of the bonds," Peabody later stated in describing this incident, "they were both anxious to accept my offer, and require me to reduce my stipulation to writing. I did so."

"The year came round," Peabody concluded in his account of his one gamble with Confederate bonds, "and Confederate bonds were worth less than even I anticipated." He held the Englishmen to their bargain and received $60,000 from them in fulfillment of it, "and this," he emphasized, "was all the money I ever made by speculating on the bonds of the Confederacy."

During the first week of March 1862, Peabody heard about the Union victory in Tennessee. General Grant had taken Fort Henry on February 6 and Fort Donelson on February 15. These Union victories, so Peabody realized, had created an opening for the advance of the Army of the West into Tennessee and Mississippi.

Peabody heard the news from his agents a few hours before it was made public. He went at once to the American Legation to inform the American Minister, Charles Francis Adams. That evening a group of American Unionists and English sympathizers met together at the legation. Peabody came with Curtis Miranda Lampson, Junius Spencer Morgan, Thurlow Weed, Bishop Charles Pettit McIlvaine, and others. It is obvious that Peabody would not have been included in this group of close friends and staunch Union supporters, had he not, despite his frequent differences with them regarding policy, been fundamentally in agreement with the North.

Some years later, in recalling this meeting at the American Legation, Thurlow Weed paid a tribute to Peabody's fundamental loyalty to the Union during the Civil War:

> I know of no more unerring test of men's real sentiment and sympathy in a season of war than their manner of receiving good news. . . . Tried by this test, Mr. Peabody's sympathies were loyal, for he voluntarily came out of his way to bring news of an important Union victory; though he never ceased as often as he had occasion to speak on the subject, to deplore the war.

The Peabody Donation Fund:
Homes for the Poor of London

IT was typical of George Peabody that, during the anxious years of the Civil War, he sought relief in considering ways and means by which he could do good in the future when hostilities would at last have ended. And so, at the height of excitement caused by the *Trent* affair, in January 1862, he began to make definite arrangements for the Peabody Donation Fund, his gift of model dwellings for London.

On January 16 and 17, 1862, he conferred with Sir Curtis Miranda Lampson, Junius Spencer Morgan, Thurlow Weed, Sir James Emerson Tennent, and Charles Francis Adams, and discussed with them his contemplated gift to Londoners. Before the scheme for this endowment could be finally settled, certain details had to be taken into consideration. Whom would Peabody choose as trustees, and when he had made his choice, would the men selected be willing to serve? What legal procedure should be adopted?

Important, too, was the timing of the announcement of this gift, for the *Trent* affair was, at the time, causing Anglo-American relations to be so strained that the proud British public might not have welcomed a philanthropic gesture by an American. The London *Times*, particularly anti-American as it was, might have scoffed at the gift, or ignored it, and this would have been a bad sendoff for the plan.

A hint of Peabody's intentions had appeared in a letter from Thurlow Weed published in the Albany *Evening Journal* earlier in January. In this letter, Weed had stated that George Peabody was contemplating a large endowment to be used for the poor of London. Weed's notice, however, did not attract much attention, and was not quoted in the London *Times* until more than a month later.

Peabody was aware that his official letter announcing the gift to London must be carefully worded before it was published in the leading newspapers in England and the United States. He decided to address this letter to Adams, Lord Stanley (president of the Board of Control), Tennent, Lampson, and Morgan and to ask these men to act as trustees for his foundation. He knew that all but Stanley would agree at once, but that Stanley's position as a member of the British Government, and the prevalent tension between England and the United States, would prevent his accepting the invitation without careful thought.

In the early evening of January 16, Peabody and Weed met in the Old Broad Street office. Peabody showed Weed the letter he had drafted. Weed approved it, and Peabody then withdrew to his inner office and carefully wrote out his founding letter on half sheets of paper with wide margins for possible corrections.

Weed had agreed with the final letter; then he and Peabody asked Curtis Miranda Lampson and James Emerson Tennent to join them. When they, too, agreed, Peabody asked his three friends to go without him to consult with the American Minister, Charles Francis Adams. Peabody left the final decision regarding the founding letter and the date of the official announcement of his plans to these four men and to Bishop McIlvaine, who was to join them at the legation.

After a lengthy discussion with Charles Francis Adams, it was decided that the announcement of Peabody's gift should be postponed, as Anglo-American relations were again very tense. Peabody agreed entirely with this decision. Peabody wrote to Weed,

Two days before, we thought it exactly the right time [to announce his gift], but one cloud between this country and ours is no sooner disposed than another appears. Today the "Times" and "Post" are at us again backed by little dogs and . . . ugly extracts from the "World" and other New York papers referring to this country makes the feeling as bad as it was before the Trent affair closed.

Peabody was referring to the friction created by a most unfortunate remark alleged to have been made by Secretary of State William Henry Seward to the Duke of Newcastle. This remark now became public knowledge. Seward, antagonistic toward England since 1850, was reported to have said to Newcastle that, in his opinion, civil war in the United States could be avoided by fomenting a quarrel, and then a war, against England. Newcastle, who was then Colonial Secretary, had taken this remark seriously—as indeed it may have been intended—and the "Newcastle Story" was published with relish by the London *Times*.

Thurlow Weed, who had some years before used his considerable political influence in New York to help Seward's election as governor of the state, made light of Seward's faux pas and called his remark to Newcastle "a bit of humour." Nevertheless, Weed agreed that the announcement of Peabody's gift should be postponed until Seward's tactlessness was forgiven if not forgotten.

It was not until March 12, 1862, that Peabody and his associates formally announced his gift. By March 15 the trustees, apart from Lord Stanley, had signed a letter of acceptance, and Stanley added his signature on March 25.

On Wednesday, March 26, 1862, the founding letter was finally published in the London *Times*, and soon other English newspapers, such as the *Post, Herald, Daily News, Advertiser*, and *Telegraph*, included the letter in their columns. Originally Peabody had planned a gift of £100,000, but he had revised his intentions and his donation was to be £150,000 (then equivalent to $750,000) instead. Later he increased this gift to £500,000.

In the long founding letter, addressed to Adams, Stanley, Lampson, Tennent, and Morgan, Peabody declared his intention of "relieving the poor and needy of this great city, and to promote their comfort and happiness." As usual, in connection with his philanthropies, Peabody gave only a few instructions to the newly appointed trustees, and he imposed only three conditions.

He stipulated first that the beneficiaries of his donation fund should be Londoners "by birth or residence"; secondly, he "excluded from the administration of this Fund the influence of sectarian religion and exclusive party politics." The third condition was that "the sole qualification for participation in the Fund was that the individual be poor, have moral character, and be a good member of society. No one should be excluded on grounds of religious belief or political bias."

The Charity Commissioners who were then, and are still, the official body responsible for the acceptance and administration of charities in Great Britain, began to arrange for the legal acceptance of Peabody's gift to London. Tennent had discussed the matter with the Commissioners, who, so he reported to Peabody, told him that "in the whole range of charities in England there is nothing to compare with the disinterestedness and magnitude of your gift."

The Charity Commissioners encountered some problems when, with the help of Sir James Emerson Tennent, they drafted the trust deed for the Peabody Donation Fund. There was no legal precedent for such a gift. The Mortmain Acts, which made provision for the legal disposition of a dead Englishman's estate, were quite clear, but Peabody was a foreigner giving away £150,000 while he lived, and in a country not his own. An understanding of international law was required to enable the Commissioners to arrange for the administration of the fund by the trustees, and it was some time before the legal difficulties had been overcome and the donation fund was formally accepted.

Another problem, too, had to be solved: whom did Peabody mean by "the poor" of London? And which of the poor were eligible for the new dwellings contemplated? Some "poor" people had no income whatsoever, some had jobs and worked, some were crippled and incapacitated, some were blind and had never worked. Finally, the trustees decided to provide inexpensive dwellings, not for people requiring charity, but for workmen and their families who were in employment but had very low incomes. This decision was obviously in accordance with Peabody's own wishes, for, throughout his life, what he desired was to assist those poor people who tried to help themselves and, with his help, were potentially able to do so.

The Charity Commissioners' discussions about the donation fund were held in private, and the general public knew only that a tremendously generous contribution to London workingclass men and women had been made by a wealthy American investment banker. News of his generosity published in many newspapers captured the imagination of ordinary Englishmen. The social reformers were naturally delighted; and in the United States and other countries there was now universal acclaim for Peabody. Apart from welcoming the donation fund itself, sensible people were made happy by any gesture which alleviated, even temporarily, the tension which was causing friction between the United States and England during the Civil War.

A few individuals, of course, such as Benjamin Moran, interpreted Peabody's munificence as "self-glorification," and thought he should have postponed the announcement until the building plans for the workers' dwellings were complete. Such criticism was in fact based on ignorance of the situation, for until the gift had been officially accepted by the Charity Commissioners no concrete arrangements were possible.

Peabody was amazed by the publicity his gift to London had evoked. He was in Bath at the time and wrote to a friend that he had not the "least conception that it would cause so much excitement over the country."

Peabody could not possibly have foreseen the tremendous scope and future of his donation fund. True, before his death he increased the fund from £150,000 to £500,000, but the growth of his project, so admirably administered by succeeding generations of trustees, was beyond his imagination. By 1882 the fund owned 3,500 dwellings and housed more than 14,600 people; by 1914 there were 6,400 Peabody dwellings, and by 1939 there were more than 8,000. Hitler's war put a temporary stop to expansion, and thirty blocks of apartments and fourteen cottages were destroyed in the bombing. As a result, at the end of the war in 1945 the number of Peabody dwellings had decreased to 7,400.

Shortage of labor and materials immediately after World War II prevented new building for some years. Then work was resumed and in 1951 the magnificent new thirteen-story Peabody flats were erected in Roscoe Street, in Finsbury, near the inner City of London. The shrewdness with which the trustees had continued to handle Peabody's original gift is indicated by the fact that these flats alone cost £650,000, considerably more than Peabody's original endowment.

On July 11, 1962, Queen Elizabeth, the Queen Mother, unveiled a plaque honoring George Peabody at another new Peabody Estate, that in Blackfriars. The speeches made on this occasion, the centenary celebration of George Peabody's Donation Fund, made it clear that a hundred years later he is remembered with profound gratitude by the people of London. Earl Jellicoe, at the time in 1962 Joint Parliamentary Secretary at the Ministry of Housing, paid tribute to George Peabody:

Few men have brought to the disbursement of a great fortune such imagination—such a sense of creative purpose—as did George Peabody. . . . We are celebrating the Centenary of one of the most striking and successful products of his wisdom and generosity, and because I believe that the wider movement which he ignited has a great role to play in the future—it is for these reasons that it is a very real pleasure for me to ask you to rise and to drink the toast of "The Founder and the Fund."

CHAPTER 17

Freedom of the City of London

THE announcement of Peabody's gift to London, establishing his fame as an international philanthropist, was welcomed by men of good will, whether supporters of the Confederacy or the Union. The donation fund was accepted as an American philanthropy, and for a moment, by social reformers at least, the conflict separating the States was ignored.

For well-educated Englishmen, a letter published in the *Times* is an expression of strong feelings about any subject of civic interest. Now, as was to be expected, the *Times* received many letters urging that some form of public thanks to Peabody be organized.

One member of the Court of Common Council, the governing body of the Corporation of the City of London, took up this suggestion. On March 31, 1862, a representative of the Court of Common Council called on Curtis Miranda Lampson asking him, as Peabody's old friend, whether he thought Peabody would accept the honor of the Freedom of the City.

I have just had a call from a gentleman connected with the Corporation [Lampson informed Peabody], who came to ask if you had any objection to have conferred on you the Freedom of the City of London. This is a compliment conferred on great and distinguished men only and I have to let the gentleman know on Wednesday as it will go before the Aldermen on Thursday. Therefore please write by return mail without fail.

Naturally Lampson had been delighted by this offer to make his old friend a freeman, for in the many centuries since the foundation of the City of London, this honor had been offered to only one American before. This American was Andrew Stevenson, American Minister in London in 1838, who had declined the honor as "being inconsistent with his official status and duties." In our own day, another famous American, General Dwight D. Eisenhower, was made a freeman. This was in 1945 after the victorious Allied campaigns in Europe.

The "gentleman connected with the Corporation" mentioned in Lampson's letter, was Sir Charles Reed, a son of Andrew Reed, a famous nonconformist minister and philanthropist. Charles Reed, a member of the City's Court of Common Council, was by profession a typefounder and by avocation a reformer. Reed was particularly interested in education. He had served as chairman of the London School Board, and it was because of his efforts that the famous Guildhall Library was expanded. He was also active in various religious and missionary societies which helped the poor.

Reed did not know Peabody personally. They had, however, once met casually in rather odd circumstances. Both men, attending a reception given by the Lord Mayor, stood waiting to leave their coats and hats in the outer hall of the Mansion House before joining the other guests.

The outer hall was lined with busts and statues of eminent men. One of the Lord Mayor's footmen who helped the arriving guests take off their hats and overcoats carelessly hung a hat on the head of one of the marble busts. Silently, without reprimanding the footman but with obvious indignation, Reed had removed the hat. Peabody, though it was not his habit to address strangers, became curious, and asked the younger man why he had done that.

"That is a bust of my father," Charles Reed replied proudly.

Peabody nodded but said nothing. He and Reed moved on into the great reception hall where they were welcomed by the Lord Mayor, but that evening they had no further contact with each other. They did not meet again until Reed became actively interested in Peabody's receiving the Freedom of the City.

Reed admired Peabody, for most Americans who lived and worked in London went home at the end of their business careers with the wealth they had accumulated in England, but here was a man sharing the fortune he had made with the poor of London, and sharing it at a critical time when so much wartime friction was dividing his country and England.

When Reed discussed giving Peabody the Freedom of the City with other members of the Common Court, there was not at first unanimous approval. Two of the aldermen called upon Reed urging him to withdraw the motion he proposed, for they believed that Peabody's gift had been incorrectly described in the press. These two aldermen, quite wrongly, thought that Peabody intended to deposit securities for the benefit of London housing and that these securities might be worth very little. To satisfy his skeptical colleagues, Reed made careful inquiries and finally convinced them that Peabody's Donation Fund was entirely genuine and was to be deposited in currency.

At the meeting of the Court of Common Council on May 22, 1862, Charles Reed moved his resolution to make George Peabody a Freeman of the City and spoke about Peabody's gift to London. In his speech he also included a brief summary of Peabody's life, emphasizing the "poor boy makes good" theme, and then continued with words that made it obvious how completely he had understood the spirit prompting George Peabody's gift.

"Here was a man," Charles Reed declared, "bound to us by no ties but those of common humanity, who at a time of jealousy and hate [during the Civil War in America] found our poorest poor objects of his bounty. This benefaction is in sympathy with the Corporation of London's vast expenditure in public works."

In a few striking phrases, Reed, though he had as yet not formally met Peabody, summarized the philosophy and outlook which prompted all of Peabody's philanthropies.

"He desires to help workingmen," Reed said, "to live better by moderate rent near their work. Mr. Peabody draws a line between the idle mendicant and the industrious poor. He strives to help those who help themselves. He safeguards their political and religious creeds."

Reed concluded his speech by asking the Court of Common Council to "confirm on Mr. Peabody its highest honor."

"I ask the Court," Reed said "to grant the Freedom of the City of London to a man who saved the credit of his country, who aided the Arctic expedition under Dr. Kane in search of Franklin, and who once rebuked a highly placed official for refusing to toast the Queen."

Alderman Benjamin Phillips seconded Reed's motion. At first there was one dissenting voice. A Councillor Anderson, not quite sure how some influential businessmen in the City would receive the news of this honor to an American, suggested that a bust of Peabody be placed in the Council Chamber instead of granting him the Freedom. Mr. Anderson was quickly silenced by a unanimous vote—a show of hands—supporting Reed's motion, and July 10 was chosen as the date on which Peabody was to be made a freeman.

Two days after Charles Reed had presented his resolution to the Court of Common Council, a visitor was announced in his place of business. The visitor was a portly, dignified gentleman with white hair who, as he entered Reed's private office, said simply that he was George Peabody. During this courtesy call Peabody only once referred to himself and that was when he expressed astonishment that Reed, a stranger to him, had known so much about his life and intentions.

Reed returned this call within a few days. He found that the great benefactor and wealthy banker lived in unpretentious lodgings with the utmost simplicity. No servant was in attendance during their talk, and the room in which Peabody received him was furnished with austerity.

Reed was deeply impressed by Peabody, "As I recognised his simplicity and real goodness," Reed remembered years later, "I became assured that his was a pure and rare benevolence." Peabody, for his part, was equally attracted by Reed's integrity, and, years later when they knew each other well, he named Charles Reed in his will as one of his British executors. After their first meetings, toward the end of June 1862, the two men met frequently. Reed helped Peabody prepare speeches and advised him on his later donations to the Peabody houses in London.

A week before Peabody was made a Freeman of the City, another distinction was conferred upon him. This was the honorary membership of the Clothworkers' Company, one of the ancient guilds of the City of London. These guilds, usually called livery companies, had their roots in medieval London and were originally formed to set standards for their particular craft. They kept the unruly elements of their workers in order, confiscated bad workmanship, and enforced regulations governing apprenticeships. At first only members of the craft were included in the guilds, but by the middle of the nineteenth century, when the livery companies were already more like clubs, it was not unusual to elect as members other distinguished citizens. The livery companies were, however, pleased when a man to be elected had some connection, however vague, with their original trade. In Peabody's case, his apprenticeship in Sylvester Proctor's drapery store was mentioned as his contact with the manufacture of cloth.

The Clothworkers' Company had originally been two guilds, the Fullers and the Shearmen, but by 1528 they had been united and granted a Royal Charter. Through the centuries many famous men had been members of the company, for example, Sir John Wattes, who served against the Spanish Armada and was later a member of the Virginia Company; Samuel Pepys, Sir Robert Peel, and Queen Victoria's husband, the Prince Consort.

One wonders how George Peabody, who in his habits remained a simple New Englander throughout his life, managed to cope with the many complicated traditions followed by members of the Clothworkers. One of these traditions, to mention an example, is typical. An Alderman Cooper, a prominent member of the Clothworkers' Company, who died early in the eighteenth century, left some money to provide for "fine cognacs" for all those present at the company's regular dinners. Cooper's wife, dying soon afterwards, left a fund "for other liqueurs" consumed at the dinners. At the banquets, therefore, guests are not asked whether they want cognac or some other drink, but, "Do you dine tonight with Alderman or Lady Cooper?"

The dinner to honor Peabody at the Clothworkers' Hall, though very formal, was a relatively quiet affair compared with the pomp and ceremony observed at the ancient Guild Hall on July 10 when he was made a Freeman of the City of London. The pageantry was regal. The proceedings took place in the Council Chamber, not a very large room, which was crowded and must have been very hot on that July afternoon. Below one wall of the chamber, adorned with portraits of George III and Queen Victoria, a raised platform had been erected with seats for the Lord Mayor, aldermen, and special guests. Members of the Common Court sat on benches running lengthwise with the hall and facing the platform. The back of the chamber was crowded with many guests standing with their ladies. The aldermen were dressed in scarlet, the councillors in violet, and all the robes were trimmed with white fur.

Precisely at three o'clock the traditional cry went up: "Pray silence for the Lord Mayor." The Right Honorable William Cubitt then slowly entered the chamber. He was dressed in the Lord Mayor's vivid scarlet robes, and wore a heavy gold chain of office studded with jewels. He was preceded by two officials bearing the mace and sword of the City.

They were followed by Peabody, who was startled by the shout of welcome from this reserved and dignified gathering. He was escorted by Charles Reed and Alderman Phillips, his sponsors. Peabody was dressed in simple black broadcloth, which stood out clearly in contrast to the colorful garments of the other men on the platform. He moved modestly forward and took his place at the left of the Lord Mayor.

The city clerk hurried through the minutes of the preceding meeting of the Common Court. Then, in a clear voice, he read aloud the resolution offering Peabody the Freedom of the City. Peabody stood quietly while he was handed a beautiful gold casket containing an illuminated parchment manuscript, the text of Reed's resolution.

Obviously moved, Peabody took the casket from the Lord Mayor, but his hands were steady, and, in response to the many speeches in his honor, he spoke clearly and firmly. He was aware that he was the first American to have been accorded honorary citizenship of the City of London, and never was there a more stately representative of his country, a man who combined such self assurance with great modesty.

In his address he emphasized that he was not a pioneer but a follower of other philanthropists and that it had always been his intention to return a portion of his fortune to those communities in which he had labored successfully. He was greeted with loud cheers when he added that he could never forget the city where he had been treated with such kindness.

He ended his speech with an indirect allusion to the Civil War. "Let me thank you," he said, "as a citizen of the United States and a resident of this city, for the honor you bestow upon me. May the difficulties in my country be resolved in the permanent triumph of liberty and good government. While I live, I will try to attain the character you give my humble name."

After the ceremony in the Guild Hall, Peabody had time for only a short rest before the banquet which was given in his honor by the Lord Mayor that evening.

This banquet was long and tiring, but to anyone during the Civil War who hoped to improve Anglo-American relations, such social occasions were of considerable importance. Three hundred guests were present in the large Egyptian Room of the Guild Hall. Many courses were served, for the Victorians enjoyed huge and heavy meals.

Peabody, as the guest of honor, sat at the right of the Lord Mayor. Near him were Lord Stanley, Sir James Emerson Tennent, and Sir Curtis Miranda Lampson, the trustees of the donation fund. Junius Spencer Morgan was present, and so were Charles Francis Adams and his wife, representing the American Legation. Charles Dickens's daughter and other prominent English and American men and women had been invited as well.

After dinner had been served, the speeches began—long speeches in which many prominent guests toasted not only George Peabody but one another as well. The Lord Mayor toasted Peabody who in turn toasted the Lord Mayor. Charles Francis Adams responded to Peabody's toast; then Lord Stanley and Sir James Emerson Tennent seemed to begin the round again by toasting the Lord Mayor. It was a veritable dance of words and speeches which finally ended when Peabody himself gave the last toast, to the Lady Mayoress.

Peabody was weary when the dinner and the speeches were over.

Nevertheless, the story was told to the day of his death that he walked home from the Guild Hall after the banquet to save the carriage fare. This tale is patently untrue, for had he wanted a carriage any one of his friends—Minister Adams, Curtis Miranda Lampson, Charles Reed, to mention only a few—would have been happy to drive him to his lodgings. If indeed, which does not seem likely, he preferred to walk home, it could only have been because he wished to pay a private call on some friend before returning to his own rooms.

The fact that the tale to illustrate his economy—his wish to save the expense of a carriage—persisted for so long, was in itself significant. It showed that he had already become a legend: the rich man who walked to save money instead of driving, who had no use for ostentation, who counted his pennies so that pounds, or dollars, would accumulate more rapidly for his charitable purposes.

Peabody's Concern with Science: Othniel Charles Marsh

PEABODY felt old and ill that summer, and after he received the Freedom of the City his friends urged him to leave London for a prolonged rest. He took their advice and spent many months away from the capital as soon as the affairs of the Donation Fund were well organized.

The trustees of the fund met in July, and Lord Stanley accepted the chairmanship. The trustees decided to postpone the appointment of the salaried officials who would manage the fund until the building plans had been further developed. The deed of trust had been prepared by the lawyers and was soon recognized by the Crown.

In the meantime, since his great donation to London had become widely known, Peabody was daily inundated with so many begging letters that he could not possibly answer them all. He finally circulated a statement to the leading newspapers declaring that, were he to respond to the hundreds of requests he was receiving, his means would soon be dissipated. The begging letters disturbed him, and the *City Press* sympathetically expressed the hope that it would not be necessary to write on Peabody's tomb, "Worried to death."

The American Legation, too, was frequently visited by individuals short of funds who asked for money from the Peabody Fund. These pathetic people were often received by Moran, who exploited their plight as a further excuse to attack Peabody in his diary.

On one occasion, when a poor woman came to the legation to ask for financial help, Moran noted in his diary that "a truly deplorable object was among the crowd this morning asking for a few shillings from the Peabody Fund." "The appropriation of this Fund," Moran continued, "arose from a selfish vanity solely, unattended by a shade of benevolence, and which will never benefit those for whose use it was so pompously announced to be intended."

Late in the summer, to get away from it all, Peabody traveled to Dalguise near Dunkeld in the Scottish Highlands, where so often before he had found rest and refreshment. Before leaving London he had entrusted important errands to Horatio Gates Somerby, who was going to the United States in August. He sent with Somerby for safekeeping in the Peabody Institute of South Danvers the gold box containing the vellum document announcing his Freedom of the City of London. For the Peabody Institute in Baltimore, Somerby took over a copy on vellum of the founding letter for the Peabody Homes in London.

In Dalguise, Peabody fished and tried to relax, but as usual he devoted many hours a day to his correspondence.

"Should the War continue," he wrote to Somerby, "I will remain in Europe, but if it ends and I am alive and well I shall be in Boston early next spring."

Peabody eagerly awaited the war news. Early in October, shortly before he returned to London, Somerby wrote from Boston that the North was obviously gathering strength and was preparing to strike quickly. Somerby had heard speeches by Charles Sumner and George Francis Train at the Faneuil Hall. Train, an erratic pro-Irish, anti-British extremist, who was rabidly against the Confederacy as well, had, early in 1862, written a scurrilous attack on Peabody. Somerby now described to Peabody how the Boston police had tangled with Train and had then led him away, handcuffed, through State Street to prison.

In October 1862, Peabody returned from Scotland to London, where he was to meet his nephew Othniel Charles Marsh.

He had not seen his nephew since his visit in America in 1856, and six years in the life of a young person is a long time. Now Othniel Marsh was a mature man with a purpose in life who stimulated his uncle's interest in science, an interest which eventually caused Peabody to help establish science museums at Harvard and Yale.

Othniel had by now taken the M.A. degree at the Sheffield Scientific School at Yale, where he had studied under distinguished professors: geology under James Dwight Dana; chemistry under Benjamin Silliman Jr.; and mathematics under Hubert A. Newton. Weak eyesight had kept young Marsh out of the Union Army, and he was now on his way to Heidelberg, one of several German universities where he planned to continue his studies under eminent scientists.

Already in the second half of the nineteenth century an upsurge of scientific interest was felt in academic circles, and the Civil War, too, saw the introduction of scientific innovations such as the repeating rifle, rudimentary machine guns, and the use of military observation balloons.

Three years before Peabody's meeting with Othniel Marsh, Darwin had published his *Origin of Species*. This great work was, of course, already being carefully studied by scientists, but its wider impact on the thinking of ordinary men was yet to come. And twenty years were to pass before Othniel Marsh's own contributions to science, made as professor of paleontology at Yale, were to be recognized by Darwin himself. "Your work," Darwin then wrote, "has afforded the best support of the theory of Evolution which has appeared in the last twenty years."

Though in 1862 Othniel Marsh was an unknown young graduate student, he had the year before produced one noteworthy paper about Nova Scotia fossils which had attracted the attention of Louis Agassiz of Harvard, the world authority on fossil fishes. The paper had also been read at a meeting of the Geological Society in London and had later been printed in the Society's *Transactions*.

When this paper was well received, Marsh had written to Peabody asking his uncle to help him during his studies in Germany. Peabody gladly consented, and he had, by sending a letter of credit for £200 directly to his nephew, and not to Judith, finally admitted that Marsh was old enough to manage his own affairs. This was a marked acknowledgment of Othniel's maturity, for he was, when he received the letter of credit, spending the summer with his aunt. She was busy with her own affairs, for she had recently remarried—her husband Jeremiah Russell had died some time before. Judith had asked Peabody whether he approved of this second marriage, and he had welcomed his new brother-in-law, especially as Judith's second husband was his very old friend Robert Shillaber Daniels.

Judith's marriage was only one of many family topics Peabody discussed with Othniel. But the two men, congenial from the first hour of their reunion, talked more about the new scientific developments and Marsh's future career than about personal affairs.

In the course of the conversation, Marsh hinted that he had a request to make. "For money, I suppose," Peabody replied, smiling indulgently at his nephew. "Not a penny for myself," Othniel replied, "but I wish you would endow scientific work at Yale College."

Othniel, obviously a tactful man, did not follow up this remark by unduly urging Peabody to consider endowing scientific research at Yale. In the first place, he realized that Peabody was always more interested in

Harvard than in Yale, and, secondly, Marsh was aware of the begging letters his uncle had received after the Donation Fund had become known. Marsh could see that these pressures were a strain for Peabody and he wanted to spare him.

Marsh wrote to Professor Benjamin Silliman Jr. at Yale that his uncle received "so many requests for aid of various kinds that were he to supply them all, the Bank of England would not cover the total." Marsh ended this letter to Professor Silliman by mentioning that, though his uncle was obviously more concerned with Harvard than with Yale, he, Marsh, "would use all his influence with Mr P. in her [Yale's] favor" and he "thought there was a fair prospect of success" in the future.

Young Othniel Marsh understood Peabody and respected his orderly and systematic mind. Marsh was quite sure that Peabody was a man who never liked to be rushed into any decision and that if, later, he tried seriously to interest Peabody in an endowment for Yale, a definite scheme for such an endowment must be submitted to his uncle.

"I did not propose any definite plan to him," Marsh informed Silliman, "as I had then none to propose, but shall hope to do so before long as I do not intend to let the matter rest until something definite is decided upon one way or the other."

One of the reasons for Marsh's optimism regarding a future donation to Yale was his appreciation of his uncle's way: "to begin with a reasonable gift and then to add to it when he saw its purpose becoming useful." Besides, Marsh's long conversations with Peabody in October 1862 had convinced the young scientist that Peabody was becoming aware of the increasing significance of science in a modern world and of its importance as a vital part of education.

Marsh's influence on Peabody is indicated by the three phases of his thinking in connection with his gift to Harvard. In 1861, a year before he met his nephew in London, Peabody was considering a donation to Harvard that would enlarge its observatory. In 1862, before he talked to Othniel Marsh, he was contemplating his Harvard benefaction in terms of a school of art. Finally, however, his donation to Harvard emerged as an endowment to be devoted to the study of American anthropology, then consisting of archaeology and ethnology.

Othniel had thus turned his uncle's thoughts for the first time to the sciences, particularly ethnology and archaeology, and had awakened his interest in endowed museums which would organize scientific expeditions to uncover animal and human remains and so reconstruct the physical and cultural history of man. Not surprisingly, when Marsh parted from his uncle and left for Germany, he was in a hopeful frame of mind.

Peabody was feeling less cheerful. His gout was more troublesome than ever, crippling his left knee and causing him great discomfort. He spent many weeks during the early part of the winter in Brighton and from there wrote to William Wilson Corcoran that Sir Henry Holland, one of Queen Victoria's doctors, had advised him to try the warm sun in the south of France.

He invited Corcoran—"you need not bring a letter of credit"—to join him early in 1863 on this journey south. Hoping that Corcoran would come too, he planned to go to Nice and perhaps to Florence and Rome, taking a courier with him who would manage travel arrangements and take charge of the dispatch of his letters and telegrams.

Peabody was disappointed when Corcoran declined because he said he could not leave Washington at that time. Peabody gently chided Corcoran for preferring his new grandchild (Loula Eustis's baby) and his Confederate associates to his old friend George Peabody, "whose views on the War were not defined and therefore suspect."

November and December in London, before Peabody left for the south in January, were dreary months. There were times when the war seemed never ending. For until Vicksburg fell in the summer of 1863, and Gettysburg was secured, the Union forces had not gained any real ascendency. From Peabody's personal point of view this meant that, in the dark, foggy winter of 1862 and 1863, the retirement for which he longed was a long way off. More and more of the day-to-day work of George Peabody and Company was now done by Junius Spencer Morgan (nine years had passed since he became a partner), by Charles Cubitt Gooch, and by the clerks in the office. Nevertheless, Peabody continued to feel the weight of his responsibility for the firm.

He had one great pleasure during this winter: he was elected, under Rule Two, to the Athenaeum (already mentioned as one of his clubs), the most distinguished club in London, then as now. Under Rule Two, a special committee annually admits nine men outstanding in science, literature, the arts, or public service. In our own day, Dwight D. Eisenhower, for example, was one of the few Americans admitted under Rule Two to the Athenaeum, the membership of which included, through the years, such famous men as John Ruskin, William Makepeace Thackeray, Sir Francis Galton, Thomas Henry Huxley, John Tyndall, John Lothrop Motley,

Robert Browning, Benjamin Disraeli, Herbert Spencer, James Clark Maxwell, and William Wetmore Story.

Before his departure for the south of France, however, Peabody had little energy to visit the Athenaeum frequently. In January he traveled first to Paris and then on to Nice via Lyons and Marseilles, arriving in Nice on February 3. His resilience was still remarkable—while in France he reached his sixty-eighth year—and after a week of "hot, sunny, cloudless weather" he was thoroughly restored. One wonders how much of his gout and other ailments were results, in part at least, of depression, for when in surroundings he enjoyed, he often recovered his vitality very quickly.

He felt strong enough in Nice to give a lavish banquet which was attended, among other well-known men, by the Prince of Wales, later Edward VII, and by King Ludwig of Bavaria. News of this banquet reached London, and Peabody's friends—especially Curtis Miranda Lampson, who had been sending him anxious letters about his health—were relieved that he was so much better. James Emerson Tennent had heard from Junius Spencer Morgan about Peabody's gala banquet in Nice. Tennent wrote to Peabody,

> You appear to have charmed all ranks, from the King and Prince to the private gentlemen. . . . Is it not a blessed thing to feel and to possess as you do, the *power to make so many people happy*? It seems to me as if no man had it on a grander scale: or ever himself enjoyed the esteem genuinely as you do. Is it not a full reward after your life of honorable and successful exertions to know that you can exercise so much power!

Peabody thoroughly enjoyed the gaiety and sociability in Nice. It was like prewar times to meet old friends, make new acquaintances, and take an active part in the carefree life of the resort. He lingered on until May before leaving via Paris for Wiesbaden, Germany. Here he took what was called an "after cure" for his gout. From Wiesbaden he wrote to Othniel, who was then attending lectures at the University of Berlin, asking his nephew to meet him for a long talk in Hamburg.

By this time, after an exhaustive correspondence with Professor Benjamin Silliman Jr. at Yale, Marsh had worked out a preliminary plan for a scientific museum at Yale. Silliman's task in connection with this plan had not been entirely simple, because the authorities at Yale had to be persuaded to accept the idea of a scientific endowment. For years, the devotees of science had been making an effort to establish firmly the teaching of scientific subjects at the college, where the liberal arts tradition was very strong, and science, particularly since the appearance of Darwin's revolutionary ideas, was suspect. Religious fundamentalists bitterly opposed the new theory of natural selection, and scientific research generally had to be defended at Yale and many other learned institutions in the United States.

Probably Peabody was aware of the difficulties the Sillimans, father and son, encountered. At any rate, when he met his nephew in Hamburg, he was obviously pleased with the plan submitted by Othniel. He told Othniel that in his will he contemplated a legacy of $100,000 to endow a museum of natural history at Yale. Actually, he decided later, while he was in America in 1866, to give Yale this gift during his lifetime, and to raise the endowment to $150,000.

One can imagine with what satisfaction Othniel heard from his uncle that his hopes for Yale were to be realized. Peabody chose Othniel Marsh, the older and the younger Benjamin Silliman, James Dixon, and James Dwight Dana as trustees of the Yale museum, and asked that these five men submit to him in due course a comprehensive plan for the proposed institution.

Othniel Marsh's report to Benjamin Silliman Sr., announcing Peabody's gift to Yale, was as restrained in the expression of his emotions as any letter written by his uncle. Othniel's report did not betray his excitement about this gift to Yale, though he was always boyishly devoted to his alma mater.

"My dear Sir," he wrote from Hamburg on May 25 to Professor Benjamin Silliman Sr., "I take great pleasure in announcing to you that Mr. George Peabody has decided to extend his generosity to Yale College, and will leave a legacy of *one hundred thousand dollars* to promote the interests of a Natural Science Museum in the Institution."

For the first time, shortly after Peabody had returned to London and Marsh had gone back to Germany, the younger man wrote and asked Peabody for financial assistance for himself. Marsh hoped to acquire while in Europe a library and a specimen collection (on a much larger scale than the one, as an undergraduate, he had mentioned to his Aunt Judith!). He wrote to Peabody,

Such a library and cabinet . . . can only be obtained in Europe. . . . The amount necessary for this object would be 3 or 4 thousand dollars. . . . I have felt some hesitation in asking for this assistance in view of all you have already done for me, but I have thought it much the best way to state the whole case frankly and leave the matter with you.

In the same letter Marsh informed Peabody that upon his return to New Haven he was to be given the chair of geology and paleontology.

"This professorship," he added with understandable satisfaction, "corresponds to that held by the great Professor Agassiz at Harvard."

Peabody was very proud of his nephew. He sent him $3,500 for his library and specimen collection. He would have considered it extravagant to send the maximum sum the young man had requested. He continued carefully to count, if no longer the pennies, at least the dollars.

The good news of his nephew's professorship was especially welcome, as the particularly wet and stormy fall in England was again depressing Peabody's spirits and causing him to suffer from rheumatism and gout. Many years had passed since, in his younger days, he had found the English climate invigorating.

In July there had been one exciting moment: George Peabody and Company were informed about the fall of Vicksburg before any other firm in London heard of this event. The news came through John Pierpont Morgan in New York, then in the firm of Dabney, Morgan, and Company, who continued to act as Peabody's agent in America. When the news of Vicksburg was received in New York, John Pierpont Morgan's cousin, James Goodwin, rushed a message by telegraph to Halifax, where an agent of Dabney, Morgan, and Company wrote out a dispatch and placed it aboard a fast steamer just leaving for England. Telegraphic communication with Halifax broke down temporarily soon after this ship left port, and George Peabody and Company were thus the first firm in London to learn about Vicksburg.

In August, Peabody was again in Scotland, in Invergarry this time, with Curtis Miranda Lampson, and during this summer he had an occasional visit from young Henry Adams and the friend with whom he was traveling. Peabody appeared to be more relaxed than he had been for some time: hopes were justified that soon the dreadful conflict in America would be over and Reconstruction would begin. Peabody already envisaged the task he must undertake in connection with Reconstruction when the time came. His contribution to Reconstruction would be educational, and though he was almost seventy, he remained forward looking. He was aware that, with the continuous growth of the population of the United States, the need for the expansion of education would become greater and more urgent.

Retirement and a Letter from the Queen

EARLY in 1864 Peabody began to make preparations for his retirement from George Peabody and Company. His partnership agreement with Junius Spencer Morgan and Charles Cubitt Gooch expired on the first of October of that year. While Peabody was in the Scottish Highlands in August, Morgan wrote urging him to continue the partnership beyond October. Morgan pointed out that many securities held by the firm would have to be sold when the partnership came to an end, and to sell these so soon would result in some loss to everyone concerned.

Peabody, however, was firm in his intentions. In six months he would be seventy, and he was convinced that he must now give his full attention to his philanthropies. When he retired he would retain enormous holdings of bonds, stocks, and other investments, and he needed leisure away from day-to-day financial affairs to consider how best to invest them for the institutions and other charities with which he was concerned.

He wrote to Morgan,

It has been my fixed determination to retire from all commercial business if I should live till the 1st of October 1864 and I can now make no change, for although the continuance of the firm for three or six months . . . may appear short to you, to me—feeling as I deeply do, the uncertainty of life at the age of seventy—months would appear as years, for I am most anxious before I die to place my worldly affairs in a much more satisfactory state than they are at present.

Morgan had to accept this decision. He was also obliged to give way to Peabody in another matter. Morgan had hoped to keep the original name of the firm, George Peabody and Company, so well known and respected in many countries, but Peabody rejected this suggestion. He did not wish to have his name used in business affairs over which he had no control. The house, therefore, became J. S. Morgan and Company. There was, however, no abrupt break in the firm's dealings, and J. S. Morgan continued to do business with the same firms which had been associated with George Peabody and Company for many years. From 1843 to 1864 the business was known as George Peabody and Company; from 1864 to 1890 as J. S. Morgan and Company; from 1890 to 1913 as Morgan, Grenfell, and Company; and from 1913 to the present day, as Morgan, Grenfell, and Company, Limited.

On the wall of the entrance hall of the firm in Great Manchester Street, in London, there are today four brass plates, five inches high and two feet, one inch long. The lowest letters are worn with time and polishing:

MORGAN, GRENFELL AND COMPANY, LIMITED

MORGAN, GRENFELL AND COMPANY

J. S. MORGAN AND COMPANY

GEORGE PEABODY AND COMPANY

Unlike many men immersed in work until their retirement, who then experience a painful slump of inactivity, Peabody had more than enough to do. After he left the business, he was as energetic mentally as ever, despite continuous bad health. His large charities required a great deal of thought, and he never, for the sake of his great philanthropic ventures, neglected smaller charitable appeals.

In the winter of 1863–64, for example, there had been a meeting of Americans in London at the Westminster Palace Hotel to organize financial aid to the United States Sanitary Commission, which had been created in 1861 by the Federal Government to help wounded soldiers and their dependents. Peabody, with Morgan, Lampson, and other prominent men, continued to the end of the Civil War to urge other Americans in London to contribute to this worthy cause; Peabody's own total contribution to the sanitary commission was $10,000.

Plans for the Peabody Donation Fund occupied much of his time. The first block of dwellings in the Spitalfields district of London was opened in 1864, and by January of 1866 he announced an addition of £100,000 to the Fund, which had now reached a total of a quarter of a million pounds (then equivalent to $1,250,000).

He also considered, and mentioned to the trustees of the fund, the possibility of setting apart rooms in the Peabody blocks of flats for the teaching of children whose homes were far away from a school. This suggestion, reflecting Peabody's consistent preoccupation with education, did not seem practical to the trustees and nothing came of the idea.

Peabody was pleased with the new Peabody flats but continued to consider his American philanthropies, rather than those in England, of major importance. Soon after his retirement he added another $25,000 to his gift to the institute in Baltimore, and he sent more books to the Peabody Institute of South Danvers.

Peabody was now more and more frequently away from London. He attended few large social gatherings, but occasionally his name was mentioned in the press when he went to some important function. In the spring of 1865, for example, he was among a group of distinguished men, including Cyrus W. Field, Sir Edward Cunard, and the Prince of Wales, who inspected the *Great Eastern*, the ship which had laid the Atlantic telegraph cable. Peabody, a director of the Atlantic Cable Company, had been aware for years of the importance of rapid communications to business of any kind.

Despite his many preoccupations, Peabody was at times restless after his retirement, waiting, one feels, for the Civil War finally to end so that he could at last revisit the United States. He obviously enjoyed traveling as much as he had when he was younger. He wrote to a friend that he could "not remain in London a week without risk of gout," and he spent many months in Scotland or Ireland. At one time, in June 1865, he rented a lake for fishing on the Scottish estate of Standish O'Grady, but by August he had gone to Ireland to fish. From there he journeyed to Liverpool to welcome John Pendleton Kennedy, who was arriving from Baltimore.

Fishing was now Peabody's great form of relaxation. It soothed his nerves, and he wrote humorously to Corcoran from Ireland that he was working very hard fishing for salmon six or ten hours a day. He claimed that fishing in the open air and "a plain diet . . . kept me free of gout and in excellent health."

In fact, his old buoyancy was returning, at least temporarily, and he began to make fresh plans for the future. Less of the "old-man-of-seventy" depression was apparent in his letters. He ventured to think further ahead, and he leased a "fine fishery" on the Shannon for five years: from April 1867 to April 1872. In July 1865, Othniel Marsh, on his way to New Haven and his professorship at Yale, visited his uncle in the Highlands and was delighted to find him in such good spirits.

Everyone, of course, even people in the unhappy and defeated South, felt intense relief when, in April 1865, before Othniel's visit to George Peabody, the dreadful war and its terrible loss of life had finally ended. The years of bitter fighting were almost over when Robert E. Lee was outnumbered in Richmond, where one hundred thousand Union troops faced his forty thousand exhausted soldiers. On April 2 General Grant had captured Petersburg, and the next day Lee evacuated Richmond. When the Union armies entered the capital of the Confederacy, Jefferson Davis fled to North Carolina. On April 9, Lee and Grant met at Appomattox Court House and the Civil War was over.

Early in 1866, Peabody's plans for a visit to the United States were settled. Formerly he had so often declared that he intended to live permanently in America after his retirement, and it has never been explained why he changed his mind. Perhaps he did have unrecorded ties in England which meant much to him as he grew older, and he could not envisage leaving England for good. Whatever his reasons for remaining in England, they reflect an emotional ambivalence. He decided to spend the rest of his life in England, and yet, so he declared, "With my advancing years my attachment to my native land has become more devoted."

Though he intended to return to England, he was eagerly looking forward to his sojourn in the United States, and from Brighton he wrote cheerfully in February 1866 to William Wilson Corcoran. He was almost seventy-one, he reminded Corcoran, but, he continued,

My feelings and disposition, I am glad to say, do not keep pace with my years, and I hope to pass my year's *visit* [Peabody's underlining of the word] in the United States in the same health and spirits. I have secured my passage in the *Scotia* on her first voyage to New York; not yet settled when she will leave, but Judson says 7th or 21st of April.

In the meantime, influential people in London had decided he should not leave without some outward expression of England's gratitude for his gift to the underprivileged citizens of the capital. Queen Victoria was familiar with the proceedings of the trustees of the Peabody Donation Fund. She had also been told about Peabody's second donation, and she herself resolved to honor him.

Had Peabody been an Englishman, the obvious way to demonstrate the royal esteem would have been to confer on him a peerage, the hereditary title of a baronet, or that of a knight, or to bestow upon him some order of decoration. There were Americans, Sir Curtis Miranda Lampson, for example, who had lived so long in England, had an English wife and English children, that they felt themselves to be English and had found it quite natural to accept a baronetcy and to become subjects of the Queen.

The Queen was undoubtedly told that Peabody in his business and personal affairs had consistently emphasized how proud he was to be an American citizen. Nevertheless, as was, and is, usual in such cases, Peabody was casually and tactfully approached by some friend of the Queen's private secretary—at the time C. B. Phipps—who asked how he would feel about being created a baronet and becoming a British subject. The answer from Peabody was definitely but politely "no." He felt his American origins too deeply. He could never change his nationality.

The Queen, therefore, through her private secretary, asked Earl Russell whether a personal letter of gratitude from her would please George Peabody, or whether Russell had other suggestions.

"The Queen is disposed to think," the private secretary wrote to Russell,

that it would be becoming that she should in some way make her affirmation of this benevolence [the Peabody Donation Fund] shown by a foreigner to the poor of the metropolis of this country, but the fact that Mr. Peabody being a citizen of the United States makes the mode of doing this rather difficult, as it is not possible to offer him any of the marks of distinction usually bestowed upon subjects.

Russell, in turn, wrote to James Emerson Tennent, a trustee of the Donation Fund and known to be a close friend of Peabody as well. Tennent, in his written reply, agreed with Lord Russell that, apart from a personal letter to Peabody, the Queen might wish to give him a miniature portrait of herself. She occasionally gave such a portrait to foreign ambassadors from countries with whom Great Britain had signed a treaty.

On March 28, 1866, the Queen dispatched her letter to Peabody. It was, of course, according to established custom, written in the third person. The paper on which the letter was written had a black border, for Queen Victoria had been in mourning since the death of the Prince Consort in 1861.

The Queen hears [she wrote] that Mr. Peabody intends shortly to return to America; and she would be sorry that he should leave England without being assured by herself how deeply she appreciates the noble act, of more than princely munificence, by which he has sought to relieve the wants of her poorer subjects residing in London. It is an act, as the Queen believes, wholly without parallel; and which will carry its best reward in the consciousness of having contributed so largely to the assistance of those who can little help themselves.

The Queen would not, however, have been satisfied without giving Mr. Peabody some public mark of her sense of his munificence; and she would have conferred upon him either a baronetcy or the Grand Cross of the Order of the Bath, but that she understands Mr. Peabody to feel himself debarred from accepting such distinctions.

It only remains, therefore, for the Queen to give Mr. Peabody this assurance of her personal feelings; which she would further wish to mark by asking him to accept a miniature of herself, which she will have painted for him, and which, when finished, can either be sent to him in America, or given to him on the return which she rejoices to hear he meditates to the country that owes him so much.

Peabody's answer to the Queen was written on April 3 at the Palace Hotel, Buckingham Gate, where he had taken rooms before his imminent departure for the United States. As a youth in Newburyport, Massachusetts, his neat handwriting had given him the chance of writing out the ballots for the Federalist Party. Now, continuous and crippling attacks of gout in his fingers had partially paralyzed his right hand, writing was painful, and he was not pleased with his handwriting.

His answer to the Queen was typical of his somewhat awkward style, an awkwardness which was often apparent when he was writing with real emotion. He first mentioned to Queen Victoria his inability to "express in adequate terms the gratification with which he had read" her sentiments transmitted to him by Earl Russell.

When he referred to the Queen's reason for honoring him—the Peabody Donation Fund for London—he wrote,

I have been actuated by a deep sense of gratitude to God, who has blessed me with prosperity, and of attachment to this great country where, under your Majesty's benign rule, I have received so much personal kindness and enjoyed so many years of happiness. [The portrait of the Queen] which your Majesty is graciously pleased to bestow on me [he would always regard as the most gracious heirloom], that I can leave to the land of my birth.

The news of the Queen's attention to George Peabody was welcomed in London as a very suitable gesture, and at the time he received other expressions of appreciation. Already his portrait, painted by a famous artist of the day, H. W. Pickersgill, hung in the Guild Hall. The Fishmongers' Livery Company, a City Company even older than Clothworkers', presented him with the Honorary Freedom of the Company, and one hundred and nineteen prominent merchants and banking firms in the City hoped to give a banquet in Peabody's honor before his departure for America. He was gratified by this invitation but declined it on the grounds that he had too much to do before the *Scotia* sailed from Liverpool.

On April 17, shortly before he left England, Peabody had been asked to distribute the prizes at the closing excerises of the Workingmen's Industrial Exhibition. Accompanied by the Lord Mayor, Peabody attended these ceremonies at the gaily decorated Guild Hall.

In his short speech at this prize-giving, Peabody referred indirectly to one of his reasons for helping at least some of the London working people to have decent homes.

"I rejoice with you," he declared at the Guild Hall that April afternoon in 1866, "in the advancement of the dignity of labor. The self-reliance and honest independence of the working people are the best guarantee of a country's prosperity and moral greatness."

America Revisited and Baltimore Institute

ON May 1, 1866, George Peabody disembarked from the Cunard liner *Scotia* in New York. This was his second visit to the United States in thirty long years. He was, in everything but his feelings, an expatriate, and he had now, as has been said, definitely given up his earlier plans to settle in America after his retirement. His sentiments, however, were to him of vital importance: he felt himself to be completely American, though he preferred, for reasons he never discussed, to live in England to the end of his days.

He had come to New York alone without a valet or a traveling companion, though so frequently, especially at night, painful attacks of gout and other ailments made it difficult for him to get about. He obviously preferred to be on his own, while other men with his immense financial resources would have traveled with at least a servant and a secretary to attend to their needs during the journey.

He appeared to be, as the New York *Times*'s reporter at the dock noticed, "in fine health and spirits" when he landed, and it was apparent that "he was grateful, after scattering blessings and bounties among the poor of London, for the privilege of again pressing the soil and breathing the atmosphere of 'his own, his native land.' "

Many friends came to welcome him at the pier when he left the *Scotia*. A decade had passed since his last visit to America, and these ten years included the disastrous Civil War, which had changed the country more than any event during the century.

Peabody was fully aware of what the war had meant to every American. He understood the grief and misery the war had caused in the North and in the South, but he refused to allow memories of the conflict to undermine his hopes for the future. Vain regrets, he was sure, would help no one; on the contrary, bitterness could only hamper Reconstruction.

He looked forward to dedicating the Peabody Institute in Baltimore; to giving a solid foundation to his gifts to Harvard and Yale, and to Phillips Academy and Kenyon College. He planned to endow libraries at Georgetown, in the District of Columbia, and in Georgetown, Massachusetts. And he was already considering his most generous and far-reaching gift: a fund to aid public education in the defeated South.

From the pier Peabody drove to the Brevoort Hotel, where he stayed for a few nights before going on to visit his sister Judith in Georgetown, Massachusetts. His rooms at the Brevoort—he had no servant to look after him—were extraordinarily untidy; papers, open trunks, newspapers, and personal belongings were strewn about everywhere, on chairs, tables, and his bed.

Here a Mr. Humphreys, about whom little is recorded except that he had known Peabody years before in Baltimore, found him when he called. To Mr. Humphreys, as his daughter claimed many years later, Peabody, when his benefactions were discussed, was reported to have said, "Humphreys, after my disappointment years ago, I determined to devote myself to my fellow beings and am carrying out that decision to my best ability."

It was this alleged remark which caused Peabody's romantically inclined friends and relatives to believe that he remembered with unhappiness his unfortunate love affair with Esther Hoppin. In fact, he had not met her for almost thirty years, and, though she was then a widow, he had shown no inclination to see her when he was in Philadelphia ten years before.

Many of Peabody's admirers had hoped to call upon him while he was at the Brevoort, but he did not stay in New York, and by the third of May he was in Georgetown with Judith. Her second marriage to Robert Shillaber Daniels was obviously happy, though Daniels, in common with Judith's first husband, was a bad manager and often in debt. Peabody had quietly taken over Daniels's indebtedness: he was never as severe with his sisters' husbands as he was with his nephews.

Judith realized that, despite the impression of good health her brother had made on the New York *Times* reporter and others, he was not well. The intense heat of that summer of 1866 did not agree with him, and he declined invitations for receptions and dinners from bankers and merchants in Boston and elsewhere. He was suffering from inflamed gums, his face was badly swollen, and naturally, as he was always careful, even a little vain, about his appearance, he disliked meeting people when he was not looking his best. He stayed indoors at Judith's, except when he went to

Boston—Georgetown was only twenty-eight miles from Boston—to see a physician, Dr. Keep, or to keep urgent business appointments.

Peabody was not idle in Georgetown. Many business and charitable affairs required his attention. The Internal Revenue collector had presented an assessment of Peabody's taxes for 1862, '63, '64, and '65. He was liable for these taxes as an American citizen, though he had resided all these years in London. It would be interesting to know exactly what tax Peabody paid for this period, but whatever it was, as the New York *Albion* pointed out, "Mr. Peabody will soon add a large sum to the Internal Revenues of the United States Government by paying his Income Tax as a citizen of the United States resident in London."

Apart from his correspondence with the Internal Revenue and his preoccupations with other business affairs, Peabody was discussing with Judith the building of a memorial church and institute in Georgetown in memory of their mother who, as has been mentioned, was born in Georgetown. There had been a split in the local Congregational Church, and eighty-five members of the congregation—not surprisingly including Judith, a born dissenter—disagreed with the doctrinal beliefs of their pastor, the Reverend Charles Beecher. The dissenting group hoped to found its own church. Thus, when Peabody agreed to finance the building of a church for the breakaway Congregationalists, Judith achieved two purposes: a new church for the dissenters and a memorial to her mother. Whenever Judith Peabody Russell Daniels appears in George Peabody's biography, one feels that one would like to know more about this determined woman.

She thoroughly approved when her brother also decided to add $100,000 to his fund for the institute in South Danvers, and $140,000 to the institute at Danvers. He also gave instructions to the institute of South Danvers to prepare a suitable strong room to house and display Queen Victoria's portrait and her letter to him along with his other honors.

While staying with Judith, Peabody was making final arrangements for the dedication of the Baltimore Institute which was to take place on October 25. John Pendleton Kennedy, the president of the Board of Trustees of the Baltimore Institute, who was leaving for Europe early in July, came to see Peabody to plan the opening ceremonies.

They also discussed the problems confronting the institute. Disharmony, not to say quarrels, had, as has been mentioned, for years caused friction between the Maryland Historical Society and the new institute to continue. In the founding letter, the historical society had been promised free quarters in the new institute building, and members of the society had been made administrators of the trust. Now the disagreements separating the institute trustees and the historical society made it clear that co-operation of the two organizations under one roof would be practically impossible. In a lengthy and diplomatic correspondence, carried on while he was visiting Judith in Georgetown, Peabody finally adjusted these differences, and, by giving the historical society a permanent publication fund of $20,000, encouraged the society to withdraw and to agree to remain a separate body.

Tact was also needed by Peabody that summer when he made final plans for his gift of a science museum to Harvard. The university was still largely liberal-arts minded, as was Yale, and many learned men in Cambridge still considered other needs more pressing than a museum, especially in prehistoric science. Harvard's general finances at the time were not flourishing, and Peabody's gift would have been welcomed by the administrators for more general use. Besides, so many believed, the library required funds, and so did Professor Louis Agassiz's Museum of Comparative Zoology.

In his approach to Harvard, Peabody was advised not only by Othniel Marsh, who, of course, came from Yale to see his uncle in Georgetown, but by Robert Charles Winthrop. In 1862, Thurlow Weed had suggested Winthrop, whom Peabody had admired for years, as the ideal man to help direct Peabody's philanthropic schemes. Winthrop's published speeches in the Massachusetts Legislature and in the Congress in Washington had always attracted Peabody's attention. Winthrop, a descendant of Governor John Winthrop, had been trained in Daniel Webster's law office, and he was now one of the outstanding public figures of the day.

When Peabody and Winthrop met—briefly early in May and later in the summer for more lengthy discussions at Tremont House in Boston and at Winthrop's home in Brookline—Winthrop agreed that Peabody's gift to Harvard should be a museum of science, specifically dedicated to ethnology and archaeology. Winthrop suggested that it would be wise to consult with James Walker, the former president of Harvard, hoping that he would influence the less scientific-minded overseers of the college and members of the faculty in favor of Peabody's museum.

Walker considered the matter carefully and then definitely supported Peabody's plan. His remarks to Winthrop on the subject might serve as a model for any spokesman expressing the views of an organization regarding an endowment from a wealthy patron.

Walker told Winthrop,

I have always been of the opinion that when a generous man like Mr. Peabody proposes a gift, we should accept it on his plans, and not on ours. Even if we could persuade him to change his plans and endow some other branch of the University he would never take the same interest, or regard it so much as his own. . . . There may be, and will be, as you say, disappointments in some quarters. But the branch of Science, to which this endowment is devoted, is one to which many minds in Europe are now eagerly turning. . . . This Museum, too, will be the first of its kind in our country.

Walker's advice was finally taken at Harvard, and Peabody's deed of gift was completed by October 8, 1866. The gift, amounting to $150,000, was to be divided as follows: $45,000 was to be invested as a fund, the income of which was to be used for the collection of objects and books relating to American archaeology and ethnology; $45,000 was to be an endowment for a professorship at Harvard on these subjects; and the remaining $60,000 was to be spent on the building of a fireproof museum.

The enthusiasm with which the news of Peabody's gift to Harvard was received by scientists in New England and elsewhere must have impressed even those who had doubted the value of this endowment. The plans for the museum had come at a propitious time; ten years before, the discovery of the Neanderthal skull had created interest in prehistoric man among scholars and laymen everywhere. Within a month of the announcement of Peabody's museum fund, historical societies, such as the famous Massachusetts Historical Society, began sending to Cambridge ethnological specimens collected through the years but never scientifically examined by trained experts.

Harvard's Professor Agassiz, the zoologist, now also welcomed the plan for Peabody's museum. Winthrop wrote to Agassiz suggesting that he come to meet Peabody early in October. Agassiz accepted this invitation. Before the meeting with Peabody, Agassiz wrote to Winthrop asking him to inform Peabody that one of the reasons science had not made more rapid progress in the United States was that the dissertations of scientists had not been widely circulated. Publishers and booksellers did not publish many scientific works because they were not profitable. Agassiz proposed to Winthrop that Peabody might consider endowing a society which would assemble and publish news of scientific research and discoveries.

Whether Peabody and Agassiz met at Winthrop's home, and Agassiz asked Peabody's help in founding the society he had in mind, is not known. At any rate, a year later, in 1867, Peabody gave $140,000 to further science in Essex County. From this endowment emerged the Peabody Academy of Science, later known as the Peabody Museum of Salem, and the scientific publications of this organization at least partially satisfied the need outlined by Louis Agassiz in his letter to Winthrop.

A few weeks after announcing his gift to Harvard, Peabody had completed his plans for Yale. On October 22, Peabody donated to Yale the same amount he had given Harvard—$150,000—to found a museum and establish a chair of natural history. This museum was to include departments of zoology, geology, and mineralogy.

Before the announcement of his gifts to Harvard and to Yale, after two months in Georgetown with Judith, Peabody was again eager for a change of scene. For some years he had been accustomed to traveling frequently, and the Daniels's quiet home and perhaps his sister's continuous and articulate solicitude for his health, had become a strain. As soon as his face was no longer swollen and he felt himself to be presentable, he decided to leave Georgetown. In July, despite the persistent heat, he set out for southern Canada with a group of relatives and friends. The George Peabody Russells, Robert Singleton Peabody, and Othniel Marsh were among the people who joined him for all or part of this journey. Uncle George was obviously giving them a treat which included a visit to Montreal as well as twelve days' fishing on the Marguerite River. Here, out of twelve days at the fishing lodge, Peabody slept in the open air under a tent for ten days and enjoyed it.

Though he was accompanied by relatives and friends and obviously enjoyed the company, he maintained the appearance that he preferred being alone. In Montreal, for example, so many people were eager to pay him their respects that he was obliged to hold a public "levee," as open house was called in Canada, so that he could receive his admirers. Nevertheless, surrounded by this crush of visitors at the open house, he said to one of the guests, Robert Bell, a Canadian Member of Parliament, that "he intended to remain in seclusion until the inauguration of the Baltimore Institute in October." And when South Danvers, in October, asked whether the town would be allowed to organize a welcome for him, he declined, but he was nevertheless happy to drive to the town with Judith and to meet twelve hundred noisy and cheering children from eight Danvers schools in the lecture hall of the Peabody Institute of the town.

He always appeared to give his full attention to immediate affairs: to the schoolchildren in South Danvers, or his companions while he fished, but a part of his mind dwelt on his philanthropies. He often surprised his friends by unexpected remarks about his future plans. On one occasion at Winthrop's house in Brookline, Massachusetts, when the two men were discussing the final arrangements for announcing Peabody's gift to Harvard, he suddenly took from his coat pocket a thick sheaf of papers.

"And now I come to the last," he said to the astonished Winthrop. "You may be surprised when you learn precisely what it [this endowment] is: but it is the one nearest my heart, and the one for which I shall do the most, now and hereafter."

Peabody then read out to Winthrop his first draft of a letter announcing the gift of one million dollars to Southern education. At the time nothing was made public of his intention, but Winthrop understood one of the reasons the opening of the Baltimore Institute was so important to Peabody: to him Baltimore was the gateway to the South.

Nine years and eight months had passed since, in 1857, Peabody had announced his endowment of the institute. The disagreements among the trustees about the site had caused so great a delay that the cornerstone was not laid until April 1859. Finally, the building had been completed in the fall of 1861, but the opening of the institute had to be postponed until 1866 because the trustees were divided into hostile camps during the Civil War. Thirteen had been loyal to the Union, while ten had supported the Confederacy. The trustees, as a result, never met as a group during the conflict. Thus, sectional and political differences had almost wrecked the institute before it was opened, and though the war was over, bitterness among the trustees continued.

Peabody's conciliatory presence at the opening ceremony was therefore of the utmost importance. It was hoped, and rightly so, that his high purpose and his compelling sincerity would reconcile the trustees at least to the point at which they would co-operate for the good of the institute which would so greatly benefit Baltimore.

The first step toward a reconciliation of the trustees was arranged during Peabody's short train journey from New York to Baltimore via Philadelphia. He arrived in Philadelphia on October 22. In Philadelphia he was met by some of the trustees, who reported on the final arrangements for the ceremony. Then, two days later, in a special railway car provided by Peabody's friend John Work Garrett, the president of the Baltimore and Ohio Railroad, he and these trustees traveled from Philadelphia to Baltimore together. The train stopped briefly at Havre-de-Grace near the Susquehanna River. Here they were joined by the other trustees, so that all of the trustees were seen to be a united group accompanying Peabody when they arrived in Baltimore.

The dedication ceremony was held in the large hall of the new institute.

Peabody, with the trustees and other prominent men, sat on a raised platform facing the audience. He seemed unperturbed as usual, and his manner
implied that the trustees had never been separated by the bitterness of the
war. He was equally calm when he received a great standing ovation from
everyone present.

Because of Kennedy's absence in Europe, his presidential address paying tribute to Peabody was read to the gathering by Judge George Washington Dobbin. When Peabody rose to respond to this speech, and after
he had again been greeted with loud applause, there was the silence of anticipation in the hall. For the first time since the beginning of the war,
Confederates and Union sympathizers were attending a meeting together.
Peabody was aware that to clear the air and to encourage Baltimoreans
to work together for the institute, plain speaking was needed. The Civil
War and the distressing friction it had caused in Baltimore could not be
ignored.

Peabody, in his speech, explained his own position in the war:

I have been accused of anti-Union sentiment. Let me say this: my father
fought in the American Revolution and I have loved my country since childhood. Born and educated in the North, I have lived twenty years in the South.
In a long residence abroad I dealt with Americans from every section. I loved
our country as a whole with no preference for East, West, North, or South.
When War came I saw no hope for America except in Union victory. But
I could not, in the passion of war, turn my back on Southern friends. I believed
extremists of both sides guilty of fomenting the conflict. Now I am convinced
more than ever of the necessity for mutual forbearance and conciliation, of
Christian charity and forgiveness, of united effort to bind up the wounds of our
nation. . . . To you, therefore I make probably the last appeal I shall ever make.
May not this Institute be a common ground, where all may meet, burying former differences and animosities, forgetting past separations and estrangements.
May not Baltimore, the birthplace of religious toleration in America, become
the star of political tolerance and charity. Will not Maryland, in place of a
battleground of opposing parties, become the field where good men may meet
to make the future of our country prosperous and glorious.

The favorable reaction to Peabody's frank speech was apparent at the
reception and festivities which followed the formal opening of the institute.
Baltimoreans who had avoided meeting for years diffidently approached
each other, and men of good will tried to make peace with their former
enemies after the long and bitter estrangement.

Peabody's great gift to Baltimore was not universally appreciated. He
was now a very famous philanthropist, and the price of fame is often anger

and jealousy on the part of smaller men. The night of the institute's opening a preposterous letter signed "S.P.Q." appeared in several newspapers. This letter accused Peabody of many transgressions: that he had feathered his nest during the war, that he never made contributions to the sanitary commission, that he gave money to the poor of London instead of helping to clothe and raise a single recruit for the Union Army.

Peabody himself and his friends did not take these attacks seriously, for as the New York *Times* pointed out, "When Lafayette revisited this country in 1825 amid honors and acclaim one voice was raised against him. Now Mr. Peabody returns to bestow his gifts amid heartfelt thanks and *one* hoarse voice attacks his patriotism."

In Baltimore, too, where the festivities connected with the institute continued for several days, people took little notice of S.P.Q.'s letter. On the day after the dedication of the institute, a crowd estimated to be twenty thousand strong crowded onto the square outside the institute while Peabody, his relatives, and friends stood on the front steps. The Fourth United States Artillery Band played stirring music, and Baltimore schoolchildren, waving flags and banners, marched past.

The next evening a huge reception had been organized for Baltimoreans in the assembly hall of the institute. Peabody moved about freely, speaking to old friends, and obviously enjoying himself. He seemed quite refreshed, though the night before he had played whist with some friends until half-past-one in the morning. Entertainments and visits with friends in Baltimore continued until Peabody left for Zanesville, Ohio, October 31, to see his relatives. He was, of course, especially looking forward to a reunion with his niece Julia, who, four years before, had married a Zanesville lawyer, Charles W. Chandler.

During the excitement and pleasurable reunion with friends in Baltimore, Peabody had appeared to be younger than his seventy-one years and he was obviously very well, but as soon as he reached the comfortable haven of the Chandlers's happy home, his gout reappeared, this time in his knees. Walking was again difficult, so he remained comfortably in bed for some days being lovingly looked after by Julia and his other relations. Bishop McIlvaine and other Ohio friends called upon him while he held court, as it were, in Julia's best bedroom in Zanesville.

The Creation of the Peabody Education Fund

SEVERAL years before his American visit in 1866, Peabody had considered establishing a fund in New York City for the benefit of "the industrious poor." When in the States, however, especially after traveling as far south as Maryland and talking to Southern friends, he was so deeply moved by the misery and poverty prevalent in the South after the Civil War that to help there became his first objective.

The pessimistic letters he received depressed him further. William Aiken, former governor of South Carolina, wrote to Peabody in care of Corcoran that the South was ruined and that nothing could save the Southern states from absolute want. "Its destruction," Aiken asserted, "is now certain."

Peabody was convinced that, in the long run, only a better standard of education would help solve the problems confronting the South. He believed that education would counteract the despair of Southerners and thus build up a new and viable society. What Peabody learned during his visit to America about Southern education, or rather the lack of it, appalled him.

During the war educational institutions everywhere in the South were destroyed or had become inactive, and few of them had been rebuilt. As a result, a whole generation of Southerners was growing up practically illiterate. Many of the boys who had been twelve when the war broke out six years before and were now young men of eighteen had never gone to school. The state governments were too poor to finance education, and this disheartening situation had worsened.

Knowledge of these conditions and his sympathy for the South prompted George Peabody to give one million dollars for the Southern Education Fund—a sum which was doubled two years later—"with which to promote and encourage the intellectual, moral, and industrial education of the destitute children of the Southern States."

Efficient men helped Peabody to organize this great enterprise, and they continued to carry out his wishes long after his death. Robert Charles Winthrop, Peabody's confidential advisor, assisted in the selection of suitable trustees for the Southern Education Fund, and for twenty-seven years he was the policy maker of the fund.

Winthrop also found and appointed the man who actually directed the administration of the fund, Barnas Sears, who had been professor of theology and later president of Newton Theological Seminary. He had succeeded Horace Mann as secretary of the Massachusetts State Board of Education, and when Winthrop approached him in connection with Peabody's Southern Education Fund, he was president of Brown University in Rhode Island.

Another man who supported Peabody's Fund for Southern Education was his old friend Thurlow Weed, with whom in London he had discusssed his various philanthropies for so many years. It was Weed, as has been said, who had suggested Winthrop as a suitable advisor.

Winthrop was in Baltimore late in January and early in February 1867, and he and Peabody met often. The excellent advice Winthrop gave Peabody is reflected in the trustees of the fund whom he and Peabody appointed. These men came from different geographical backgrounds and had such divergent interests that together they were bound to become a team with a broad outlook. They were

> Robert Charles Winthrop, Massachusetts
> Hamilton Fish, New York
> Bishop Charles Pettit McIlvaine, Ohio
> General Ulysses Simpson Grant, United States Army
> Admiral David Glasgow Farragut, United States Navy
> William Cabell Rives, Virginia
> John Henry Clifford, former governor of Massachusetts
> William Aiken, former governor of South Carolina
> William Maxwell Evarts, New York
> William Alexander Graham, former governor of North Carolina
> Charles Macalester, Pennsylvania
> George Washington Riggs, Washington, D.C.
> Samuel Wetmore, New York
> Edward A. Bradford, Louisiana

George N. Eaton, Maryland

George Peabody Russell, Massachusetts

After these men had been invited by letter to become trustees and had accepted, Peabody and Winthrop went to Washington to meet them in a group at Willard's Hotel. In the meantime, with Winthrop's help, Peabody had drafted his founding letter, which was dated February 7, 1867, and was addressed to the sixteen trustees.

In this letter he emphasized that to be a really great country, the United States's "moral and intellectual development should keep pace with her material growth." Without good education in the South as well as in the North, such a well-balanced development could never take place. And, as he declared in this founding letter, "the impoverished people of the South cannot, without aid, advance themselves in knowledge and power" and thus contribute to the growth of the nation.

The meeting of the trustees on February 8, 1867, was an emotional affair. It was not quite two years since Appomattox, and for the first time former governors of Northern and Southern states came together for a peaceful purpose. Before beginning their conference, the trustees and Peabody knelt in prayer led by Bishop McIlvaine.

In a Founder's Day address given on February 18, 1916, President Bruce Ryburn Payne of George Peabody College for Teachers in Nashville, Tennessee, presented a touching description of the scene. With Winthrop in the chair, President Payne stated, Peabody, standing between General Grant and Bishop McIlvaine, read the deed of gift, which was "the first guarantee of a reunited Country and of perpetual Union."

At the meeting at Willard's Hotel, Peabody and his trustees could not possibly have foretold the future importance of the Peabody Education Fund. At the time it was clear that no gift was more needed by the Southern states, but no one could yet envisage the beneficial consequences of the fund, or know that for thirty years it would echo and re-echo and inspire the John F. Slater Fund, the Anna T. Jeanes Fund, and influence the founding of Tulane University and the Johns Hopkins University and Medical School.

The fund awakened the public school movement in the Southern states and caused legislators to vote for free public schools. The fund made possible the training of teachers and gave great impetus to normal schools. And in 1914, when the fund's chief task had been completed, its main resources were concentrated on the Peabody Normal College, Nashville,

Tennessee, an outgrowth in 1875 of the moribund literary department of the University of Nashville, which has since 1908 achieved renown as George Peabody College for Teachers.

At the first meeting with the trustees, Peabody was conscious only of the immediate and desperate need of a revival of education in the South. Before the trustees parted, they decided to meet again in New York on March 19.

In the meantime, Winthrop and Barnas Sears, who was appointed a little later, began working out detailed plans for the disposal of the fund. Sears was aware that Peabody wanted Southern communities to help themselves rather than to receive charity. Sears declared that, as the agent of the Peabody Education Fund, he would grant financial aid to such Southern schools as were already established and which were supported and administered by the Southern people. Other schools, which were threatened by suspension because of a lack of funds, would be given financial assistance until such time as they could be self-supporting. Sears also announced that some money would be given to communities where no schools existed so that new schools could be built, but these grants were to be made on condition that these communities themselves be responsible for the support of the schools.

Sears also mentioned normal schools in his early announcements. He said that donations from the Peabody Fund would be concentrated on a few well-run institutions rather than on a large number of less efficient normal schools. But the normal schools, too, were expected to become self-supporting or be financed by their own state or community.

Sears and Peabody were frequently asked whether some Southern states would not benefit more than others from the fund. Peabody, who had delegated decisions to the trustees, answered such questions by deferring to them.

"I leave absolute discretion to the Board of Trustees," he wrote, "as to the localities in which the Fund will be expended. I hope all the Southern States which have suffered from the war will ultimately receive benefits according to their needs."

For when George Peabody had contributed to any cause and had handed over the administration to a body of trustees, he was often impatient when he was asked about details concerning the trustees' activities. Besides, immediately after the first meeting of the Peabody Education Fund trustees in Washington, he was preoccupied with other developments.

On the day after the meeting, he was surprised and gratified when President Andrew Johnson and his secretary, Colonel William G. Moore, called upon him at Willard's Hotel.

President Johnson had welcomed Peabody's gift to the South, which, he hoped, would be a factor in reuniting the country. Johnson was not experiencing an easy term of office. He faced a hostile Congress, both Houses of which were controlled by Radical Republicans with strong desires to punish the former Confederate States. With a threat of impeachment hanging over Johnson at this time, he was a worried man.

His political advisor, Francis Preston Blair, was recommending strong measures, such as a complete change of the Cabinet, and Peabody had been mentioned as a possibility for Secretary of the Treasury. It is not known whether in their meeting on February 9 President Johnson discussed Blair's suggestion with Peabody, but he would without a doubt have refused an invitation to become a member of the Administration. He knew that he was far too old to launch forth on a new career, even had it interested him. And it did not interest him because he was concentrating on his philanthropies. In fact, he now appeared to be in a hurry to complete plans for his various charities. He gave the impression of a man who realized that he had not much more time.

Before returning to Salem toward the end of February, he gave an additional $15,000 to the public library in Newburyport and wrote the instrument of trust which created the Peabody Academy of Science (after 1915 called the Peabody Museum of Salem).

These gifts and above all his enormous donation to Southern education caused him once more—as he had been in London—to be overwhelmed by hundreds of begging letters. He asked Judith to sift through his mail, and one can imagine with what relish, perhaps a little self importance, she conscientiously assumed this task. Finally Peabody was obliged, in a letter to leading newspapers, to announce that he had delegated others to attend to his correspondence, and he added that about four thousand begging letters had been burned in his presence.

Early in March, resolutions were passed by both Houses of Congress praising Peabody, thanking him for his gift to the South, and requesting that the President have a gold medal struck in his honor. About the same time Queen Victoria's portrait painted especially for Peabody arrived in Washington and was presented to him by the British Ambassador, Sir Frederick Bruce. The news of this portrait added to Peabody's renown, and the newspapers, already full of stories about him, included reports about this portrait.

If this adulation of a citizen had happened in the nineteen-seventies instead of the eighteen-sixties, Peabody would undoubtedly have been eligible to become "the man of the year," and his picture might have been displayed on the cover of one of the glossy news magazines. Reporters were not very different a hundred years ago. An interview with Peabody, quoted in the Newark *Journal*, reflects the approach of the press to him as well as Peabody's modest reaction to fame.

REPORTER: What are your views on those who suggest you as President of the United States?

PEABODY: It is a kind and complimentary reference. If I were forty and could be elected unanimously, not as a partisan, I would like it. But I am seventy-two and my main concern is to preserve my health. The English climate suits me, but I will return to the United States in three years.

REPORTER: What will you do in the next three years?

PEABODY: Fish for salmon. I need the exercise and I enjoy it. It is good for my lungs and circulation.

REPORTER: Have you accomplished all you set out to do?

PEABODY: All the plans I made in London before I came have been accomplished with slight modification. Only the gift of $140,000 for science in Essex County was not then contemplated. In all my charities Robert Charles Winthrop gave me valuable advice. If I could choose the President of the United States he would be my choice.

Having accomplished what he intended to do during his visit to the United States, Peabody had booked his return voyage to England on the *Scotia*, sailing from New York on May 1, 1867. During the last months of his stay in America, though he was feeling very tired, he did not rest. On March 22 in New York he gave a large banquet for more than seventy guests in honor of General Grant and the trustees of the Education Fund. A few weeks later he was in both parts of Danvers, where he was welcomed by the citizens and the schoolchildren, and after that he went to Georgetown to attend a farewell reception.

His last visit to Baltimore before sailing was equally strenuous, especially as he went from there for a day to Washington to be received by President Johnson in the White House. While visiting Baltimore toward the end of April he stayed for a few days at the home of his friend John Work Garrett, who lived outside the city in Oakland. Many visitors arrived at the Garrett home while Peabody was there, but he was unruffled and re-laxed, obviously enjoying himself. He attended a large wedding party in Baltimore when Reverdy Johnson's daughter was married. He appeared to be indefatigable and people were impressed by his vigor. Actually, he was doing too much. He lost twenty pounds during this visit to America, and his spurts of energy were bad for his ailing constitution.

The visit of one of Garrett's friends in Oakland had far-reaching re-sults. This visitor was Johns Hopkins, Baltimore merchant and financier who had casual contact with Peabody in 1856. Now Hopkins came to Garrett's home to have a quiet discussion with Peabody. Garrett was aware that Hopkins, married but childless, was wondering what to do with his great wealth and wanted Peabody's advice. Garrett was present when Pea-body and Hopkins conferred in his study after dinner.

As Garrett later reported the conversation, Peabody, explaining the basis of his philanthropies to Hopkins, said,

When aches and pains made me realize that I was not immortal, I felt, after tak-ing care of my relatives, great anxiety to place the millions I had accumulated, so as to accomplish the greatest good for humanity. I . . . formed the conclusion that there were men who were just as anxious to work with integrity for the . . . suffering and the struggling poor as I had been to gather fortune. . . . I called a number of my friends . . . and proposed that they should act as my trustees. . . . I then, for the first time, felt there was a higher pleasure and a greater happi-ness than accumulating money, and that was derived from giving it for good and humane purposes.

Hopkins was obviously so carried away by Peabody's personality and his educational interests that he made his will the very next day, and two months later bills to incorporate his benefactions were in the Maryland Legislature. Thus Peabody, apart from his own great charities, may honor-ably stand in the shadow of what has been achieved by the Johns Hopkins University, Medical School, and Hospital.

Peabody himself did not appreciate the extent to which he had influ-enced Hopkins, who had been only one among the many men he had met during this visit to the United States. Peabody was now eager to be gone and hoped for a rest on the *Scotia* during his return journey to England. He was an upright, impressive figure when Winthrop and other friends saw him off at the Cunard pier in New York. On board was a Philadelphia newspaper owner, John Wien Forney. In common with the other passengers on the *Scotia*, Forney was interested in the famous philanthropist. Forney wrote,

As I studied the venerable philanthropist yesterday as he lay dozing on one of the sofas in the forward saloon, I confessed I had never seen a nobler or more imposing figure. Never has human face spoken more humane emotions. The good man's soul seems to shine out of every feature and lineament. His fine head, rivalling the best of the old aristocracy, and blending the ideals of benevolence and integrity, his tranquil and pleasing countenance, and his silver hair, crown a lofty form of unusual dignity and grace.

Return to England

As the *Scotia* approached Queenstown in Ireland where Peabody was to disembark, he exchanged farewells with the other passengers. The Americans on board presented him with a resolution praising his philanthropies and extolling him as being greater than James Smithson or Stephen Girard. Peabody, the resolution stated, "had given his wealth away during his lifetime while he could watch and plan for its wise use." Peabody listened carefully as the resolution was read and then asked the reader to strike out this comparison with Smithson and Girard, which, he said, "might be construed as a criticism of those two illustrious men."

Before leaving the boat at Queenstown, Peabody gave John Wien Forney, the Philadelphia newspaper owner, letters of introduction to people in London. Forney intended to write a long report about the Peabody housing estates in London, and his articles became an important source of information for future generations concerned with housing reform in England and the United States.

Peabody traveled direct from Queenstown by way of Dublin to Castle Connell on the Shannon River near Limerick, for his doctor had advised him not to spend the summer in London. At Castle Connell he had leased fishing rights for six months and expected to fish for trout and salmon eight or ten hours a day. He had paid a large sum for these rights, $25,000, and, as his English friends would have expressed it, he was jolly well going to get his money's worth.

Fishing had become, for him, a kind of cure-all. He believed that the open air and the exercise involved in this sport might alleviate his "gouty bronchitis"—the diagnosis for his persistent cough and cold given by his physician. Fishing did indeed offer him distraction for hours at a time, but the evenings in Castle Connell would have been lonely had not several of his friends, Curtis Lampson and others, come to stay with him. As he never derived any pleasure at all from reading, he was very dependent on the company and conversation of his friends, especially now, when, after being continuously surrounded by people in America, he was suddenly very much alone.

One of his guests that summer at Castle Connell was John Bright, who was in special prominence just then because of his association with the Reform Act of 1867. Bright found pleasure in these visits—on one occasion he stayed a whole week—though "the weather was intensely hot; the river low, and fishing very bad."

Bright thoroughly enjoyed his talks with Peabody, whom he considered "a remarkable and generous man." Bright was particularly struck by Peabody's intelligence and knowledge in view of the fact that he never studied or read, and yet was obviously so well informed.

"Peabody," Bright noted in his diary, "has had almost no schooling and has not read books, but has had much experience, and is deeply versed in questions of commerce and banking. He is a man of strong will, and can decide questions for himself."

While Peabody was fishing in seclusion on the Shannon, he was notified that various honors were being prepared for him. In 1867 and 1868 he was the reluctant recipient of several distinctions. He wrote from Ireland to Robert Winthrop, who was in England in the summer of 1867, "I reluctantly agreed to receive these honors. . . . My friends told me I could not refuse them."

In 1868 the town of South Danvers was renamed Peabody in his honor. A year before, Harvard University made him, *in absentia*, an honorary Doctor of Civil Law. By some critics this degree from Harvard was considered untimely, as it followed too soon after Peabody's donation for the Harvard Museum; there are always individuals who accuse academic institutions of "selling honorary degrees."

In New York another honor for Peabody was well under way. Craftsmen of the famous silversmith firm of Starr and Marcus were making the elaborate medal to be presented by Congress. It was said to be the most distinctive gold medal ever produced in the United States. The central piece, an intricate pattern with several figures, was a round design, three inches in diameter and one half inch thick. Peabody's left profile was modeled on this golden circle; his head and shoulders were carved in bold relief. The reverse bore the inscription: "The People of the United States to George Peabody, in Acknowledgement of his Beneficial Promotion of Universal Education."

This medal, handmade and resembling a piece of small statuary rather than a medal, was not completed and exhibited to Congress until May 1868, and Peabody himself did not see it until early the next year. It is now in the Peabody Institute Library in Peabody, Massachusetts. Peabody's own taste had always remained austere and very simple, and one wonders what he really thought of the intricate pattern of this medal.

In England, too, people were eager to honor the aging Peabody. Oxford University invited him to accept, *honoris causa*, a doctorate of Civil Law. The degree-giving in Oxford was on June 26, 1867, and Peabody traveled from Castle Connell to London, where he was joined by the Tennents, the Lampsons, and Robert Winthrop, who accompanied him to Oxford.

Anyone who has recently witnessed a degree-giving in the old Sheldonian Theatre in Oxford will realize that this ceremony has not changed since Peabody's day, nor had it been altered before that for hundreds of years. Five other distinguished men presented themselves that June day in 1867 for degrees, but Peabody was undoubtedly the center of attention.

"The lion of the day," *Jackson's Oxford Journal* recorded, "was beyond a doubt Mr. Peabody."

A mathematics don at Christ Church and an amateur photographer, Charles Lutwidge Dodgson, better known to posterity by his pen name of Lewis Carroll, was equally impressed. He wrote in his diary,

Went to the [Sheldonian] Theatre as an extra proctor and took half the lady's gallery; it was a troublesome business to get them to move on and sit close. Freemason's fête in the afternoon, where I was introduced to the hero of the day, Mr. Peabody, who kindly consented to sit for a photograph in the morning.

Peabody has been pleased with the festivities in Oxford, but they had tired him and he was glad to return to Castle Connell for more quiet fishing. He did not stay in London long enough to await John Pendleton Kennedy, who was shortly to arrive from the United States. Peabody and Kennedy, however, met in Nice during Peabody's continental journey early in 1868.

When the cold rainy weather made fishing in Castle Connell unattractive, Peabody returned to London to prepare for this tour. In London one of his greatest honors was in its early stages. A statue of Peabody was to be erected in the City in remembrance of his housing endowments. A committee had been organized in 1866 to raise funds for this statue by popular subscription. The site selected for the statue was Threadneedle Street near the Royal Exchange in the heart of the business and banking district.

The response to the appeal for contributions to the statue fund was impressive. There were as many contributions in shillings as in pounds, for a large number of poor men and women welcomed this opportunity to express their gratitude to Peabody. Years later, after the Second World War, Londoners showed a similar gratitude to President Roosevelt, when they contributed toward his statue in Grosvenor Square.

William Wetmore Story, in whose work through the years Peabody had always been interested, was chosen as the sculptor to make the statue. Peabody was pleased with this choice, for he and Story understood each other well. Story had been born in Salem and had attended Harvard University and Harvard Law School before he became a full-time artist and settled in Rome in 1850.

While Peabody was in London in the fall of 1867, he was a guest in the home of Curtis Miranda Lampson and his wife at 80 Eaton Square. In their house he sat for Story's preliminary sketches for the statue. Lady Lampson had invited the sculptor, who had come from Rome for a few weeks, to use her back drawing room as a studio.

Peabody stayed with the Lampsons for the early part of the winter, but by the middle of January he and Robert Winthrop, who was to be his companion on this European tour, left for Rome. Here Peabody again sat for Story, this time in the sculptor's own studio.

The statue, unveiled two years later by the Prince of Wales, later Edward VII, shows Peabody wearing the ordinary clothes of the period, sitting relaxed and looking utterly benevolent in a heavy Victorian chair. Even today this statue, unlike so many Victorian monuments, does not seem dated. It gives the impression of a benevolent yet shrewd and firm elderly gentleman who knew exactly what he wanted from life.

Much of Peabody's time during his and Winthrop's visit to Rome was spent in Story's studio, but he and Winthrop did some sightseeing, and they were also received by Pope Pius IX. Peabody's Puritan ancestors would no doubt have been shocked had they known that, after the audience, he sent a contribution to Cardinal Antonelli for the hospital of San Spirito and some of the Vatican's other charities.

Winthrop stayed in Rome longer, but Peabody left toward the end of February, stopping at Genoa and then going on to Nice by boat. This time he did not anticipate with pleasure his visit to the south of France, for early in December his friend "Loula" Corcoran Eustis had died in Cannes after a long and painful illness, leaving three young children. Peabody's chief purpose in Cannes was to stay with the unhappy young widower. He planned to meet John Pendleton Kennedy in Nice before going on to Cannes.

Kennedy, on his way to Rome, had time for a short call on Peabody. He found the old gentleman in bed in a small hotel room on the third floor of a second-class hotel. Peabody was in an unhappy mood and suffering with gout in his hand. Kennedy must have wondered whether Peabody would ever learn to spend money on greater comforts for himself.

Despite his ill health, Peabody soon traveled to Cannes to give what comfort he could to the distracted George Eustis. Peabody's next stop was Paris, where he was joined again by Winthrop. In Paris he was received by the Emperor Napoleon III and the Empress Eugenie, who had the year before expressed her respect for him in an admiring letter. By March, Peabody had returned to London and was again surrounded by comfort and care in the Lampsons's hospitable home.

Here he was often confined to his bed because he felt too tired and unwell to get up, but his old restlessness, even after the exhausting trip to the Continent, had not left him, and he welcomed visitors who could offer him some distraction. Many interesting callers came to see him at Eaton Square, including Kennedy who was then in London, but soon even good companionship no longer gave him relief, and when the weather improved in the spring he was off again to Castle Connell. Shortly, however, he returned to England to see Winthrop, who was preparing to leave for the United States.

By September, Peabody had again returned to Ireland, this time as the guest of James Emerson Tennent and his wife at Tempo Manor, in Enniskillen. Here they were joined by Reverdy Johnson, now United States Minister to England. In November the same old friends were Peabody's guests in Brighton. The Brighton Corporation gave a dinner in honor of the Americans late in November, but Peabody was too ill to be present. He could now rarely cope, without undue fatigue, with formal social engagements.

There were many days in this long cold winter when Peabody was deeply depressed; his gout was worse, he suffered from lack of appetite and often felt very weak. His painful hand frequently made it impossible for him to write letters; he had to dictate them to a clerk. This was a considerable deprivation; his personal correspondence had always been a source of great satisfaction to him.

His low state of mind was further affected early in 1869 by the death of his old friend Sir James Emerson Tennent at the age of seventy-eight. Tennent had been with Peabody so recently in Brighton that his death was a great shock. Robert Winthrop, at home in Brookline, was justifiably anxious about Peabody.

"Recent advices from Mr. Peabody," he wrote to Hamilton Fish, "make me very apprehensive that he is more ill than we anticipated."

Peabody himself had become aware that he was a very sick man, and he was determined to pay one more visit to the United States before he died.

"I fear," he wrote to Kennedy, "if I postpone this visit until next year, it will be too late."

He therefore booked passage on the *Scotia* which sailed from Liverpool on May 29, 1869. It was a sad small group which saw him off at the docks, for Lampson was the only one of his old London friends and contemporaries who was now left.

Last Visit to the United States

PEABODY's last visit to the United States saddened his relatives and friends; his appearance was a shock to them. He was obviously aging fast; his old vigor was gone. Two of his nephews who lived in New York and some of the trustees of the Peabody Institute in Peabody had come to meet the *Scotia* when he disembarked. They escorted him to the home of Samuel Wetmore in Waverly Place where he stayed while he was in the city. Peabody had always preferred the complete independence of hotel rooms, and this visit must have been a trial to him, especially as his innate courtesy and his gratitude to Wetmore for his hospitality required him, outwardly at least, to be an appreciative guest. At any rate, it was a short visit.

A few days later in Boston he was met at the train by John Clifford, governor of Massachusetts; by his old friend and travelling companion of the year before, Robert Charles Winthrop; and by Dr. Barnas Sears, the general agent of the Peabody Education Fund.

In Boston, where he was the guest of Samuel T. Dana, he immediately consulted Dr. Putnam, a well-known Boston physician, who was unfortunately unable to do much for him. Nevertheless, Peabody exerted himself and took an interest in the life of Boston, where that summer a great Peace Jubilee and Music Festival was being held. In the middle of June, he attended a choral concert. He had not announced in advance that he would be present and was taken aback when the Mayor of Boston came onto the stage during an intermission and told the large audience that "Mr. Peabody, the friend of the whole world," was present. There was a deafening applause, and Peabody rose shakily to thank the Mayor and to say "that he loved the new world as much as he loved the old."

He soon left Boston and hoped for a quiet visit in Salem with his nephew George Peabody Russell and his wife, and with Judith and her family. George Russell acted as his secretary and helped him arrange the further donation of a second million dollars to the Peabody Education Fund.

The brief rest in Salem had apparently refreshed him, for early in July he was well enough to travel to Newport, Rhode Island, to meet the trustees of the Peabody Education Fund. He had prepared a letter which he read to them himself and in which he announced his new gift to the fund. The letter was gracious and in his usual style, and he emphasized how much the work of the fund owed the trustees and Dr. Barnas Sears, the general agent.

Peabody was obviously determined no matter how ill he felt to get about as usual, for, a few days after meeting the trustees in Newport, he was in Peabody, Massachusetts, conferring with the librarian of the Peabody Institute; then on to Georgetown to stay with his sister Judith and to see the new church and library building. Finally on July 14 he attended the official opening of the new Peabody Institute in Danvers.

Here his friends observed with anxiety that he appeared to be strikingly feeble as he sat on the platform during the opening ceremonies. His hands trembled painfully, and stimulants had to be given him. With tremendous will power he rose, slowly addressed the meeting, and announced that he was giving the institute another $45,000, bringing the total gift up to $100,000.

What worried the gathering in Danvers was not only his shakiness and his hesitant speech but that this usually calm old gentleman lost his temper. In an irritable voice he complained that the trustees had spent too much money on the lecturers invited to address the members of the institute. He nervously repeated several times, "You spend too much money," but soon regained his composure and praised the work of the institute.

When Peabody returned to Salem, his nephew, George Peabody Russell, urged him to go for a change of air to White Sulphur Springs, West Virginia, to join William Wilson Corcoran who had invited him. This visit to White Sulphur Springs had been considered by Peabody some weeks earlier, and on his behalf his nephew had written to Corcoran. Corcoran must have understood the seriousness of Peabody's condition when he was informed by George Peabody Russell that his uncle would be traveling under the care of himself and his wife. In the old days Peabody had always preferred to travel alone and to move about from place to place at his own pace.

The resort hotel at White Sulphur Springs, then known as "Old White" (today as the "Greenbrier") was surrounded by cottages where groups of guests could have more privacy. People who came for their health drank the waters, walked in the surrounding woods, or talked to their friends, sitting comfortably on the wide verandas or on the lawns. Younger visitors to the springs hunted, rode the mountain trails, or rolled ninepins in the lovely gardens.

White Sulphur Springs was a famous meeting place for Southern society, and in the Reconstruction period Southern culture revived and revolved about these Virginia springs. That summer of 1869 when Peabody was there, a record number of one thousand visitors had come to the Springs, among them many prominent men including General Robert E. Lee and other distinguished former Confederate generals.

Peabody shared a cottage with General Lee, William Wilson Corcoran, Johns Hopkins, and others. Peabody was not well enough to join his friends in the dining room or parlor in the main building of "Old White," but he received many of his fellow guests at the Springs in his cottage. A number of them, at the suggestion of Governor Henry A. Wise of Virginia, drew up a resolution expressing their respect for him, for in the South, as elsewhere at the time, such resolutions were *de rigueur*.

"Mr. Peabody's manners," General John Eaton, Superintendent of Education in Tennessee, a guest at the Springs, observed, "are singularly affable and pleasing, and his countenance one of the most benevolent we have ever seen. It is also indisputably handsome."

The Southerners at White Sulphur Springs wished to emphasize their admiration for Peabody, the Northerner in their midst, so they organized a great ball in his honor. This seems a most peculiar function with which to celebrate the presence of a sick old gentleman who was not well enough to attend himself. In bed in his cottage he could hear the echoes of this merrymaking. It is not recorded whether these happy sounds filled him with pleasure or with nostalgic memories of his own youth and vigor.

To those who attended the ball, however, it apparently meant a great deal, for there had not been many functions on this elaborate scale in the South since the war. It was said that in some strange way this ball held in Peabody's honor revived the Southerners' self respect. Percival Reniers, an authority on the history of the springs of Virginia, expressed in 1941 what appears to be a very odd and not entirely respectful attitude toward Peabody in connection with this ball. Reniers wrote in his *Springs of Virginia*,

The affair that did most to revive their [the Southerners'] esteem was the Peabody Ball . . . [that] was given to honor the king of philanthropists, Mr. George Peabody, the Yankee-born millionaire of London. Everything was ripe for the Peabody Ball, everybody was ready for just such a climax, the background was a perfect build-up. Mr. Peabody appeared at just the right time and lived just long enough. A few months later it would not have been possible, for Mr. Peabody would be dead.

Peabody's friends at the Springs in 1869 did not regard his presence in this cold-blooded manner. On the contrary, eager to revive the South and Southern education, they understood and were grateful for what he had done for their cause. A famous photograph taken at the Springs on one of the days when Peabody was well enough to leave his bed reflects the respect with which he was surrounded.

There were thirteen persons in this photograph, five of whom sat on cane-bottom chairs, while the other eight stood in a row behind. Peabody sat in the center of the seated men between General Lee and William Wilson Corcoran, and the others in the photograph included some of the most famous generals of the Confederacy, such as P. G. T. Beauregard of Louisiana, James Conner of South Carolina, and Alexander R. Lawton of Georgia.

This early picture is not merely a photographic curiosity; it symbolizes the real desire felt by these more enlightened Southerners to promote the educational possibilities offered by Peabody for the Southern states.

The presence at White Sulphur Springs of Barnas Sears and of Jabez Lamar Monroe Curry—later to succeed Sears as the general agent of the Peabody Education Fund—and of Judge Lyons and other Southern advocates of public education, made that summer the occasion for informal and fruitful conferences on the work of the fund and on Southern education generally.

General Lee's concern with Southern education was stimulated by these talks. He was the president of Washington College (now Washington and Lee) in Lexington, Virginia, and it was at this time Peabody gave the Virginia bonds already mentioned, valued at $60,000, to Washington College.

Naturally, Peabody's gift to Washington College and his persistent interest in his Education Fund were not approved of by some shortsighted people in the North. These people continued to hate the South and did not want to understand how vital it was for the future of the whole country to build up a new unity. William Lloyd Garrison's attack on Peabody in the *Independent*, for example, was venomous. Peabody was described as a man "not mentally or morally gifted," and Garrison wrote that "his first notable gift was made to Maryland when that State was rotten with treason," that "he doesn't go to a Northern mineral spring, but to White Sulphur Springs in Virginia where the *élite* of rebeldom welcome him

with congratulatory resolutions." The record of the South, Garrison concluded, "is one of lust and blood, of treachery and cruelty, of robbery and
oppression, of rebellion and war. . . . These are the people Mr. Peabody
praises."

It was just as well that Peabody did not see Garrison's article, for he
no longer remained as calm as formerly under unfair attack. His health
had not improved at the Springs despite the excellent care of Dr. J. J.
Moorman, the physician who attended him. By August 30, however, he
was well enough to travel and he left the Springs in a special railroad car
accompanied part of the way to Baltimore by General Lee. In Baltimore
he spent the day with John Work Garrett, then went on to Philadelphia,
where he seemed better. His cough had subsided and his appetite had improved, but it was apparent to his friends that his condition was worse
than when he arrived in the United States.

After his arrival in New York, his first task was to write a new will,
which read as follows:

First: My remains shall be sent to Peabody, Massachusetts, United
States of America, and buried in Harmony Grove Cemetery,
Salem, Massachusetts.

Second: I give to Henry West, 22 Old Broad Street, London, £2,200,
or to his wife, Louise West, in case of his death.

Third: I give to Thomas Perman of 22 Old Broad Street, London,
£1000, or to his wife, Annette Emma Perman, or to her child
in case of his or her death.

Fourth: I give to the Trustees of the Peabody Donation Fund in London £150,000 for homes for the poor of London, to be allo-
cated in two sums: £100,000 in 1873 and £50,000 any time
after that. If it is necessary to add another trustee I suggest
the name of Mr. Charles Reed.

Fifth: I constitute Sir Curtis Miranda Lampson and Mr. Charles
Reed executors of my British possessions. George Peabody
Russell, Robert Singleton Peabody, and Charles W. Chandler [the husband of his niece Julia] will constitute the executors of my United States possessions. It is my wish that
both groups always act in harmony.

Sixth: I give to each British executor £5,000, and to each American executor $5,000.

Seventh: The residue of my estate now and hereafter due I give to the
family trust already established. This is my last Will and

Testament written in my hand and sealed this ninth day of September 1869.

Soon after Peabody had signed his will, he left New York and made plans to return to New England. He was obviously eager to settle certain affairs as soon as possible. In Salem he ordered a granite sarcophagus for his own grave; he then hurried on to Boston, and from there to Newport, Rhode Island, to meet John Pendleton Kennedy, who was at the time "very much out of health" to come to Salem or Boston. From Newport, Peabody took the night boat for New York and went on the next morning to Baltimore. Soon he returned to New York by way of Philadelphia. He visited these cities in quick succession because he had a strong desire, almost a compulsion, once more to see old friends, to revisit his institutes, and to take leave of his trustees.

When he embarked on the *Scotia* on September 29, 1869, he must have known that he would never see America again.

Death

DR. MOORMAN in White Sulphur Springs had urged Peabody on his return to England to remain there for only a short time and to go on to the south of France where the climate would suit him better. When Peabody landed in Queenstown on October 8, he traveled to London to the home of the Lampsons in Eaton Square; from there he hoped to leave shortly for the south.

Unfortunately, however, he was not strong enough to contemplate another journey, and despite the affectionate and constant care given him by the whole Lampson household, his condition did not improve. He was very ill, and news bulletins were published daily in the press reporting his condition. The *Anglo-American Times*, published in London, stated on October 30 that

Mr. Peabody has been lying all week very ill at 80, Eaton Square where he had stopped on his way to the South of France. . . . There has been no improvement, and the latest report was that, though easier on Thursday night, his condition remained the same. Everyone, from the Queen downward, has been making inquiries about the eminent American philanthropist.

There was a constant stream of callers at Eaton Square. Men and women from all walks of life came to inquire about Peabody and to leave messages of respect. Lady Lampson and her staff were kept busy receiving these visitors and assuring them that when Mr. Peabody was well enough these messages would be conveyed to him.

Before Queen Victoria realized how ill Peabody was, she had hoped he would come to Windsor for a few days to recuperate. Arthur Helps, one of her Privy Councillors, wrote to Curtis Miranda Lampson to say that if Mr. Peabody would come to Windsor "he could rest [there]—and need not come to dinner, or any meals if he feels unequal to it; but be where the Queen could see him quietly at any time of the day most convenient to him." And when Queen Victoria had been told of the seriousness of Peabody's illness, she sent a telegram of inquiry and sympathy and one of her secretaries called at Eaton Square.

By October 27 it was obvious to his physician, Dr. Gull, and a medical attendant, Mr. Covey, that Peabody's condition was precarious. They held out virtually no hope for his recovery. There were hours at a time when he was unconscious.

Strangely enough, on this very day, October 27, when the bulletins regarding his condition were extremely pessimistic, he rallied sufficiently to send Horatio G. Somerby, the old friend who was acting as his secretary, to the American Legation to ask his old enemy, Benjamin Moran, to come to Eaton Square. One can only assume that, throughout the years of Moran's bitter attacks in his diary, Peabody must somehow have been aware of the man's hatred and that now, before he died, he hoped to make peace with his enemies. In his diary for that day (October 27) Moran noted laconically,

Horatio G. Somerby came and said Mr. Peabody wished to see me. I promised to call and sent the old man my regards. But Somerby did not know how ill the old man is. The *Times* of today says he is in a dangerous state and Mr. Motley [John Lothrop Motley, then American Minister to London] tells me he is really dying. A few hours must close his earthly career.

For days before his death Peabody lay quietly, apparently unconscious of his surroundings. He did not respond to anything said to him until a clergyman, Dr. Nolan, with whom Peabody had once made an ocean crossing, came to his bedside and prayed. After the prayer Peabody was heard to mutter "Amen" and then whisper, "It is a great mystery, but I shall know all soon."

Peabody died peacefully, in the presence of a few loyal friends, including the Lampsons and Charles Reed, at 11:30 in the evening of November 4, 1869. He was seventy-four years old.

Upon Sir Curtis Miranda Lampson fell the responsibility of supervising Peabody's funeral arrangements in England and of having the body embalmed and prepared for transportation to America. Lampson was familiar with Peabody's will and knew that he was to be buried in the Harmony Grove Cemetery in Salem.

Lampson telegraphed to George Peabody Russell informing him of his uncle's death. George Russell replied that he would leave immediately for England and return as soon as possible to America with his uncle's body.

Lampson appreciated that there must be a funeral service in England before the nephew reached London. There had been many letters to the Lampsons and so many tributes to Peabody in the press that, obviously, his admirers in London were determined to have a service at which they could show him their last respects.

In the meantime, Arthur Penrhyn Stanley, the famous Dean of Westminster, who was in Italy when he heard of Peabody's death, felt that "by reason of his benefactions to the City of London, Peabody was entitled to a burial in Westminster Abbey." Burial in the Abbey was, and is, the greatest honor that can be conferred upon a British subject, and to confer this honor on a foreigner is rare.

As a result of the Dean's wishes, which were supported by the Chapter of Westminster, by the public, and by Queen Victoria, Sir Curtis Lampson was asked to have the great philanthropist buried in the Abbey. Lampson then explained that, according to Peabody's will, he was to be buried in Salem, Massachusetts. Finally, after lengthy consultations with John Lothrop Motley, with Arthur Helps for the Queen, and with members of the Chapter at Westminster, it was decided to have a temporary burial in Westminster Abbey on November 12.

Prime Minister William E. Gladstone promised to attend the Abbey service and at a Cabinet meeting decided to send Peabody's remains back to America in the newest and largest warship of the British Navy, the *Monarch*.

The suggestion of sending the *Monarch* on this peaceful mission was an important gesture, for it eased the current Anglo-American controversy about the *Alabama*, a disagreement then worrying statesmen in both countries. The *Alabama* was a British-built Confederate warship which had sunk millions of dollars worth of Union cargo during the Civil War. Now the United States was demanding reparations. England bitterly resented this demand, and Anglo-American tension was again at a high pitch at the time of Peabody's death. Gladstone's conciliatory gesture, therefore, offering the *Monarch*, was welcomed in both England and in America. Even in death, Peabody's efforts to maintain good relations between the two countries were being strengthened.

At noon on Friday, November 12, Peabody's hearse, drawn by four horses and followed by five mourning coaches, began the slow procession from Eaton Square to Westminster Abbey. The procession moved along streets lined with silent crowds, and at the entrance of the Abbey, too, people had congregated.

"It was touching," the American Minister, John Lothrop Motley, wrote to Hamilton Fish, then Secretary of State, "to observe upon the faces of the vast crowd a general air of respect and earnest sympathy. . . . The silence and decorum in the midst of the chief thoroughfares of this immense city were impressive."

The funeral party and dignitaries followed the coffin past the crowds through the Abbey entrance into the nave. The beautiful singing of the choristers blended with the organ and filled the Abbey with music. From the small high windows oblique shafts of the sun drifted down into the somber Abbey.

Even Benjamin Moran, who was present, was impressed. He "mentally remarked," as he wrote in his diary,

that I could now forget that I had ever warred with the dust before me. . . . I reflected on the marvellous career of the man, his early life, his penurious habits, his vast fortune, his magnificent charity; and the honor that was being paid to his memory by the Queen of England in the place of sepulchre of twenty English kings. . . . George Peabody having received burial in Westminster Abbey, an honor coveted by nobles and not always granted kings.

The London correspondent of the New York *Times* was more sincerely moved than Moran. This correspondent was fully and wholeheartedly aware of Peabody's greatness. "My transatlantic heart," he wrote, echoing the sentiments of the other Americans present in the Abbey,

beat rather quicker at the thought of clergy and nobility, Prime Minister and people, of this great realm gathered to lay our citizen countryman among sleeping kings and statesmen. The crowd outside was, if possible more interesting than that within. The gaunt, famished London poor were gathered in thousands to testify their respect for the foreigner who had done more than any Englishman for their class, and whose last will contains an additional bequest to them of £150,000.

On the Sunday after the funeral, Peabody memorial services were held in many English churches. The Bishop of London was the preacher at the service in the Abbey. In the United States, too, Peabody's passing was noted with great respect. In Boston and Baltimore church bells were tolled, and the Tennessee Legislature passed a resolution "deploring this loss of a benefactor of all mankind."

While Peabody's coffin rested in the Abbey, plans were under way for the transport of his remains to the United States. George Peabody Russell had arrived from Salem, but as his uncle had been a public figure of such prominence, the young man had to leave final arrangements to the authorities in England and America.

Two messages concerning the transport of the coffin to the States reached the American Legation at the same time. One was from Lord Clarendon of the Foreign Office expressing Queen Victoria's desire to transport Peabody's coffin on the *Monarch*. The other was from Hamilton Fish, stating that Rear Admiral William Radford, U.S.N., would send an American vessel from Marseilles to Portsmouth for the same purpose.

According to Benjamin Moran, "these two communications threw Mr. Motley into one of his fits of indecision," and he hardly knew what to do. He communicated with Hamilton Fish asking for advice. Fish consulted the President, and Grant decided to accept the Queen's suggestion but requested that an American warship escort the *Monarch* on her crossing to America.

So on Saturday, December 11, Peabody's coffin was taken from the Abbey to begin the long journey to America. In a cold, drenching rain, carriages followed the hearse to Waterloo station where a special train was ready to take the remains to Portsmouth. Here, at the dock, a double line of marines forming an honor guard stood stiffly at attention. Hundreds of spectators waited in the pouring rain, and the members of Portsmouth City Council stood out from the crowd in their scarlet robes of office. The many umbrellas held up by the assembled people mingled oddly with lines, spars, and beams of the many British ships in the port.

A gun salute went up from the *Excellent*. The bow battery of the *Monarch* echoed the boom, and bugles sounded a funeral dirge. The British vessels lowered their ensigns to half mast and raised the American ensign abreast foretopmast crosstrees. The U.S.S. *Plymouth* lowered her ensign from her peak. The guns of the *Duke of Wellington* fired at minute intervals. The rain became heavier, and a fresh gale blew the wind vigorously through the rigging of the assembled ships.

Minister Motley went aboard the *Monarch*, which had been transformed into a slate-gray funeral ship, as soon as the booming of the cannon had stopped. He stood facing Captain John E. Commerell beside the coffin on the *Monarch*'s quarterdeck. Motley made a brief speech concluding with the words, "As Minister of the Republic at the Court of Her Majesty I deliver to your safe keeping, at the request of the relatives and executors of Mr. Peabody, his revered remains." Captain Commerell's formal reply concluded with his acceptance of "this sacred trust."

On account of the stormy weather, the coffin was moved from the quarterdeck to the captain's cabin, which had been made over into an impressive mortuary chapel. The coffin rested on a black-covered dais in the middle of the cabin, and sentinels from among the crew stood continuous guard during the crossing.

It was a slow journey. The vessels stopped at Madeira to refuel and in Bermuda to take on dispatches and provisions. They then steamed on toward Portland. This small Maine harbor had been chosen instead of Boston in Peabody's home state as the landing port because the *Monarch* drew too much water for Boston harbor and the Portland water was deeper.

Many Bostonians were disappointed and angry and did not believe that the people of "little Portland" would be sufficiently experienced or worldly wise to cope with the proper reception of the largest and newest ship of the British Navy. Provincial Portlanders would blunder, Boston merchants wrote despairingly to George Peabody Russell, and "nothing would be in worse taste" than to have the reception of Peabody's coffin in Portland.

To some extent, the Bostonians were proved right when, in the Maine Legislature, a controversy ensued concerning the attendance of the entire legislature in Portland for the arrival of the warships. Some of the members of the House in Augusta did not, at first, agree to attend, because, unable to forget the war, they were antagonistic to Peabody for his generosity to the "rebels."

A reconciliation committee of the Maine Legislature finally persuaded its members to attend in a body. From the beginning of the controversy, however, all the members had been gratified to welcome to Portland Admiral David Glasgow Farragut, who was to be in charge of the naval reception. His selection was suitable in every way, for he had been one of the original trustees of the Peabody Education Fund, quite apart from being so outstanding an officer in the United States Navy. Actually, Peabody's funeral reception was Farragut's last tour of duty; he was already a sick man and he died six months later.

Portland was filled with young members of the Marine Corps, the state militia, sailors, and hundreds of curious visitors. No one knew just when the funeral fleet would arrive, and it suddenly occurred to someone to hold a ball for the young men in uniform. This ball, given in a town already draped in mourning for the great occasion, was indeed in startlingly bad taste; perhaps the Bostonians had been right about Portland. At any rate, while the ball was in full swing, a messenger hurried into the Fluento Hall and announced that the *Monarch* had arrived in port.

As soon as the vessel had docked, Captain Commerell called on Admiral Farragut requesting that Peabody's coffin remain two more days on board the *Monarch* as a final mark of respect. This delay enabled Portland citizens to visit the great British warship, and silent crowds moved past the bier in the captain's cabin.

January 29, 1870, the day on which the coffin was taken off the *Monarch*, was cold and stormy. Uniformed men were drawn up in ranks on the wharf, and onlookers stood close together to ward off the wind. Drummers sounded a muted roll and the ship's band played a somber death march. Marines stood at attention, and officers and crews of the ships bared their heads. The boatswain's whistle piped shrilly. The coffin, made fast with a roped rig, was swung over the *Monarch*'s side to the deck of a small, waiting ship and then transported to the Eastern Wharf. From there it was taken to the Portland City Hall, where for two days Peabody lay in state.

On February 1, after a service of remembrance, twelve sailors from the U.S.S. *Plymouth*, under falling snow, placed the coffin aboard the funeral train which carried Peabody home to Peabody, Massachusetts. Here his body lay in state in the library of the Peabody Institute before the burial.

Again, as he lay in state, a controversy almost marred the occasion. It was rumored that General Robert E. Lee planned to attend the service at the graveside. Robert Charles Winthrop, who was to give the final eulogy, feared that the presence of Lee might "cause something unpleasant to occur at the funeral which might be unpleasant for him [Lee] as for us." Winthrop was afraid of demonstrations, for the anti-Confederate feeling remained strong in New England. In fact, this problem solved itself, because Lee was ill and unable to come to Peabody for the funeral.

Thousands of respectful people from Salem, Danvers, and other towns in the vicinity had braved the stormy weather and come to Peabody for the funeral, though there was room for only a few of them in the South Congregational Church. There were well-known men, too, in the procession which, in carriages or on foot, followed the hearse to Harmony Grove Cemetery. Queen Victoria's son, Prince Arthur, on a visit to Canada and the United States that year, attended the service, and so did, of course, the governors of Maine and Massachusetts, the mayors of nearby towns, Charles W. Eliot of Harvard, and the captains of the *Monarch* and the *Plymouth*.

Judith, her husband, Othniel Marsh, and other members of Peabody's family stood a little apart from these famous people. To them, George Peabody was the brother and uncle whom they had loved and revered as a man and whom they would have loved and revered had he remained throughout his life an obscure New Englander, known and respected only by his own community. As they listened at the graveside to Winthrop's moving eulogy of George Peabody, they remembered that, in Peabody's boyhood, Harmony Grove Cemetery, lying on the boundary between Peabody and Salem, had been a thick walnut grove where he had often played. Here, in memory of his youth, he had built the family tomb, where his father and mother and other members of his family had already been buried. When George Peabody himself was laid to rest in Harmony Grove Cemetery on that cold and windy winter's day in 1870, he had indeed returned home.

CHAPTER 25

George Peabody's Legacy

REMARKABLE BUSINESS ACUMEN, spectacular financial success, and an indomitable faith in his fellow man made George Peabody's philanthropy possible. When Peabody retired in 1864, in ill health and wanting to put both his estate and his philanthropies in good order, his personal worth was at least $6.1 million.

A basic accounting of Peabody's total philanthropy, during his lifetime and after his death, indicates gifts of almost $10 million, an amount that would be far greater, of course, if adjusted to current inflated values. That total includes $2.5 million for low-income housing in London; $2 million for rebuilding public education in the southern United States after the Civil War; $1,828,120 distributed among seven U.S. libraries and institutes; $551,000 for science education; $20,000 each for the Maryland Historical Society and the Massachusetts Historical Society; and $10,000 for Arctic Exploration. The total also includes $71,850 for several patriotic causes, $70,740 for churches and other charities, $81,000 for personal legacies in England and the United States, a small donation to the Historical Society of Philadelphia, an additional unknown sum to the Maryland Historical Society, and for his own Family Trust an amount variously estimated between $1.5 and $4 million.

In this concluding chapter, I hope to provide a summary appreciation of the lasting contributions made by George Peabody in a number of social and cultural realms and to emphasize the importance and influence of his legacy even in our own times.

Housing for Working Poor

Even before George Peabody became widely known in this country as a philanthropist keenly interested in the endowment of schools, libraries, and museums, this wealthy international entrepreneur made his largest single gift, $2.5 million, to establish a housing trust for the benefit of the London poor. The nature of this outstanding act of generosity reflected the fact that George Peabody never forgot his own origins and unmet needs as one of eight children in a poor family. Before his retirement, Peabody had discussed with friends a suitable gift for the working poor families of London. Carefully soliciting advice from trusted sources, he considered and rejected possibilities that included establishing a network of badly needed fountains of clean drinking water to help alleviate periodic outbreaks of cholera and other serious diseases and a program of aid to charity schools for indigent children, a project dear to the influential social reformer Lord Shaftesbury. It was also Shaftesbury who suggested to Peabody the greater need for low-cost model apartments for the working poor.

In March of 1862, Peabody officially established the Peabody Donation Fund (later known as the Peabody Trust) in London. The event was, in itself, remarkable for its generosity and for the level of social concern it represented on the part of a wealthy tycoon. The context and circumstances of this extraordinary gift made it all the more amazing to the British. The great conflagration of the U.S. Civil War, an ongoing catastrophe for North America, forced Britain and other European states into specific, side-choosing political postures of their own. England's basic position often placed it in harmony with Confederate aims, and tension between the United States and Britain were palpable in 1862. Yet amid such animosities, the American businessman George Peabody—a "Yankee" who had already been blackballed in certain London social and financial circles because of the number of U.S. failures to honor international debts following the 1837 financial panic—was spending his own fortune for the benefit of London's poor.

Of all Peabody's philanthropic activities, none continues to draw more admiration from the British than this well-conceived and much-needed model of low-income housing. To this day, the Peabody Trust of London remains very active in the field of affordable housing by providing homes for some 26,000 individuals as well as through other means of alleviating poverty among the people of London.

The Peabody Education Fund (PEF, 1867–1914)

To citizens of the United States, Peabody is more generally known for his establishment and endowment of educational institutions, including libraries, lyceums, museums, and schools. A reasonable estimate of the total he gave for such purposes amounts to $6,868,800. The largest single block of that total, $2,004,700, went to the general field of education, and $2,000,000 of that was distributed by the Peabody Education Fund, from 1867 to 1914. On a smaller scale, Peabody also provided for best scholars' medals at what is now the Peabody High School, in Peabody, Massachusetts ($2,600 from 1854 through 1867) and the Holton High School, in Danvers, Massachusetts ($2,000 in 1867). He also donated $100 to a London School, in 1864.

Perhaps the most important aspect of George Peabody's legacy in the United States, however, rests on the effect and influence of the $2 million post–Civil War fund that he established to promote tax-supported public schools and teacher education in the eleven former Confederate states and West Virginia. At the time this seminal gift was made in 1867, three significant events dramatized its importance: President Andrew Johnson's personal visit to an ailing George Peabody in Washington, D.C., on February 9 of that year; a unanimous Congressional resolution of gratitude and a gold medal that were presented to Peabody on March 16; and, less than one week later, an impressive banquet jointly honoring General Grant and the other trustees of the Peabody Education Fund. In addition, Southern political and military leaders, including Robert E. Lee, also showed grateful acceptance of the PEF as a practical means to heal Civil War wounds.

By the end of the nineteenth century, a strong consensus had developed around Peabody's notion that fostering education at all levels in the South was the surest way to heal the nation. Out of this realization the Southern Education Board held four conferences on education in the South, from 1898 to 1901, with J. L. M. Curry and other PEF trustees playing important roles in these efforts. John D. Rockefeller's General Education Board also included Curry and others from the Southern Education Board. Over the years, the PEF, the John F. Slater Fund for Negro Education in the South, Conferences for Education in the South, the Southern Education Board, the General Education Board, the Rosenwald Fund, and the Anna T. Jeanes Foundation all worked together to achieve Peabody's earlier vision. The common problem was to advance public education in the South, to encourage state and local laws that perpetuated tax-supported public schools, and to found and sustain both teacher institutes and teacher training normal schools.

In spite of its noble and well-charted purposes, the operations of the

PEF were not entirely smooth or without controversy. Because the need was great and PEF resources were limited, first administrator Barnas Sears exercised what some believed were overly restrictive policies concerning how its funds were to be distributed. He required that all schools aided by the PEF come under state control, that they meet at least nine months a year, have at least one teacher for every fifty pupils, and that townspeople match PEF funds or exceed them, often by as much as two or three times the amount awarded by the PEF. This strategy forced citizens to become involved in underwriting tax-supported schools under state supervision. Sears thus used the Fund's limited resources as a sometimes provocative lever, coercing recipients toward the goal of permanent tax-supported schools.

Some criticized the PEF for aiding black schools at only two thirds the rate set for white schools, a policy which Sears formulated after he found that black schools were actually often better provided for than white schools. Rightly or wrongly, Sears's justification was that during Reconstruction black schools were given massive amounts of aid by the federal government, as well as assistance from Northern missions and Northern teachers. He also observed that black schools cost less to maintain. After 1871, however, many white communities met Sears's aid requirements while black communities were increasingly less able to do so.

Sears was faulted especially for aiding private white schools in Louisiana. The PEF dilemma there was that the state-mandated, racially mixed schools in Louisiana in fact served mainly black students because middle class and wealthy white parents chose to send their children to private fee-based schools. Many poor white parents, on the other hand, unable to afford such fees, refused to send their children to the integrated state schools. Sears felt that his only option in Louisiana was to support private white schools for the benefit of poor whites or else see most white children go unschooled altogether. Many have criticized this decision. Historian William P. Vaughn charged in 1964 that Sears and the PEF perpetuated racial segregation in Southern schools. Historian Henry J. Perkinson later wrote that, by going along with racially separate schools, the Peabody Fund "prevented the South from attaining educational equality with the North for the next seventy-five years." Whether such hindsight is accurate or not, the PEF's influence in Louisiana was less successful and more controversial than in the other PEF-aided Southern states.

On balance, however, the PEF was considered then, and is praised now, as a great benefactor of public and higher education in the United States, particularly in the South. The weight of historical judgment lies heavily on the side of admiration for the PEF. The view of Southern historian Thomas D. Clark is that the PEF "has worked as educational leaven," and Edgar W. Knight speaks for many historians when he says that "the Peabody Fund . . . was not only the earliest manifestation of a spirit of reconciliation on the part of the Northern man toward the Southern states, but it was also one of the largest educational blessings which ever came from the outside to that section of the country."

The PEF, governed by a board of trustees from both North and South, was the first multimillion dollar foundation in the United States that exercised a positive attitude toward solving social ills. It was this nation's first educational foundation without religious conditions, the first whose influence was national, the first to provide for modifications as conditions changed, and the first to set a pattern of selecting trustees from the professions and business. These precedent-setting policies, many of which were adopted by later foundations, thus influenced all subsequent philanthropic efforts in the South and the nation. J. L. M. Curry's history of the PEF credits Peabody's philanthropic example with directly influencing Paul Tulane to found Tulane University, in New Orleans, and Anthony Drexel to found Drexel University, in Philadelphia. The Anna T. Jeanes Foundation also drew inspiration from the PEF, and the arguments put forward by Peabody in support of education as a national solidifying agent were the very arguments that Cornelius Vanderbilt found so convincing when he was led to endow Vanderbilt University, in Nashville, Tennessee.

George Peabody College for Teachers

George Peabody's instructions to the PEF trustees allowed them to end the trust after thirty years. At its 1914 dissolution, the PEF gave $468,000 to fourteen Southern university departments of education, and $346,797 to the John F. Slater Fund (the latter now used by the Southern Education Foundation for African American education).

In 1914 the PEF also gave $1.5 million to establish George Peabody College for Teachers, in Nashville, which was to be a model for the South. Peabody College's academic lineage of over two hundred years began with Davidson Academy, chartered by the North Carolina legislature in 1785, when Tennessee was still part of North Carolina. Davidson Academy, 1785–1806, was rechartered as Cumberland College,

1806–26, then rechartered as the University of Nashville, 1826–75, as State Normal College (commonly called Peabody Normal College, with funding from the PEF), 1875–1909, and then as George Peabody College for Teachers, 1909–79, located across Hillsboro Road from Vanderbilt University. On July 1, 1979, after decades of academic competition and cooperation between these two institutions, George Peabody College for Teachers finally merged with Vanderbilt University and was renamed Peabody College of Vanderbilt University.

Throughout this century, the college has enjoyed a role of leadership in teacher preparation and educational research. In the normal-school era of teacher education, Peabody Normal College led the South and the nation with the most highly trained faculty of any comparable school. In the early 1960s Peabody College pioneered in innovative areas of preschool research. Three years before the 1964 establishment of the federal Office of Economic Opportunity's first Head Start program, Peabody College psychology professor Susan Gray and local educator Rupert Klaus began an Early Training Program of enrichment intervention to improve the later learning of ninety low-income black Middle Tennessee preschoolers.

Today, as Vanderbilt University's ninth college, Peabody is a national leader in the fields of educational leadership, learning technology and multi-media applications, service learning and experiential education, and special education. Peabody College was a national leader in special education research even before the 1963 dedication of its John F. Kennedy Center for Research in Education. Since 1979, under deans Willis D. Hawley and James W. Pellegrino, Peabody College has advanced its small but excellent teacher education and research programs and has continually enhanced its national reputation. Among Peabody College's 29,000 living alumni are more than thirty college and university presidents, 175 school superintendents, and countless well-prepared teachers in many American and overseas classrooms, all of whom have made enormous contributions to society through scholarly research, innovative practice, new programs of study, and influence on public policy. Peabody College in the 1990s continues to prepare leaders in education and human development in the South and the nation, a leadership role begun in 1867 with the pioneering impetus of the Peabody Education Fund.

Music Education

Having lived and worked in Baltimore for twenty-two of his seventy-four years (from 1815 to 1837), George Peabody honored his youthful attachments there by gifts totalling $1.4 million, which made possible the establishment of the Peabody Institute of Baltimore. The idea for this cultural center had preoccupied the philanthropist's mind for fifteen years prior to its founding. Its four parts—an academy (later conservatory) of music, an art gallery, a scholars' library, and a lecture hall and lecture series—were a model for all of Peabody's endowments in the United States.

The Baltimore Institute's Conservatory of Music was the first music conservatory founded in the United States, in 1857, and the fourth to offer instruction, beginning in 1868. It announced its role in the cultural life of Baltimore as the Peabody Academy of Music with a series of twelve concerts in 1866. It was renamed the Peabody Conservatory of Music in 1874, under its Danish-born and European-trained director Asger Hamerik, who developed a nationally acclaimed professional orchestra, one of only four in the country at this time. Unlike European music conservatories, which had church origins and received state support, the Peabody Conservatory of Music pioneered in performing contemporary compositions and in promoting American music, despite a barrage of criticism from the press. It added its own liberal arts courses and later developed affiliations with nearby liberal arts colleges and the Johns Hopkins University.

During its long history, the Conservatory has seen periods of expansion as well as financial distress. A Preparatory School for musically talented children, begun in 1894 by music conservatory graduate May Garrettson Evans, became part of the Peabody Conservatory of Music in 1898 and has had a successful growth. The Conservatory weathered the 1930s Depression and expanded after World War II, adding to the number of distinguished European musicians on its faculty. When fiscal deficits threatened in the 1970s, however, the Conservatory began an official affiliation with the Johns Hopkins University, with which it had cooperated in joint academic programs since the 1920s. It has been closely involved with the Baltimore Symphony Orchestra and the Baltimore Opera and the training and promoting of American conductors through the American Conductors Project, the first program of its kind in this country. Today, the Conservatory enrolls over six hundred carefully selected and talented students from around the world. Its Preparatory Department boasts an enrollment of nearly three thousand students in every age bracket, with musical course-offerings stretching from early childhood to dance to adult education.

For nearly a century and a half, graduates of the Peabody Conservatory of Music have been among the most important performers, composers, and music educators in the country. Through its distinguished faculty, the Conservatory has brought both cultural enjoyment and a distinguished program of music education to Baltimore and the nation.

Art Education

Begun in 1873, the Peabody Institute Gallery of Art was one of the first art museums in the nation. It began with a small collection of sculptures, two donated by Peabody Institute trustees John M. McCoy and George S. Brown. The Gallery also developed into something of an art school because, with permission, art students could copy its works.

By 1879 the Gallery had begun regular exhibitions of paintings and sculptures, owned by the Gallery or borrowed for display, which gradually increased the audience for fine art in Baltimore. An 1881 exhibition of casts of antiques, bas-relief, and statuary, which trustee John Work Garrett bought for the Peabody Gallery in London and Paris, was so popular that demand for the exhibition catalogue required three printings. In 1884, Garrett lent the Peabody Gallery fifty-two paintings he owned for a showing, attracting 13,464 visitors, and in 1885 T. Harrison Garrett exhibited his collection of Rembrandt's etchings. In 1893 the Peabody Gallery received trustee Charles James Madison Eaton's art collection, and Eaton's nieces also presented to the Peabody Gallery the considerable art collection of Baltimore merchant Robert Gilmore, Jr., which their uncle had purchased to prevent its sale to buyers outside of Baltimore. In 1908, trustee John W. McCoy gave the Peabody Gallery his art collection, which included works by Maryland sculptor William Henry Rinehart, along with paintings by Thomas Hovenden and Hugh Bolton Jones. Later, in 1911, the Peabody Gallery received the art collection of Baltimore stock broker George Carter Irwin, which included works by Scacciati, Casmicache, Sirani, Volkmar, and Bonheur. Irwin's sisters established a fund used by the Peabody Gallery to purchase paintings by such distinguished American artists as Winslow Homer, George Innes, Frederick Childe Hassam, and Jonas Lie.

The Peabody Gallery continued its growth over the next decade, both by adding to its own collection and by expanding the scope of its exhibitions. Notable exhibits included those by many well-known local artists, such as Charles H. Walther, the members of the Charcoal Club of Bal-

timore, and the group of Baltimore women calling themselves "The Six."
The gallery also attracted visitors and students to view the work of nationally prominent American painters and, in 1914, held an especially
successful, internationally flavored exhibit of modernist paintings.

In the mid-1930s, the expanding Peabody Conservatory of Music's
need for space prompted a decision to close the Peabody Gallery. Its over
one thousand art pieces were placed on extended loan in the Baltimore
Museum of Art (opened in 1914) and in Baltimore's Walters Art Gallery
(which became public in 1934). The Peabody Gallery of Art collection,
still largely owned by the Peabody Institute of Baltimore, is exhibited
regularly in the Baltimore Museum of Art, Walters Art Gallery, Peale
Museum, Maryland Historical Society, and in other significant exhibitions, both in this country and abroad. The art collection is well documented in the Peabody Institute Archives, which tell the history and
public showings of its major art items.

Public Libraries

George Peabody's total gifts of $1,828,120 to seven libraries in the United
States included endowments for four Peabody Institutes, each with a
library to be freely used by townspeople in addition to a lecture hall and
lecture fund. Among the models Peabody had in mind for these Institutes
were the British Museum and the New England lyceums (named after
Aristotle's school), the first organized by Josiah Holbrook in Millbury,
Massachusetts, in 1826.

In 1852, the town fathers of Danvers, Massachusetts, invited Peabody
to visit his hometown during its centennial celebration. Too busy with his
duties and business interests in London, he decided instead to send a
check in the amount of $20,000 to found his first institute, with its
accompanying library, lecture hall, and lecture fund. It was with this gift
that he penned the phrase that is still closely associated with his vision as
a philanthropist: "Education, a debt due from present to future generations." With this initial gift for library support, Peabody joined Joshua
Bates, whose grant of $50,000 established the Boston Public Library at
about the same time, as one of the earliest supporters of free public
libraries. George Peabody's endowment of libraries in the seven communities in the United States where he lived and worked (or, in the case of
Georgetown, Massachusetts, where his mother was born and lived) was
an exemplary expression of the value of a community library, a precedent

that was highly influential in promoting the idea of tax-supported public libraries throughout the country.

Among the libraries that Peabody endowed, the Peabody Library of Baltimore was unique both for its singularly rich research and reference collection and for its location in one of America's most architecturally striking library buildings. During the formative years in the library's history (1860 to 1867), John G. Morris, its first librarian, developed a coherent plan for the purchase of books, working closely with the trustees' library committee and seeking the advice of scholars and scientists in the United States and abroad, and comprehensively catalogued the list of the library's holdings in 1861 and 1863. Provost-Librarian Nathaniel H. Morison, who headed the library from 1867 to 1890, further listed and cross-referenced the contents of the Peabody Library in the five-volume *Catalogue of the Library of the Peabody Institute of the City of Baltimore*, published between 1883 and 1893, and subsequently in a second eight-volume catalogue in 1905. These important listings were widely used as buying guides and for interlibrary loan purposes before the library's use of card catalogues.

This rapidly increasing reference collection was housed in the Peabody Institute building, designed in the grand new Renaissance style by Edmund G. Lind, a British-born architect practicing in Baltimore. A library building had been planned from the outset in 1857, but the trustees asked that the construction of the Institute be accomplished in two symmetrical phases. By 1878, need for additional space led to the completion of the spectacular new library building, also designed by Lind and built on the east side of the original structure, so expertly joined that they appear as one. Inside, five balconies and six tiers of stacks soar fifty-six feet to a skylit ceiling supported by pillars and cast-iron, gilt-covered railings, creating an effect often described as "a cathedral of books." For decades the Peabody Library reference collection was exceeded in quality only by the Harvard Library and the Library of Congress.

In his own *Autobiography*, Andrew Carnegie suggests the influence of Peabody's example, and one can readily infer Carnegie's keen interest in Peabody's endowment of libraries. Peabody's direct philanthropic influence in Baltimore, however, is more than a matter of inference. Although the Peabody Library in Baltimore served both scholar and generalist, librarian Nathaniel Morison was concerned about the reading needs of Baltimore's broader public. In this concern, his ally was the Baltimore merchant Enoch Pratt, a Peabody Institute trustee and treasurer. Aware of the need for a public library and encouraged by Morison, Enoch Pratt endowed the Enoch Pratt Free Library, which opened in 1886, with Morison's assistance in both building design and book selection.

George Peabody also directly influenced fellow Baltimore merchant Johns Hopkins to found the Johns Hopkins University, Hospital, and Medical School. The Johns Hopkins University was built in 1876 four blocks from the Peabody Institute so that faculty and students could use the Peabody Library's rich resources. Good relations continued after the Johns Hopkins University moved in 1916 three miles north to its Homewood campus. Johns Hopkins scholars long used the relatively close Peabody Library rather than the more distant Library of Congress, knowing that in some fields the Peabody Library collections were superior.

By the 1950s, income from the original endowment could no longer cover the modern budgetary needs of the Peabody Library. Merging the Peabody Library with one of its sister institutions in Baltimore was discussed for thirteen years before an agreement was reached that joined the Peabody with the Enoch Pratt Free Library on July 2, 1966. Though much was done to refurbish the facility during the next several years, budget cuts in the late 1970s and early 1980s forced the City of Baltimore to discontinue supporting the Peabody Library as part of the Enoch Pratt Free Library. In the summer of 1982 trustees from the Enoch Pratt, the Peabody Institute, and the Johns Hopkins University agreed to transfer the Peabody Library to the Johns Hopkins University. Shortly after July 1, 1982, Enoch Pratt Librarian Evelyn L. Hart began skillfully supervising the transferral of a quarter million volumes into the Peabody Library department of the Milton S. Eisenhower Special Collections Division of the Johns Hopkins University.

Thus, it was through the cooperation of the Enoch Pratt Free Library and the Johns Hopkins University that the Peabody Library of Baltimore was able to remain an active research and reference library. It is fitting that these institutions have helped to sustain the Peabody Library, since their founders had been George Peabody's fellow merchants and friends and his philanthropic example had influenced them so deeply.

Science Education

George Peabody's designated gifts in support of science totaled $551,000. The science museums he helped to establish at Yale, at Harvard, and in Salem, Massachusetts, were influenced partly by his nephew, Othniel C.

Marsh, whose Yale education, paid for by his uncle, enabled Marsh to become the first American professor of paleontology and the second such professor in the world. Knowing of his uncle's desire to make a gift to Harvard, Marsh encouraged Peabody to contribute to both Harvard and Yale in the fields of archaeology, ethnology, and paleontology. In October 1866, Peabody gave $150,000 each for museums at Harvard (the Peabody Museum of Archaeology and Ethnology) and at Yale (the Peabody Museum of Natural History).

Peabody's support of these museums and of his nephew's scientific work greatly affected the study of archaeology and anthropology in the United States. While the first Peabody Museum building at Yale was being completed, in 1876, Marsh and his assistants made scientific history, collecting rail-car loads of fossils and assembling entire dinosaurs, toothed birds, and extinct mammals. Marsh's enormous collection at Yale is still being catalogued. During the same period, Frederic Ward Putnam, Curator of the Peabody Museum of Archaeology and Ethnology at Harvard (from 1874 to 1909), linked research and academics by establishing a Department of Anthropology in 1902. He also helped establish the Anthropology Department at the American Museum of Natural History in New York City as well as the Department and Museum of Anthropology at the University of California. Known as the "Father of American Anthropology," Putnam also served as secretary of the American Association for the Advancement of Science, from 1873 to 1898.

Since the inception of Harvard's Peabody Museum, its personnel have won international respect, especially in the study of Central American Mayan culture, and have led several hundred expeditions worldwide to study early human life. Expeditions continue: on archaeology throughout the Americas, ethnography of the Old World, and paleoprimatology of southern Asia. Renovated exhibition halls attract 120,000 visitors annually. Research has blossomed to include trace element and microwear analyses on artifacts and DNA studies of living primates.

In addition to the establishment of the Harvard and Yale museums, Peabody also provided endowments for the already well-established East India Marine Society (founded in 1799) and the Essex County Natural History Society (founded in 1833). Upon accepting the endowment of $140,000 on February 26, 1867, these two cooperating institutions of Salem, Massachusetts, designated their science holdings as the core collection for the Peabody Academy of Science, renamed the Peabody Museum of Salem in 1915.

These two collections thus combined to form one of the outstanding science museums in North America. The East India Marine Society's ethnological and marine history collections were brought to Salem by acquisitive shipmasters from China, Sumatra, India, and the Pacific islands. The Essex County Natural History Society (which had merged in 1848 with the Essex Historical Society to form the Essex Institute) had been founded to collect New England's natural history antiquities. Soon after the Peabody Academy of Science housed and displayed the East India Marine Society's ethnological and maritime collections together with the Natural History Society's collections, other New England societies began to donate their ethnological and maritime objects to the new Peabody Academy of Science. Edward Sylvester Morse, first director of the Peabody Academy of Science (from 1880 to 1916) and a student of the famous naturalist and scholar Louis Agassiz at Harvard, worked assiduously to organize and develop the Peabody Academy of Science collections.

In 1984 the Peabody Museum of Salem absorbed the China Trade Museum of Milton, Massachusetts, which housed the finest collection of Asian export art in the world. Then, in July 1992, after nearly two hundred years of public showing of Asian and Pacific ethnological and marine history treasures, the Peabody Museum of Salem and the Essex Institute consolidated into the Peabody and Essex Museum.

Today, science education for the public, especially young people, is the focus of the Peabody and Essex Museum's 127-member staff. The museum's collections illuminate Salem's history from its founding as the third oldest colonial village to its zenith as a nineteenth-century seaport, when its ships transferred goods, culture, and artifacts between America and the then little-known Oriental and Pacific worlds. The museum now consists of six departments: Maritime History, American Decorative Arts and Essex County Historical Collections, Asian Export Art, Ethnology, Natural History, and Archaeology. The nine buildings of the museum contain the largest collection of Japanese arts and crafts outside Japan; a splendid collection of Chinese and other Asian porcelain, furniture, and decorative art; the largest collection of marine paintings and drawings in the United States; two libraries holding 2.5 million items, including the George Peabody papers and the world's largest collection of Hawthorne's papers and works; and the Essex County collection of furniture, decorative arts, costumes, military uniforms, dolls, and toys, dating from the seventeenth century to the present.

Over 150,000 visitors study at or wander through the Peabody and Essex Museum each year, and over 13,000 schoolchildren participate in its programs annually. The museum publishes *Peabody Essex Museum Collections*, the oldest continuously published historical journal in the United States; *The American Neptune*, the oldest journal of maritime history in this country; *Quarterly Review of Archaeology;* and catalogues and books on exhibitions and the permanent collection. In 1993 the museum hosted an exhibit, *The Great Age of Sail: Treasures from the National Maritime Museum of England*, containing over one hundred marine paintings and navigational objects, said to be the most important maritime exhibition ever held in the United States.

Clearly, in the era before state and federal aid to science made a difference, George Peabody's gifts of these three museums of science significantly advanced our knowledge of anthropology, natural science, and maritime history.

* * *

It is unfortunate that George Peabody's legacy and influence are now so dimly remembered and so little appreciated. We know much more about John D. Rockefeller, Andrew Carnegie, and other great philanthropists: who they were, how they made their fortunes, the foundations and institutions they created and sustained, their successes and failures. George Peabody's achievements and lasting influence are not so fully recognized. Much publicized and honored at his death, he is now largely forgotten except by those who work in and use his institutions and by scholars in fields he endowed.

The modern viewpoint does not easily take in, from a single perspective, the enormity of Peabody's contribution, both as entrepreneur and as philanthropist. So successful were his business efforts and so influential his company's example—in marshaling the essential capital for canals, railroads, and other improvements necessary for Western commercial expansion—that he had much to do with preserving the whole system of industrial capitalism at the turn of the century. And, as we have seen in this chapter, Peabody was no less influential in the conception and development of the uniquely American institution of philanthropy.

Indeed, it is George Peabody, not his better-known successors in that field, who originated the very practice of modern philanthropy, the results of which are still evident and thriving in social and cultural institutions as diverse as homes for London's poor, an outstanding college of education, a leading music conservatory and art collection, seven libraries, and three museums of science. These and other enduring expressions of Peabody's magnanimity still exist, still serve, still stand as models of faith in human worth and in the values of culture and education that are and will remain George Peabody's principal legacy.

George Peabody's Honors

Honors Bestowed During His Lifetime

(In England and Europe):

- Honorary membership in the ancient guild of the Clothworkers' Company of London, July 2, 1862; four years later, honorary membership in the ancient guild of the Fishmongers' Company of London, April 19, 1866.

- The first American to receive the Freedom of the City of London, on July 10, 1862, an honor also given to General Dwight D. Eisenhower in 1945.

- A handwritten letter of thanks from Queen Victoria and a priceless miniature portrait of herself, given through the British ambassador to Peabody, then in the United States, March 1867.

- A private audience with Pope Pius IX and another with French Emperor Napoleon III and Empress Eugénie, both in 1868.

- Sculptor W. W. Story's seated statue of George Peabody erected near the Royal Exchange, Threadneedle Street, London, paid for by popular subscription and unveiled July 23, 1869. A replica erected in front of the Peabody Institute of Baltimore in 1890.

(In the United States):

- A proposed appointment to become Secretary of the Treasury in President Andrew Johnson's cabinet, February 1867, respectfully declined by Peabody because of his age and ill health.

- A unanimous Congressional resolution of praise and the presentation of a gold medal to George Peabody, March 1867, in gratitude for the 1867 establishment of the Peabody Education Fund.

- An honorary doctor of laws degree from Harvard University, in absentia, July 17, 1867 (for the Peabody Museum of Harvard); and an honorary doctor of civil law degree from Oxford University, June 26, 1867.

• The renaming of his hometown of South Danvers, Massachusetts, which became Peabody, Massachusetts, on April 13, 1868.

Honors Bestowed Posthumously

• A funeral service and temporary burial, unprecedented for a non-British subject, in Westminster Abbey, November 12–December 11, 1869.

• The return and presentation of Peabody's remains to the United States aboard HMS *Monarch*, December 11, 1869–January 29, 1870, accompanied (by special order of President Grant) by the USS *Plymouth*.

• U.S. Naval reception, commanded by Admiral David Farragut, of Peabody's remains, Portland, Maine. Lying-in-state honors held in Portland, Maine, and in Peabody, Massachusetts. Final burial in Harmony Grove Cemetery, Salem, Massachusetts, February 1870, attended by Queen Victoria's third son, Prince Arthur, who was then on a Canadian tour.

• A proposal in 1896, though unsuccessful, by Virginia and South Carolina legislatures to erect a statue of George Peabody in Statuary Hall, United States Capitol.

• Election to the New York University Hall of Fame, 1900. A bust of George Peabody, by sculptor Hans Schuler unveiled on May 12, 1926.

• Peabody's image, along with those of Thomas Jefferson, Benjamin Franklin, Ralph Waldo Emerson, Horace Mann, and Johns Hopkins, included in Louis Amateis's design of two bronze doors and a transom panel tableau (completed in 1904), "Apotheosis of America," symbolizing intellectual development in the United States, for the west entrance, United States Capitol.

• An unsuccessful proposal by Tennesseans in 1941 for a commemorative United States postage stamp. A similar proposal initiated in 1993 by Massachusetts citizens for issue of a commemorative stamp at the bicentennial of Peabody's birth in 1995.

• An international celebration scheduled for 1995 of the bicentennial of his birth, in cooperation with the Peabody Trust, London, and other Peabody institutions in the United States.

An Essay on Sources

George Peabody's business and personal papers in the Peabody and Essex Museum (hereafter abbreviated GP-P&EM), Salem, Massachusetts, were brought from London in the early 1870s by nephew Robert Singleton Peabody, stored and sorted in the early 1930s at Phillips Academy, Andover, Massachusetts, deposited in 1935 in the Essex Institute (now Peabody and Essex Museum), and reorganized in 1985 in 140 boxes of manuscript material, 42 letter books, 180 account books, and 16 boxes of newspapers, scrapbooks, and manuscripts (identified as MSS#: 181, George Peabody [1795–1869] Papers, 1815–1927).

Other George Peabody–related letters and papers are in the Boston Public Library; Chicago Historical Society; Cornell University; Peabody College of Vanderbilt University; Greenbrier Hotel, White Sulphur Springs, West Virginia; Harvard University; Historical Society of Pennsylvania; the Johns Hopkins University Library; Library of Congress; Maine Historical Society; Maine State Library; Maryland Historical Society; Maryland State Library; Massachusetts Historical Society; Morgan Guaranty Trust Company of New York; National Archives; New York Historical Society; New York Public Library; Peabody Historical Society of Peabody, Massachusetts; Peabody Library Archives of the Johns Hopkins University Library; Peabody Institute Library of Peabody, Massachusetts; Peabody Library Association of the Public Library of Washington, D.C.; Peabody Museum Libraries of Harvard and Yale universities; Pierpont Morgan Library of New York; Salem Courthouse, Massachusetts; University of Rochester; and Yale University.

George Peabody-related papers in England are at the British Library; Clothworkers' Company; Cunard Steamship Co., Ltd.; Fishmongers' Company; Guildhall Library; Leicestershire County Record Office; Morgan, Grenfell & Co., Ltd.; Royal Archives at Windsor Castle; Public Record Office; Somerset House; Treasurer-Solicitor's Office; and Westminster Abbey.

News clipping albums are at the GP-P&EM; Peabody Library Archives of the Johns Hopkins University Library; and Maryland Room, Enoch Pratt Free Library; Peabody Institute Library, Peabody, Massachusetts; Peabody Historical Society, Peabody, Massachusetts; and Peabody Museums of Harvard and Yale universities. Local contemporary Massachusetts newspapers are indexed in the Peabody Institute Library, Peabody, Massachusetts. George Peabody entries are indexed in *New York Times* and London *Times*. Hitherto unrecorded George Peabody entries in U.S. and British newspapers in the Library of Congress and the British Library Newspaper Collection (Colindale) are listed in my 1956 dissertation.

Chapter 1

Peabody's genealogy is in my dissertation, as are references to courthouse records from Haverhill, Rowley, Newburyport, Danvers, and Salem, Massachusetts. Peabody's boyhood years are filled in largely from Peabody family letters and from reminiscences scattered in news accounts occasioned by his death, the transportation of his body across the Atlantic, the various lying-in-state ceremonies, and the final burial. See also Edwin Ponder Hoyt, *The Peabody Influence: How a Great New England Family Helped to Build America* (New York: Dodd, Mead & Co., 1968).

Chapter 2

George Peabody's War of 1812 military service and land-bounty warrant application, February 25, 1857, are in the National Archives. Peabody's June 28, 1813, letter to his sister Judith is in the Peabody Institute Archives, Peabody, Massachusetts; a newspaper clipping of this letter is also mounted on the back of a Peabody portrait in the Peabody and Essex Museum Print Department. Peabody's flashy uniform is described in John Pendleton Kennedy's Journal, LXXIII, Peabody Library Archives of the Johns Hopkins University Library. Peabody's first drygoods advertisements were in Georgetown, D.C., *Federal Republican and Commercial Gazette* issues of September, October, November, and December, 1812. The Riggs & Peabody advertisement is in the Baltimore *American and Commercial Daily Advertiser,* June 8, 1818.

Retiring from Riggs, Peabody & Co. in 1829, Elisha Riggs became a prominent New York banker. Riggs family members joined William Wilson Corcoran in banking and did much business with Peabody in London. The Riggs National Bank in Washington, D.C., is the modern descendant of the Corcoran-Riggs connection. See the Riggs Papers in the Library of Congress, records of the Riggs National Bank, and John Beverley Riggs, *Riggs Family of Maryland; A Genealogical and Historical Record, Incl. A Study of the Several Families in England* (Brookeville, Maryland: privately printed, 1939). Peabody's 1827 passport and will are in the GP-P&EM.

Chapter 3

Peabody's first arrival (November 25, 1827) and subsequent arrivals in England are listed in the Aliens Entry Books, Public Record Office, London. His *Florida* seasickness is described in a letter in the Peabody Papers, Boston Public Library. His second European trip (1831) is described in a letter to his sister Judith in the Peabody Papers, Yale University. The letter about the value of education to his brother David's son, George Peabody (1815–1832), dated May 18, 1831, is in the GP-P&EM, quoted in Charles Schuchert and Clara Mae LeVene, *O. C. Marsh, Pioneer in Paleontology* (New Haven: Yale University Press, 1940), 21. The death of Peabody's younger sister Mary Gaines Marsh and the career of her son O. C. Marsh are in the Peabody Papers and the O. C. Marsh Papers, Yale University, and in Schuchert and LeVene, *O. C. Marsh.* The Panic of 1837 and other aspects of Peabody's business affairs in this and later chapters are in Muriel Emmie Hidy, "George Peabody, Merchant and Financier, 1829–1854" (Ph. D. diss., Radcliffe College, 1939; published: New York: Arno Press, 1978).

Chapter 4

The broken engagement with Esther Elizabeth (Hoppin) Lardner and a photograph of her portrait by Thomas Sully are in my article, "The Girl George Peabody Almost Married," *Peabody Reflector*, XXVII, No. 8 (October 1955), 215, 224–225; reprinted in *Peabody Notes*, XVII, No. 3 (Spring 1964), 10–14.

George Peabody's partner in 1854, Junius Spencer Morgan, was John Pierpont Morgan's father. J. P. Morgan began his banking career as New York agent for George Peabody & Co. J. P. Morgan's son, John Pierpont Morgan Jr.'s "Reminiscences," March 1938, is in the Morgan Guaranty Trust Co., New York, and Morgan, Grenfell & Co., Ltd., London, and is mentioned in Frederick Lewis Allen, *The Great Pierpont Morgan* (New York: Harper & Bros., 1949), 234; and in Kathleen Burk, *Morgan Grenfell 1838–1988: The Biography of a Merchant Bank* (Oxford: Oxford University Press, 1989), 23, 287–288. Other documents on the allegation are in Somerset House, London, and the Hamilton Fish Papers, Library of Congress.

Frank N. Jones, *George Peabody and the Peabody Institute* (Baltimore: Peabody Institute Library, 1965), 7, described Peabody's alleged proposal during his Baltimore years (1815–37) to Elizabeth Knox, daughter of Samuel and Grace (Gilmore) Knox. At her father's urging that she marry a banker, she married George Carson, a Baltimore bank teller, who died after the birth of their fourth child. In the Carson family tradition, on Peabody's return to Baltimore in 1857, he again proposed to the widow Carson, then managing a boarding home. She declined, saying that people would believe she had married Peabody solely for his money (from an undated manuscript by J. W. Leakin, "Family Tree of the Knoxes and Their Connections," Peabody Library Archives of the Johns Hopkins University Library, deposited in 1958 by Mrs. Charles Rieman (née Elizabeth Taylor Goodwin), a descendant of Elizabeth [Knox] Carson).

Chapter 5

Peabody's difficulties in selling Maryland's bonds are explained in Muriel Hidy's dissertation; her husband Ralph W. Hidy's *The House of Baring in American Trade and Finance; English Merchant Bankers at Work 1763–1861* (Cambridge: Harvard University Press, 1949. Reprinted. New York: Russell and Russell, 1970); Hugh Sisson Hanna, *Financial History of Maryland, 1789–1848* (Baltimore: The Johns Hopkins University Press, 107); and U.S. Senate Document No. 610 (1840), 174–194. Henrietta M. Larson, *Guide to Business History* (Cambridge: Harvard University Press, 1948), 163, wrote of Gustavus Myers's bias: "Marxian in its thought framework and not concerned with a careful analysis of the men's business administration." Peabody's vindication and Maryland's praise are contained in Governor Thomas Pratt's 1847 message to the Maryland Assembly;

Maryland House of Delegate's *Proceedings* (1847), 420; and *Bankers' Magazine and State Financial Register*, III, No. 7 (January 1849), 394–397.

Chapter 6

The Peabody-Melville meeting is described in Melville's *Journal*, (Cambridge: Harvard, 1948), 47, and Jay Leyda, *The Melville Log, a Documentary Life of Herman Melville, 1819–1891* (New York: Harcourt, Brace & Co., *1951*), 338. Peabody's aid to Kossuth is described in letters from David Hoffman and Dudley Coates Stewart, November 4 and 10, 1850, GP-P&EM. Peabody's help in the search for Sir John Franklin is recounted in GP-P&EM; John Pendleton Kennedy Papers, Peabody Library Archives of the Johns Hopkins University; British Library Manuscript Division, London; and in my "George Peabody and the Search for Sir John Franklin, 1852–1854," *American Neptune*, XX, No. 2 (April 1960), 104–111. A White House desk from the Franklin search came about as follows: Captain Buddington of the U.S. whaler *George Henry* extricated H.M.S. *Resolute*, a British ship abandoned in the Arctic ice in the search for Sir John Franklin. The U.S. government purchased the damaged *Resolute*, repaired it, and returned it to Britain as a gift. When the *Resolute* was broken up, Queen Victoria had a massive desk made from its timbers and given to the U.S. President. First Lady Jacqueline Kennedy found the desk in a storeroom in 1961 and had it refurbished for President Kennedy's use. Famous photos show President Kennedy's young son, "John-John," playing under that desk. President Clinton returned the desk to the Oval Office in 1993.

Chapter 7

Peabody's loan (difficult to collect) is recorded in *Proceedings of the 23rd Congress, 1st Session, House of Representatives*, Tuesday, August 1, 1854. Richard O. Cummings, "The Growth of Technical Cooperation with Governments Abroad, 1849–1853," *Pacific Historical Review*, XVIII, No. 2 (May 1949), 199–212, described Peabody's loan to the U.S. exhibitors at the 1851 Exhibition and Peabody's part in the U.S. help in the search for Sir John Franklin.

Accounts of Peabody's first Fourth of July banquet are in the London *Times*, July 9, 1851; and London *Ladies' Newspaper and Pictorial Times*, July 26, 1851. The book describing the October 27, 1851, dinner was compiled by Henry Stevens, *An Account of the Proceedings at the Dinner Given by Mr. George Peabody to the Americans Connected with the Great Exhibition, at the London Coffee House, Ludgate Hill, on the 27th October, 1851* (London: William Pickering, 1851).

Chapter 8

Peabody's contribution to the Maryland Institute is described in the Garrett Papers, Library of Congress. For the Danvers centennial see *Centennial Celebration at Danvers, Massachusetts, June 16, 1852* (Boston: Dutton and Wentworth, 1852). Peabody's relation with Thurlow Weed is recorded in the Weed Collection, University of Rochester; Corner Collection, Maryland Historical Society; Weed's

Albany *Evening Journal* for the period; and Harriet A. Weed, ed., *Autobiography of Thurlow Weed* (Boston: Houghton, Mifflin & Co., 1884). George Peabody's romantic interest in Miss Wilcocks, ambassador-to-Britain Joseph Reed Ingersoll's niece, is in the GP-P&EM and the Corcoran Papers, Library of Congress; and in Elise Tiffany, daughter of Baltimore businessman Osmond Capron Tiffany (1794–1851), is in the GP-P&EM.

Accounts of others receiving Peabody's financial help, including sculptor Hiram Powers, explorer John Charles Frémont, and writer Delia Salter Bacon, are all in the GP-P&EM; that of editor Horace Greeley is in the GP-P&EM and the Chicago Historical Society. U.S. Legation Secretary (London) Benjamin Moran's animosity to Peabody cited in this and later chapters is described in his forty-one-volume manuscript diary (1857–1865), Library of Congress, partly published in Sarah Agnes Wallace and Frances Elma Gillespie, eds., *The Journal of Benjamin Moran, 1857–1865* (Chicago: University of Chicago Press, 1948), I and II.

Chapter 9

Junius Spencer Morgan's papers are in the Pierpont Morgan Library. His career is described in Herbert Satterlee, *The Life of J. Pierpont Morgan* (New York: privately printed, 1937), which also contains young John Pierpont Morgan's early remarks about Peabody found here and in Chapter 11. The George Peabody-J. S. Morgan partnership (August 10, 1854) accounts are in the GP-P&EM; the Pierpont Morgan Library; and Morgan, Grenfell & Co., Ltd.; and in Vincent P. Carosso, *The Morgans: Private International Bankers, 1854–1913* (Cambridge: Harvard University Press, 1987); Richard Kenin, *Return to Albion; Americans in England, 1760–1940* (New York: Holt, Rinehart and Winston, 1979); Ron Chernow, *The House of Morgan: An American Banking Dynasty and the Rise of Modern Finance* (New York: Atlantic Monthly Press, 1990), Chapter One; Kathleen Burk, *Morgan Grenfell 1838–1988: The Biography of a Merchant Bank* (Oxford: Oxford University Press, 1989); and Fritz Redlich, *The Molding of American Banking: Men and Ideas* (New York: Johnson Reprint Corp., 1968). Notice of Peabody's $1,000 contribution to the Washington Monument is in the GP-P&EM and the National Archives.

Reverdy Johnson, whom Peabody consulted about the Peabody Institute of Baltimore, was in London to argue U.S. claims arising from the Clayton-Bulwer Treaty. Intimation that Peabody was originally proposed as an arbiter is in Nathan G. Upham's letter, September 30, 1853, to George Peabody, GP-P&EM. John Pendleton Kennedy's original plans for the Peabody Institute of Baltimore are described in his Journal in the Peabody Library Archives of the Johns Hopkins University Library. George P. A. Healy's portrait of Peabody and Peabody's help in Healy's career are mentioned in GP-P&EM; George P. A. Healy, *Reminiscences of a Portrait Painter* (Chicago: A. C. McClurg & Co., 1894); and *A Souvenir of the Exhibition Entitled Healy's Sitters* (Richmond: Virginia Museum of Fine Arts, 1950).

Chapter 10

The George Peabody-Daniel Edgar Sickles affair is in GP-P&EM; Peabody Papers, Library of Congress; Somerby Papers, Massachusetts Historical Society; Boston *Post*, August–November, 1854; and New York *Times*, September 6, 7, and November 6, and 28, 1854. James Buchanan's ambivalent position in the affair led to strained relations with Peabody, mentioned in Chapter 11. All this is also covered in Nat Brandt, *The Congressman Who Got Away with Murder* (Syracuse: Syracuse University Press, 1991), 30–31.

Chapter 11

Peabody's arrival on the *Atlantic* is in New York *Times* and New York *Herald*, September 16, 1856. His declining of the New York City honors is in New York *Times*, September 24, 1856. The Danvers celebration is in *Proceedings at the Reception and Dinner in Honor of George Peabody, Esq., of London, by the Citizens of the Old Town of Danvers, October 9, 1856* (Boston: H. W. Dutton and Son, 1856); New York *Times*, October 10 and 11, 1856; and seventeen-year-old Alice L. Putnam's recollections in "The Peabody Celebration in Danvers. From a Letter in Possession of Col. Eben Putnam," *The Historical Collections of the Danvers Historical Society*, XX (1932), 63–64. The critical New York *Herald* articles appeared on October 3, 6, 10, 11, and 13, 1856. Family letters and accounts, kept by sister Judith (Peabody) Russell Daniels, are in the GP-P&EM.

Chapter 12

Peabody Institute plans and events are described in GP-P&EM and in John Pendleton Kennedy's Journal, Peabody Library Archives of the Johns Hopkins University Library; Roseann Kahn, "A History of the Peabody Institute Library, Baltimore, Maryland, 1857–1916" (Master's thesis, Catholic University of America, 1953) ACRL Microcard Series No. 16; and Peabody Institute of Baltimore, *The Founder's Letters and Papers Relating to its Dedication and its History up to the 1st January, 1868* (Baltimore: William K. Boyle, 1868).

Peabody's tour, speeches, and honors in February, March, and April, 1857, in this chapter, Chapter 11, and in "George Peabody's Honors," are in these 1857 newspapers: Richmond (Va.) *Dispatch*, March 13; Mobile *Daily Tribune*, March 15; New Orleans *Daily Picayune*, March 20, 24, 25; New Orleans *Daily Delta*, March 20, 21; St. Louis *Daily Missouri Republican*, April 4; St. Louis *Daily Evening News*, April 3; Indianapolis *Daily Journal*, April 8; Cincinnati *Daily Gazette*, April 11; Pittsburgh *Evening Chronicle*, April 14; Oswego (N.Y.) *Daily Times*, April 25; and Springfield *Illinois State Journal*, April 6.

Chapter 13

The Bank of England loan account is in GP-P&EM; Benjamin Moran's diary, Library of Congress; The Pierpont Morgan Library; Corcoran Papers, Library of Congress (many relevant letters are in William Wilson Corcoran, *A Grandfather's Legacy; Containing a Sketch of His Life and Obituary Notices of Some Members of His*

Family, Together with Letters from His Friends [Washington, D.C.: Henry Pol-kinhorn, 1879]); Herbert Satterlee, *The Life of J. Pierpont Morgan* (New York: privately printed, 1937); J. L. M. Curry, *A Brief Sketch of George Peabody and a History of the Peabody Education Fund Through Thirty Years* (Cambridge: Harvard University Press, 1898); and New York *Times*, February 9 and 18, 1858. Pea-body's differences with the "new Americans" in London over Fourth of July dinners are in Moran's diary, Library of Congress, printed in Sarah Agnes Wal-lace and Frances Elma Gillespie, eds., *The Journal of Benjamin Moran, 1857–1865* (Chicago: University of Chicago Press, 1948).

Chapter 14

Rumor of a rift between Peabody and Morgan and its denial are in New York *Herald*, September 20 and October 12, 1859; New York *Times*, January 12, 1860; and GP-P&EM. Peabody Donation Fund (Peabody Homes of London) events here and in Chapter 16 are in John Pendleton Kennedy's Journal, Peabody Li-brary Archives of the Johns Hopkins University Library; and GP-P&EM.

Chapter 15

O. C. Marsh's career mentioned here and in Chapter 18 is described in his papers at Yale University; GP-P&EM; and in Charles Schuchert and Clara Mae LeVene, *O. C. Marsh, Pioneer in Paleontology* (New Haven: Yale University Press, 1940).

Critics of Peabody's stand in the Civil War include Benjamin Moran (see his diary), whose enmity was of long standing, and John Bigelow, Consul General in Paris, who did not present evidence. Samuel Bowles's unsubstantiated condem-nation in the Springfield (Ill.) *Daily Republican*, October 27, 1866, was uncritically repeated by Matthew Josephson, *The Robber Barons* (New York: Harcourt, Brace & Co., 1934 and 1962), 60; and by Carl Sandburg, *Abraham Lincoln, The War Years* (New York: Harcourt, Brace & Co., 1939), III, 124–125; and by Leland D. Baldwin, *The Stream of American History* (New York: American Book Co., 1952), II, 121. Two of President Lincoln's three emissaries to counter pro-Confederate sentiment in England stated that while Peabody did not publicly take sides, he privately aided them to promote the Union cause. Thurlow Weed's "The Late George Peabody; A Vindication of his Course During the Civil War," is in the New York *Times*, December 23, 1869; reprinted in *Historical Collections of the Danvers Historical Society*, XIX (1931), 9–15; and affirmed in Episcopal Bishop Charles Pettit McIlvaine's letter to Thurlow Weed, December 24, 1869, quoted in New Haven (Conn.) *Daily Palladium*, January 6, 1870. Peabody's refusal to sell Confederate bonds in Europe is in New York *Times*, May 23, 1861; and his bet of $60,000, which he won, arguing that Confederate bonds would depreciate, is described in New York *Times*, January 27, 1870. The Allen S. Hanckel incident and the *Trent* affair are in the Liverpool (England) *Daily Post*, January 8, 1862; and GP-P&EM.

Chapter 16

Besides Peabody Donation Fund sources cited for Chapter 14, see the Weed Collection, University of Rochester, also quoted in Thurlow Weed Barnes, *Memoir of Thurlow Weed by his Grandson* (Boston: Houghton, Mifflin & Co., 1884); Benjamin Moran's diary, Library of Congress; Somerby Papers, Massachusetts Historical Society; London *Times*, March 26, 1862; and other newspapers, some excerpts of which are in *The Peabody Donation* (London: E. Couchman & Co., 1862). Subsequent developments are in *Mr. Peabody's Gift to the Poor of London* (London: Spottiswood & Co., 1866). The centenary celebration is in *The Peabody Donation Fund, 1862–1962* (London: George Berridge & Co., Ltd., 1962).

Chapter 17

British public demand to honor Peabody is in the London *Times*, March 29, 1862. Honorary membership in the Clothworkers' Company is in "Court Orders of the Clothworkers' Company, London," July 2, 1862. Charles Reed's relations with Peabody are recorded in his *Memoir of Charles Reed* (London: Macmillan & Co., 1883). Granting of the Freedom of the City of London to Peabody (he was the first American to receive this honor) is in The Corporation of London, *London's Roll of Fame, 1757–1884* (London: Cassell & Co., Ltd., 1884), 263–266; London *Times*, July 11, 1862; Boston *Daily Advertiser*, July 26, 1862; and New York *Herald*, July 26, 1862. The Lord Mayor's Guild Hall banquet is in "Journals of the Court of Common Council," July 10, 1862, Guildhall Record Office, London. Peabody's walk home from the banquet is in the Brighton (England) *Observer*, November 12, 1869.

Chapter 18

The begging letters are mentioned in London *Times*, August 23, 1862. Peabody's election to the Athenaeum Club is recorded in GP-P&EM, and Humphrey Ward, *History of the Athenaeum, 1824–1925* (London: William Clowes and Sons, 1926), 195–198. References to O. C. Marsh are cited in Chapter 15 notes.

Chapter 19

Peabody's retirement and the subsequent history of his firm are in the records of Morgan, Grenfell & Co., Ltd.; Morgan Guaranty Trust Co.; GP-P&EM; Pierpont Morgan Library; and in works on John Pierpont Morgan cited above in Chapters 4 and 9 notes. Peabody's $10,000 donation to the U.S. Sanitary Commission is recorded in the Kennedy Papers, Peabody Library Archives of the Johns Hopkins University Library; and New York *Albion*, May 7, 1864. Peabody's second gift to his London Donation Fund is in these London newspapers: *Times*, February 12, 1866; *Leisure Hour*, XV, No. 761 (1866), 474; *Court Journal*, April 7, 1866; *Fun*, February 24, 1866; and in New York *Times*, March 15, 1866. Queen Victoria's letter and letters about the Queen's portrait, together with Peabody's reply, are in the Royal Archives, Windsor Castle. The originals of these widely reprinted letters are in the Peabody Institute Library, Peabody, Massachusetts. Peabody's appearance at the prize-giving ceremony of the Workingmen's Industrial Exhibition is recorded in *Illustrated London News*, XLVIII, No. 1368 (April 28, 1866), 409; New York *Times*, May 1, 1866; London *Times*, April 18, 1866; and New York *Herald*, May 2, 1866. His honorary membership in the Fishmongers' Company is in "Extracts from Court Minutes," April 19, 1866, Fishmongers' Company, Fishmongers' Hall, London; and London *Times*, April 23, 1866.

Chapter 20

Peabody's arrival is recorded in New York *Times*, May 3, 1866. His remark to Mr. Humphreys is quoted in J. L. M. Curry, *A Brief Sketch of George Peabody and a History of the Peabody Education Fund Through Thirty Years* (Cambridge: Harvard University Press, 1898), 12. Peabody's taxes are referred to in London *Times*, May 31, 1866; and New York *Albion*, May 19, 1866. His confiding to philanthropic advisor Robert Charles Winthrop about his intended gifts is recorded in Winthrop's *Eulogy Pronounced at the Funeral of George Peabody, at Peabody, Massachusetts, 8 February, 1870* (Boston: John Wilson and Son, 1870); and Curry, *A Brief Sketch*. The codicil to Peabody's will about 1860 leaving $100,000 to the Harvard Astronomical Observatory is in GP-P&EM. His second thought was to endow at Harvard a "School of Design" (probably art or architecture). Peabody Museum of Harvard founding is recorded in GP-P&EM; Marsh Papers, Yale University (pertinent parts in Marsh's biography by Schuchert and LeVene; Charles G. Willoughby, "The Peabody Museum of Archaeology and Ethnology, Harvard University," *Harvard Graduates' Magazine*, XXXI, No. 124 (June 1923), 495–503; and Ernest Ingersoll, "The Peabody Museum of American Archaeology," *Lippincott's Magazine*, X (November 1885), 474–487. Louis Agassiz's connection with Peabody's gifts to science is mentioned in the Winthrop Papers, Massachusetts Historical Society, with the pertinent letter quoted in R. C. Winthrop, *Addresses and Speeches on Various Occasions* (Boston: Little, Brown & Co., 1879), II, 312–315.

The Peabody Institute of Baltimore-Maryland Historical Society difficulties are recorded in Maryland Historical Society, *Maryland Historical Society and the Peabody Institute Trustees. A Report from a Special Committee of the Maryland Historical Society, Read and Adopted at the Society's Monthly Meeting, April the 5th, 1866* (Baltimore: John Murphy & Co., 1866). Peabody's $20,000 for the society's publication fund is referred to in James Morrison Harris, *Address by the Hon. J. Morrison Harris, Upon the Occasion of the Celebration of the Fiftieth Anniversary of the Organization of the Maryland Historical Society, Delivered March 12, 1894* (Baltimore: J. Murphy & Co., 1897).

Peabody's arrival in Baltimore and the ceremony and speeches at the dedication are recorded in Baltimore *Sun*, October 23, 24, and 25, 1866; New York *Herald*, October 26, 1866; New York *Times*, October 27, 1866; Peabody Institute of Baltimore, *The Founder's Letters and Papers Relating to its Dedication and its History up to the 1st of January, 1868* (Baltimore: William K. Boyle, 1868); and John Pendleton

Kennedy, "Sketch of the Peabody Institute, Baltimore," *Occasional Addresses; and the Letters of Mr. Ambrose on the Rebellion* (New York: G. P. Putnam and Son, 1872), 305–327.

The "S.P.Q." letter was in New York *Evening Post*, October 25, 1866; New York *Times*, October 27, 1866; and New York *Albion*, October 27, 1866. Replies and defenses were in New York *Evening Post*, October 26, 1866; and New York *Times*, October 27 and 31, 1866.

Chapter 21

Weed stated that money from the Peabody Education Fund was originally intended for New York City's poor but that Civil War devastation turned Peabody's mind toward education in the South. Weed credited R. C. Winthrop as the architect of the Peabody Education Fund (Harriet A. Weed, ed., *Autobiography of Thurlow Weed* [Boston: Houghton, Mifflin & Co., 1884] and New York *Times*, December 23, 1869). The first meeting of the PEF trustees is described in the New York *Herald*, February 9, 1867; the GP-P&EM; Hamilton Fish Papers and Corcoran Papers, Library of Congress; in J. L. M. Curry, *A Brief Sketch of George Peabody and a History of the Peabody Education Fund Through Thirty Years* (Cambridge: Harvard University Press, 1898), 26–27; and Bruce R. Payne, *George Peabody; Founder's Day Address, February 18, 1916* (Nashville: George Peabody College for Teachers, 1916). The PEF is covered in Curry, *A Brief Sketch;* Peabody Education Fund, *Proceedings* (Boston: John Wilson and Son, 1875–1916), 6 vols.; and several dissertations about the fund in the library of Peabody College of Vanderbilt University.

President Andrew Johnson's personal call on Peabody is described in New York *Herald*, February 10, 1867; and in St. George L. Sioussat, "Notes of Colonel W. G. Moore, Private Secretary to President Johnson, 1866–1869," *American Historical Review*, XIX, No. 1 (October 1913), 105. For the proposed reconstituted Johnson Cabinet, see letters from Blair to Johnson, February 12 and 24, 1867, Andrew Johnson Papers, Library of Congress; quoted in part in Ellis Paxton Oberholtzer, *A History of the United States Since the Civil War* (New York: Macmillan Co., 1917), I, 469–470. Peabody's visit to the White House is described in the New York *Herald*, April 29 and May 1, 1867; and the Baltimore *Sun*, April 27, 1867.

The begging letters are mentioned in New York *Tribune*, March 11, 1867; and London *Times*, March 30, 1867. Republican Senator Charles Sumner (Massachusetts) introduced the Congressional resolution; the debate is contained in *Congressional Globe, 40th Congress, 1st Session, March 4–December 2, 1867* (Washington: Rives and Bailey, 1867), LXXXIX, 28–30, 38–75, 83, 94, 108; *Journal of the United States Senate, 40th Congress, 1st and Special Session* (1867), 6, 19, 20, 40, 45, 47, 63, and Index 228.

Queen Victoria's portrait made especially for Peabody is described in London *Times*, May 24 and June 16, 1866. Its deposit in a specially built vault, Peabody Institute Library, Peabody (then named South Danvers), Massachusetts, was reported in London *Times*, March 18, 1867; and New York *Times*, April 1, 1867.

Peabody's predeparture interview is in Newark (N.J.) *Daily Journal*, April 29 and 30, 1867. The Peabody-Hopkins conversation was described by eyewitness John Work Garrett sixteen or seventeen years after the event in his *Address Delivered on the 30th of January, 1883, Before the Young Men's Christian Association of Baltimore on the Occasion of Their Thirtieth Anniversary* (Baltimore: News Steam Printing Office, 1883), 9–10, copies in the Johns Hopkins University Library and the Garrett Papers, Library of Congress; also quoted in Baltimore *Sun*, January 31, 1883, and mentioned in "Johns Hopkins, Bachelor Father to a Great University," Baltimore *Sun*, December 23, 1973. Evangelist Dwight L. Moody's hearing of this interview from Garrett about 1879 is mentioned in Curry, *A Brief Sketch*, 17–18; and Henry Mitchell MacCracken, *The Hall of Fame* (New York: G. P. Putnam's Sons, 1901), 180. D. C. Gilman quoted the conversation in his *The Launching of a University and Other Papers: A Sheaf of Remembrances* (New York: Dodd, Mead & Co., 1906), 10–12. Peabody's influence on Hopkins is referred to in Kathryn A. Jacob, "Mr. Johns Hopkins," *Johns Hopkins Magazine*, XXV, No. 1 (January 1974), 13–17; and Broadus Mitchell, "Hopkins, Johns," *Dictionary of American Biography*, edited by Dumas Malone (New York: Charles Scribner's Sons, 1943), IX, 213–214. The Peabody-Hopkins meeting at Garrett's home may have occurred October 30, 1866; or November 12–13, 1866 (most likely); or February 3, 1867; or April 25, 1867, when Peabody was in Baltimore.

John Wien Forney's description of Peabody aboard the *Scotia* and the resolutions in Chapter 22 are contained in his *Letters from Europe* (Philadelphia: T. B. Peterson, 1867), 19–31; New York *Herald*, May 28, 1867; and London *Times*, May 22, 1867.

Chapter 22

John Bright's observations are in his *Diaries of John Bright* (London: Cassell & Co., 1930), 308, 330, 334. The Congressional gold medal is described in Joseph Flourimund Laubat, *Medallic History of the United States, 1776–1876* (New York: J. W. Boulton, 1878), 1, 421–426; New York *Times*, May 26, 1868, and January 29, 1869; New York *Herald*, May 29, 1868, and January 31, 1869; London *Times*, August 25, 1868, and February 12, 1869.

The Harvard honorary degree is recorded in Harvard University, *Quinquentennial Catalogue of the Officers and Graduates of Harvard University 1636–1905* (Cambridge: Harvard University Press, 1905), 571; Harvard University, *Baccalaureate Sermon, and Oration and Poem. Class of 1867* (Cambridge: John Wilson and Son, 1867), 32–33; Boston *Daily Advertiser*, July 18, 1867; and criticized in the Worcester (Mass.) *Daily Spy*, July 26, 1867.

The Oxford honorary degree is documented in Oxford University, *Oxford University Calendar, 1868* (Oxford: James Parke & Co., 1868), 163; *Oxford University Journal*, June 27, 187; *Oxford University Herald*, June 29, 1867; *Oxford Times*, June 29, 1867; *Oxford Chronicle and Berks and Bucks Gazette*, June 29, 1867; and *Jackson's Oxford Journal*, June 29, 1867. Lewis Carroll's remarks are in his (Charles Lutwidge Dodgson's) *The Diaries of Lewis Carroll*, edited by Roger Lancelyn Green (New York: Oxford University Press, 1954), I, 261.

For opposition to changing the name of South Danvers to Peabody, see South Danvers *Wizard*, April 1, 22, and May 6, 1866. Accounts of W. W. Story's statue of Peabody, unveiled July 23, 1869, by the Prince of Wales, are in GP-P&EM; Corcoran Papers, Library of Congress; "Dispatches from United States Ministers, Great Britain," National Archives; "Minutes of the Committee for Erecting a Statue to Mr. George Peabody, 1866–1870," Manuscript 192, Corporation of London, Guildhall Library; James Macauley, ed., *Speeches and Addresses of H.R.H. the Prince of Wales: 1863–1888* (London: John Murray, 1889), 78–79; the London *Times*, May 22, 25, 26, 1866; April 20 and 23, May 16, 1867; July 14 and 22, 1869.

Peabody's audience with Pope Pius IX is mentioned in South Danvers *Wizard*, March 25, 1868; Robert Charles Winthrop, *Reminiscences of Foreign Travel; a Fragment of Autobiography* (Boston: John Wilson and Son, 1894), 97, 100; Andrew Dickson White, *Autobiography of Andrew Dickson White* (New York: Century Co., 1906), II, 424; *Massachusetts Historical Society Proceedings*, X (1867–1869), 339; New York *Herald*, March 21 and 22, 1868; and Baltimore *Times*, November 6, 1869. Peabody's being received by Napoleon III and Empress Eugénie is mentioned in the Winthrop Papers, Massachusetts Historical Society; and *Massachusetts Historical Society Proceedings*, X (1867–1869), 340.

Chapter 23

Peabody's New York arrival is recorded in New York *Herald*, June 10, 1869. His remarks at the Boston Musical Festival are in P. S. Gilmore, *History of the National Peace Jubilee and Great Music Festival Held in the City of Boston, June, 1869, to Commemorate the Restoration of Peace Throughout the Land* (Boston: Lee and Shepard, 1871), 598; and Boston *Post*, June 21, 1869.

Peabody's White Sulphur Springs meeting with Lee and other former Confederate officers and politicians is referred to in the GP-PEM; Corcoran Papers, Library of Congress; John Eaton, *First Report of the Superintendent of Public Instruction in the State of Tennessee, Ending Thursday, October 7, 1869* (Nashville: George Edgar Grishman, 1869), Appendix T; Perceval Reniers, *The Springs of Virginia; Life, Love, and Death at the Waters 1775–1900* (Chapel Hill: University of North Carolina Press, 1941), 218–219; and these 1869 newspapers: Richmond (Va.) *Daily Whig*, July 28, August 13, and August 17; New York *Times*, July 31; New York *Herald*, August 1 and August 17; and London *Anglo-American Times*, August 14. Photographs of Peabody, Lee, and the other former Confederate generals are described in the Richmond (Va.) *Daily Whig*, August 20, 1869, and New York *World*, September 14, 1869; and appear in Alfred Lawrence Kocher and Howard Dearstyne, *Shadows in Silver, a Record of Virginia, 1850–1900, in Contemporary Photographs taken by George and Huestis Cook with Additions from the Cook Collection* (New York: Charles Scribner's Sons, 1954), 189, 190; Francis Trevelyan Miller, ed., *The Photographic History of the Civil War* (New York: Review of Reviews Co., 1911), X, 4; Roy Meredith, *The Face of R. E. Lee* (New York: Charles Scribner's Sons, 1947), 84–85; Douglas Southall Freeman, *Robert E. Lee, a Biography* (New

York: Charles Scribner's Sons, 1947), IV, 438; and Charles William Dabney, *Universal Education in the South* (Chapel Hill: University of North Carolina Press, 1936), I, facing 83.

Peabody's gift to Lee's Washington College of Virginia bonds lost on the *Arctic* in 1854 is recorded in Richmond (Va.) *Daily Whig* and New York *Herald*, both August 17, 1869; New York *Albion*, August 21, 1869; and Freeman, *Robert E. Lee*, 438. The value of the bonds, redeemed by the State of Virginia, with interest, was paid in 1883 to Washington and Lee University. Peabody's last will appeared widely in the press after his death.

Chapter 24

Peabody's last illness is reported in London *Anglo-American Times*, October 23, 1869. The Queen's concern is expressed in a letter from Helps to Lampson, October 30, 1869, Royal Archives, Windsor Castle. Benjamin Moran's diary entries for late 1869 and early 1870 in the Library of Congress offer rare details. Peabody's last words and death are reported in a letter from McIlvaine to Winthrop, November 20, 1869, quoted in William Carus, ed., *Memorials of the Right Reverend Charles Pettit McIlvaine, Late Bishop of Ohio in the Protestant Episcopal Church of the United States* (London: Elliot Stock, 1882), 294–296; and repeated in Winthrop's *Eulogy Pronounced at the Funeral of George Peabody, at Peabody, Massachusetts, 8 February, 1870* (Boston: John Wilson and Son, 1870), 21–22. Another account of Peabody's last days and death is in a letter from Motley to Fish, November 6, 1869, Dispatch No. 142, "Dispatches from United States Minister, Great Britain," National Archives. The General Register Office, Somerset House, London, has Peabody's official death certificate. The use of Westminster Abbey for temporary burial is described in Arthur Penrhyn Stanley, "Recollections by Dean Stanley of Funerals in Westminster Abbey 1865–1881," 21–22, Westminster Abbey, London. The decision to use H.M.S. *Monarch* as the funeral ship is contained in the Gladstone Cabinet Minutes, November 10, 1869, Gladstone Papers, British Library.

Complicated U.S. and British government decisions regarding Peabody's death, transatlantic crossing, and attendant events are, for the U.S., contained in "Dispatches from United States Ministers, Great Britain," National Archives; "Admirals and Commodores' Letters," National Archives (which include the log of the U.S.S. *Plymouth*); Hamilton Fish Papers, Library of Congress; and for Britain: Gladstone Papers, British Library; Royal Archives, Windsor Castle; and "Log of H.M.S. *Monarch*," Admiralty Records, Public Record Office, London.

The Boston-Portland controversy, the Portland disembarkation, and attendant events are recorded in *Mortuary Honors to the Late George Peabody in Portland, Me.* (Portland: Loring, Short and Harmon, 1870). The controversy over Robert E. Lee's attendance at the funeral is recounted in the Corcoran Papers, Library of Congress, and the Kennedy Papers, Peabody Library Archives of the Johns Hopkins University Library. Prince Arthur's decision to attend the funeral is recorded in the Royal Archives, Windsor Castle. A brief account of the funeral with photographs is in "Historical Funerals, George Peabody, 1795–1869, Philanthropist and Financier," *American Funeral Director,* LXXV, No. 5 (May 1952), 46–48. Winthrop's laudatory *Eulogy* has insights into Peabody's character and influence. The funeral is described in my article, "The Funeral of George Peabody," *Essex Institute Historical Collections,* XCIX, No. 2 (April 1963), 67–87.

Partially known funeral costs to the town of Peabody ($240), the State of Maine ($2,890.55), Westminster Abbey ($653.50), and other costs ($240) are listed in GP-P&EM (total known funeral costs, $8,584.05). See also Peabody (Mass.) *Press,* March 23, 1870; State of Maine Executive Council, "Register of the Council," XXXIV (1870), 110, 180–181, 314, 318–319, 598–599, Maine State Library, Augusta; and Westminster Abbey Muniments, "Funeral Fee Book 1811–1899," 231. British and U.S. Government costs are not known.

Chapter 25

Peabody's wealth in the 1850s–1860s and his Bank of England loan are mentioned in Kathleen Burk, *Morgan Grenfell 1838–1988: The Biography of a Merchant Bank* (Oxford: Oxford University Press, 1989). British and U.S. honors are in my 1956 dissertation and my *George Peabody, a Biography,* 1971, Appendix, and in "George Peabody's Honors" in this revised edition.

Peabody Education Fund (PEF)

Historians praising the PEF: E. Merton Coulter, *The South During Reconstruction, 1855–1877* (Baton Rouge: Louisiana State University Press, 1947), 327; Harvey Wish, *Society and Thought in Modern America* (New York: Longmans Green & Co., 1952), II, 37; Edgar W. Knight, *Public Education in the South* (New York: Ginn & Co., 1922), 383–414; Edgar W. Knight, *Education in the United States* (New York: Ginn & Co., 1951), 555; Paul H. Buck, *The Road to Reunion, 1865–1900* (Boston: Little, Brown & Co., 1937), 164, 166; Abraham Flexner, with collaborator Esther S. Bailey, *Funds and Foundations: Their Policies Past and Present* (New York: Harper and Brothers, 1952), 11; William Knox Tate, "Elementary Education in the South," *The South in the Building of a Nation, A History of the Southern States* (Richmond, Virginia: Southern Historical Publication Society, 1909), 291; J. L. M. Curry, "The Peabody Education Fund," *Educational Review,* XIII (March 1897), 226; Daniel Coit Gilman, "Five Great Gifts," *The Outlook,* LXXXVI, No. 13 (July 27, 1907), 648–652 and 657; Thomas D. Clark, *The Southern Country Editor* (New York: Bobbs-Merrill Co., 1948), 30; Charles William Dabney, *Universal Education in the South,* 2 Vols. (Chapel Hill: University of North Carolina Press, 1936), I, 101, 104; William Torrey Harris is quoted in J. L. M. Curry, *A Brief Sketch of George Peabody and a History of the Peabody Education Fund Through Thirty Years* (Cambridge: John Wilson and Son, 1898), 230; Jesse Brundage Sears, *Philanthropy in the History of American Higher Education;* Bulletin No. 26 (Washington, D.C.: United States Bureau of Education, 1922), 91; and John F. Kasprzak, "George Peabody and the Peabody Education Fund: A Study in Reconciliation" (Master's thesis, American University, June 1966).

The PEF's influence and leaders are in Peabody Education Fund, *Proceedings of the Trustees of the Peabody Education Fund From Their Original Organization on the 8th of February, 1867* (Boston: John Wilson & Sons, 1875), I, 1867–74 (plus 6 volumes of *Proceedings*, 1875–1916); J. L. M. Curry, *A Brief Sketch of George Peabody and a History of the Peabody Education Fund Through Thirty Years* (New York: Negro Universities Press, 1969, reprint of 1898 edition); Leonard P. Ayres, *Seven Great Foundations* (New York: Russell Sage Foundation, 1911); Ullin Whitney Leavell, *Philanthropy in Negro Education* (Nashville: George Peabody College for Teachers, 1930); Hoy Taylor, *An Interpretation of the Early Administration of the Peabody Education Fund;* Contributions to Education No. 114 (Nashville: George Peabody College for Teachers, 1933); Daniel C. Gilman, "Thirty Years of the Peabody Education Fund," *Atlantic Monthly*, LXXIX (February 1897), 161–166; Joseph Walter Brouillette, "The Third Phase of the Peabody Education Fund, 1904–1914" (Ph.D. diss., George Peabody College for Teachers, 1940); Thomas Michael Drake, "The Impact of the Peabody Education Fund on the Development of Tax-Supported Education in Tennessee, 1867–1880" (Ed.D. diss., Tennessee State University, 1990); Earle H. West, "The Peabody Fund and Negro Education, 1867–1880," *History of Education Quarterly*, VI (Summer 1966), 3–21; Earle H. West, "The Life and Educational Contributions of Barnas Sears" (Ph.D. diss., George Peabody College for Teachers, 1961); and Howard Turner, "Robert M. Lusher, Louisiana Educator" (Ph.D. diss., Louisiana State University, 1944).

Second PEF agent J. L. M. Curry's work and influence is described in William J. Lewis, "The Educational Speaking of Jabez L.M. Curry" (Ph.D. diss., University of Florida, 1955); Richard Connelley Peck, "Jabez Lamar Monroe Curry: Educational Crusader" (Ph.D. diss., George Peabody College for Teachers, 1942); Jessie Pearl Rice, *J. L. M. Curry, Southerner, Statesman and Educator* (New York: King's Crown Press, 1949); J. L. M. Curry's educational philosophy about black education is in Donald Spivey, *Schooling for the New Slavery: Black Industrial Education, 1868–1915*. Contributions in Afro-American and African Studies, No. 38 (Westport, Connecticut: Greenwood Press, 1978), 28, 32, 37, 77–84.

Criticism of the PEF's black education policy is in William P. Vaughn, *Schools for All: The Blacks and Public Education in the South, 1865–1877* (Lexington: University Press of Kentucky, 1974); William P. Vaughn, "Partners in Segregation: Barnas Sears and the Peabody Fund," *Civil War History*, X, No. 3 (1964), 260–274; Kenneth R. Johnson, "The Peabody Fund: Its Role and Influence in Alabama," *Alabama Review*, XXVII, No. 2 (April 1974), 101–126; F. Bruce Rosen, "The Influence of the Peabody Fund on Education in Reconstruction Florida," *Florida Historical Quarterly*, LV, No. 3 (1977), 310–320; Hugh Victor Brown, *A History of the Education of Negroes in North Carolina* (Raleigh: Irving Swain Press, 1961); Henry Allen Bullock, *A History of Negro Education in the South From 1619 to the Present* (Cambridge: Harvard University Press, 1967); Horace Mann Bond, *Negro Education in Alabama: A Study in Cotton and Steel* (New York: Octagon Books, 1969); Horace Mann Bond, *The Education of the Negro in the*

American Social Order (New York: Octagon Books, 1966, revision of 1934 edition), 29; Willard Range, *The Rise and Progress of Negro Colleges in Georgia 1865–1949* (Athens: University of Georgia Press, 1951); Robert G. Sherer, *Subordination or Liberation? The Development and Conflicting Theories of Black Education in Nineteenth Century Alabama* (University: University of Alabama Press, 1977); and Henry J. Perkinson, *The Imperfect Panacea: American Faith in Education 1865–1990* (New York: McGraw Hill, 1991), 29.

George Peabody College for Teachers

Peabody Normal College's transition to Peabody College of Vanderbilt University is described in Paul K. Conkin *et al.*, *Gone with the Ivy: A Biography of Vanderbilt University* (Knoxville: University of Tennessee Press, 1985), 177–179, 470–473, and 706–715; Sarah K. Bolton, *Famous Givers and Their Gifts* (Freeport, New York: Books for Libraries Press, 1971 reprint of 1896 edition), 307–308; Jack Allen's two articles: "The Peabody Saga," *Peabody Reflector*, LIII, No. 2 (Summer 1980), 4–13; and "Peabody: A Tale of Two Centuries," *Peabody Reflector*, LVIII, No. 2 (Spring 1986), 19–23.

William W. Force, *Payne of Peabody: An Apostle of Education* (Nashville: privately printed, 1985), is useful, as is his *A Short History of George Peabody College for Teachers, 1974–1979* (Nashville: Williams Printing Co., 1986), which criticized *Design for the Future: A Report from the Select Committee on Peabody's Second Century to President John Dunworth and the Board of Trustees* (Nashville: George Peabody College for Teachers, August 29, *1974).*

Early Peabody-Vanderbilt connections are in Wallace Beasley, The Life and Educational Contributions of James D. Porter (Nashville: Bureau of Publications, George Peabody College for Teachers, 1950); Harvie Branscomb, *Purely Academic: An Autobiography* (Nashville: Vanderbilt University, 1978); George A. Dillingham, *The Foundation of the Peabody Tradition* (Lanham, Maryland: University Press of America, 1989); Edwin Mims, *Chancellor Kirkland of Vanderbilt* (Nashville: Vanderbilt University Press, 1940); Edwin Mims, *History of Vanderbilt University* (Nashville: Vanderbilt University Press, 1946); and Vanderbilt University, *Vanderbilt University Centennial: The Program and Addresses Given on October 3, 1975, Celebrating the One Hundredth Anniversary of the Ceremonies that Opened the University* (Nashville: Vanderbilt University, 1976).

The Peabody-Vanderbilt 1979 merger is described in "Boards Vote Peabody Merger," *Vanderbilt Gazette*, No. 111 (May 16, 1979), 1, 12; "The Committee of Visitors," *The Peabody Reflector*, LII, No. 3 (Autumn 1979), 10, 12; Alexander Heard, "A Vanderbilt Perspective on the Merger," *Peabody Reflector*, LII, No. 2 (Summer 1979), 4–5; Bill Hiles, "A New Era Dawns . . .," *Peabody Reflector*, LII, No. 1 (Spring 1979), 4–5; "How Students See the Merger," *Peabody Reflector*, LII, No. 3 (Autumn 1979), 13–14; "Peabody-Vanderbilt Merger Information," *Peabody Reflector*, Special Section, LI, No. 4 (Winter 1979), 98 a–h; and Hardy C. Wilcoxon, "Continuing Our Mission," *Peabody Reflector*, LII, No. 2 (Summer 1979), 2–3.

Other Peabody College-Vanderbilt University sources are John Dale Russell, *Report of the Study of Closer Cooperation Between George Peabody College for Teachers and Vanderbilt University* (Nashville, May 1962); "President Claunch Dies," *Peabody Reflector*, LXII, No. 1 (Spring 1991), 2; Edward Neely Cullum, "George Peabody College for Teachers, 1914–1937" (Ed.D. diss., George Peabody College for Teachers, 1963); George A. Dillingham, *The Foundation of the Peabody Tradition* (Lanham, Maryland: University Press of America, 1989); and Mary S. Hoffschwelle, "The Science of Domesticity: Home Economics at George Peabody College for Teachers, 1914–1939," *Journal of Southern History*, LVII, No. 4 (1991), 659–680.

Peabody College psychology Professor Susan Gray's leadership in Head Start is described in "Head Start Program Marks Anniversary: Has Peabody History," *Peabody Reflector*, LXII, No. 1 (Spring 1991), 7.

Peabody College progress since 1979 under Dean Willis D. Hawley is in Alexander Heard, "A Vanderbilt Perspective on the Merger," 4–5, and Hardy C. Wilcoxon, "Continuing Our Mission," both in *Peabody Reflector*, LII, No. 2 (Summer 1979), 2–3; Willis D. Hawley, "From the Dean," Peabody Reflector, LVIII, No. 2 (Spring 1986), 2, and LIX, No. 2 (Fall 1987), 2; "Centuries of Influence: A Celebration of Library Science at Peabody," *Peabody Reflector*, LIX, No. 2 (Fall 1987), 9, 11; Nelson Bryan, "The Dean and the Decade: Willis Hawley, Completing His Deanship, Reflects on Peabody's First Ten Years as a School of Vanderbilt University," *Peabody Reflector*, LXI, No. 1 (Fall 1989), 12–15; "Technology Can Reconstruct Classroom Instruction," *Vanderbilt Register*, December 8, 1989, n.p.; "Peabody gets $80,000 Grant," *Vanderbilt Register* (December 8, 1989), 7; Jean Crawford, "Learning with Jasper," *Peabody Reflector*, LXI, No. 2 (Summer 1990), 26–27; "VU's Peabody Holds Top Ranking Again," *Nashville Banner*, February 18, 1991, B-5; and "Peabody Top Choice in Education," *Peabody Columns*, I, No. 7 (March 1991), 2.

Peabody College's progress under Dean Pellegrino is described in "New Peabody Dean Eager to Help State Change Face of Education," *Tennessean*, December 26, 1991, B-3; "Pellegrino Announces Faculty Searches in Each Department," *Peabody Columns*, II, No. 45 (January 1992), 1; Marcelle Robertson, "New Dean to Work for 'Answers,'" *Vanderbilt Hustler*, CIV, No. 1 (January 14, 1992), 1, 11; James Pellegrino, "From the Dean," *Peabody Reflector*, LXIII, No. 2 (Fall 1992), inside front cover; "Campus Links to National, Metro K–12 Alliances," *Vanderbilt Register* (September 17 and 21, 1992), 1, 6; "New Initiatives Strengthen VU/Metro Ties," *Peabody Columns*, III, No. 5 (January 1993), 2; "SR Building to Return as Focal Point for Campus," *Peabody Columns*, III, No. 7 (March 1993), 1–2; and *Vanderbilt Register* (May 3–16, 1993), 1, 5.

Peabody Institute of Baltimore (PIB)

PIB is described in Roseann Kahn, "A History of the Peabody Institute Library, Baltimore, Maryland, 1857–1916" (Master's thesis in library science, Catholic University of America, 1953), published as ACRL Microcard Series No. 16

(Rochester, New York: University of Rochester Press for the Association of College and Reference Libraries, 1954); Elizabeth Schaaf (compiler), *Guide to the Archives of the Peabody Institute of the City of Baltimore 1857–1977* (Baltimore: Archives of the Peabody Institute of the Johns Hopkins University, 1987); *The Peabody: An Illustrated Guide* (Baltimore: Peabody Institute of the Johns Hopkins University, 1977); and Sherry H. Olson, *Baltimore: The Building of an American City* (Baltimore: The Johns Hopkins University Press, 1980), 105, 168, 192.

John Pendleton Kennedy's shaping of the PIB is in Charles H. Bohner, *John Pendleton Kennedy: Gentleman from Baltimore* (Baltimore: Johns Hopkins Press, 1961), 214–215, 234, 235, 238, 239. George Peabody's influence on Johns Hopkins and the placing of his seated statue near the Peabody Institute are in Harold A. Williams, *Robert Garrett & Sons Incorporated: Origin and Development: 1840–1965* (Baltimore: 1965, 27, 30, 32–33, 52–53, 56, 65.

Sources on early PIB librarians and administrators are George Harvey Genzmer, "Morris, John Gottlieb (Nov. 14, 1803–Oct. 10, 1895)," *Dictionary of American Biography*, edited by Dumas Malone (New York: Charles Scribner's Sons, 1934), VII, 212–213; "Morris, John Godlove," *National Cyclopedia of American Biography* (New York: James T. White & Co., 1893), III, 61; and John G. Morris, *Life Reminiscences of an Old Lutheran Minister* (Philadelphia: Lutheran Publication Society, 1896).

Early PIB librarians: Samuel Eliot Morison, *Nathaniel Holmes Morison, 1815–1890: Provost of the Peabody Institute of Baltimore, 1867–1890, An Address . . . February 12, 1957* (Baltimore: Peabody Institute Library, 1962); "Morison, Nathaniel Holmes," *Biographical Cyclopedia: Representative Men of Maryland and District of Columbia* (Baltimore: National Biographical Publishing Co., 1879), 323–324; [Morison, Nathaniel Holmes], *Peabody Bulletin* (Baltimore), May 1936; N. H. Morison, *et al.*, compilers, *Catalogue of the Library of the Peabody Institute of the City of Baltimore* (Baltimore: Peabody Library, 1883–93); John Parker, "Reminiscences of Fifty Years in the Library of the Peabody Institute of the City of Baltimore," *Peabody Bulletin* (Spring 1922), 4–8; Francis T. Barrett, "A Great Catalogue, Being an Appreciation of the Catalogue of the Library of the Peabody Institute, Baltimore," *The Library*, VI (1894), 69–73; Samuel Swett Green, *The Public Library in the United States, 1853–1893* (Boston: Boston Book Co., 1913), 118; and Richard H. Hart, *Enoch Pratt, the Story of a Plain Man* (Baltimore: Enoch Pratt Free Library, 1935).

PIB librarians continued: "Uhler, Philip Reese," *Who Was Who in America* (Chicago: A. N. Marquis Co., 1943), I:1263; "Uhler, Philip Reese," *Dictionary of American Biography*, edited by Dumas Malone (New York: Charles Scribner's Sons, 1943), XIX, 106–107; "Uhler, Philip Reese," *Biographical Cyclopedia of Representative Men of Maryland and District of Columbia* (Baltimore: National Biographical Publishing Co., 1879), 576–577; "Uhler, Philip Reese," *National Cyclopaedia of American Biography Being the History of the United States* (New York: James T. White & Co., 1900), VIII, 251; and "Uhler, Philip Reese," *Appletons' Cyclopaedia of American Biography*, edited by James Grant Wilson and John Fiske (New York: D. Appleton & Co., 1889), VI, n.p.

PIB continued: [Dielman, Louis Henry], *Baltimore News-Post*, May 30, 1942; "Dielman, Louis Henry," *Maryland History Notes*, XVII, No. 1 (May 1959), 2; and Robert G. Breen, "A Carroll Colloquy: College Left Its Cachet," *Sun* (Baltimore), February 8, 1952; Peter Young, "Back to the Stacks: Lloyd Brown to Assemble Historical Annapolis Data," *Evening Sun* (Baltimore), November 30, 1960; "Kerr Gets Post in Annapolis," *Evening Sun* (Baltimore), October 31, 1960; Naomi Kellman, "Mr. Peabody's Pet Project," *Sun* (Baltimore), February 9, 1947; (for Frank N. Jones), "New Peabody Librarian," *Gardens, Houses and People* (Baltimore), July 1957; and "New Library Director," *Sun* (Baltimore), June 17, 1957. The Peabody Library during 1947–1952 is described in "Fifty Turn Out for First Sunday Open-Day at Peabody Library," *Sun* (Baltimore), January 14, 1952; and James H. Bready, "Peabody Institute Library," *Sun* (Baltimore), January 6, 1952.

Legal and other controversies on the Peabody Library-Enoch Pratt 1966 merger are in Arthur Joseph Gutman, Letter, "Peabody Library," *Morning Sun* (Baltimore), June 14, 1966; Gerald W. Johnson, Letter, "The Real Question About the Library," *Sun* (Baltimore), April 22, 1966; George Rodgers, "Some of Peabody Library Books Set for Disposal," *Evening Sun* (Baltimore), June 23, 1966; Frank P. L. Somerville, "Peabody-Pratt Tie-Up Weighed," *Sun* (Baltimore), January 22, 1966; Frank P. L. Somerville, "Peabody's Shift of Books Fought," *Sun* (Baltimore), October 1, 1966; Frank P. L. Somerville, "Pratt Board is Silent on Peabody Plan," *Sun* (Baltimore), January 22, 1966; John Dorsey, *Mr. Peabody's Library: The Building, The Collection, The Neighborhood* (Baltimore: Enoch Pratt Free Library, 1978); Lawrence J. McCrank, "The Centennial Celebration of the Foundation of the Peabody Library, Baltimore, Maryland: A Report and Review," *Journal of Library History*, XIV, No. 2 (Spring 1979), 183–187; and "Pratt Takes Over Peabody," *News American* (Baltimore), July 3, 1966, B-9.

The Peabody Library 1977 restoration is in "Soot Hides Treasures. Peabody Library Spruced Up," *Sun* (Baltimore), February 19, 1977. The 1966 Peabody Library-Enoch Pratt and the 1982 Peabody Library-Johns Hopkins mergers are also in Eric Garland, "Has Baltimore Put Its Library on the Shelf?" *Baltimore Magazine*, LXXVI, No. 2 (February 1983), 46–51, 102–106; James H. Bready, "What's Ahead for Peabody Library Now That Hopkins Owns It?" *Sun* (Baltimore), July 4, 1982; "The Peabody Library," *Sun* (Baltimore), July 5, 1982; "The Peabody Library Returns," *Peabody News* (August/September 1982), 4; Ann Gwyn, "Changing Hands: Johns Hopkins Acquires Peabody Library," *Wilson Library Bulletin*, LVII, No. 5 (January 1983), 401–404; and Gunther Wertheimer, "Disgrace at the Peabody," *Evening Sun* (Baltimore), June 9, 1989.

H. L. Mencken's use of the Peabody Library is in John Dorsey, ed., *On Mencken* (New York: Alfred A. Knopf, 1980), 54; William Manchester, *Disturber of the Peace: The Life of H. L. Mencken* (New York: Harper & Brothers, 1950), 292; *Letters of H. L. Mencken; Selected and Annotated by Guy J. Forgue* (Boston: Northeastern University Press, 1981), 422; and John Dos Passos's research in the Peabody Library is in Townsend Ludington, *John Dos Passos: A Twentieth Century Odyssey* (New York: E. P. Dutton, 1980), 456.

The Peabody Library 1957 centennial celebration is in Lawrence J. McCrank, "The Centennial Celebration of the Foundation of the Peabody Library, Baltimore, Maryland: A Report and Review," *Journal of Library History*, XIV, No. 2 (Spring 1979), 183–187; and John Dorsey, *Mr. Peabody's Library: The Building, The Collection, The Neighborhood* (Baltimore: Enoch Pratt Free Library, 1978).

The Peabody Library is also in "Gifts to the Peabody Double Last Year's," *Sun* (Baltimore), July 7, 1978; *The Peabody Institute and Its Future* (Baltimore: Peabody Institute [1957]); "Peabody to Join Hopkins," *Sun* (Baltimore), December 21, 1976, A-1 (c. 1), A-8 (c. 2–c. 5); William T. Snyder, Jr., "Peabody Institute of Baltimore," *Baltimore*, XXXVI, No. 6 (March 1943), 37–38; "Peabody Library Starts 260,000-Card Index," *Evening Sun* (Baltimore), January 10, 1952; and Zoë Ingalls, "The Soaring Splendor of the Peabody Library," *Chronicle of Higher Education*, XL, No. 15 (December 1, 1993), B-5.

For George Peabody's likely influence on Carnegie, see Andrew Carnegie, *Autobiography of Andrew Carnegie* (New York: Doubleday, Doran & Co., 1933), 270. For Peabody's gifts to Maryland, see my articles, "George Peabody and Maryland," *Peabody Journal of Education*, XXXVII, No. 4 (November 1959), 150–157; and "Maryland's Yankee Friend—George Peabody Esq.," *The Maryland Teacher*, XX, No. 5 (January 1963), 4–7, 24 (reprinted in *The Peabody Notes* [Spring 1963], 4–7, 10).

The PIB's Gallery of Art holdings are described in Elizabeth Schaaf, "Baltimore's Peabody Art Gallery," *The Archives of the American Art Journal*, XXIV, No. 4 (1984), 9–14; "Rinehart, William Henry," *Appletons' Cyclopaedia of American Biography*, edited by James Grant Wilson and John Fiske (New York: D. Appleton & Co., 1888), V, 256; William S. Rusk, "Notes on the Life of William Henry Rinehart, Sculptor," *Maryland Historical Magazine*, XIX, No. 4 (December 1924), 309–338; [William Henry Rinehart], *Sun* (Baltimore), January 5, 1936; Lynn D. Poole, "Mantle of Success," *Sun* (Baltimore), May 16, 1948; and William S. Rusk, "Rinehart, William Henry," *Dictionary of American Biography*, edited by Dumas Malone (New York: Charles Scribner's Sons, 1943), XV, 615–617.

For the PIB Conservatory of Music, see *Peabody Conservatory of Music, Academic Years 1993–95* (Baltimore: Peabody Institute of the Johns Hopkins University, 1993); "Peabody Institute, Baltimore," *The International Cyclopedia of Music and Musicians*, edited by Oscar Thompson (New York: Dodd, Mead & Co., 1975), 1640; Elizabeth Schaaf, "From Idea to Tradition: The Peabody Prep," *Music Educators Journal*, LXXII, No. 1 (September 1985), 38–43; Margie H. Luckett, "May Garrettson Evans," *Maryland Women* (Baltimore: 1937), 106; [May Garrettson Evans], *Evening Sun* (Baltimore), November 29, 1934; "Peabody Preparatory School Founder to be Honored Sunday," *Sun* (Baltimore), May 21, 1947; [May Garrettson Evans], *Evening Sun* (Baltimore), November 29, 1934; and [May Garrettson Evans], "Baltimore," Chapter XXXVII in Ishbel Ross, *Ladies of the Press: The Story of Women in Journalism by an Insider* (New York: Harper and Brothers, 1936), 493–497.

See also "Lanier, Sidney," *Appletons' Cyclopaedia of American Biography*, edited by James Grant Wilson and John Fiske (New York: D. Appleton & Co., 1888), III,

613; Brian McGinty, "A Shining Presence: Rebel Poet Sidney Lanier Goes to War," *Civil War Times Illustrated*, XIX, No. 2 (May 1980), 25–31; Weimer Jones, "The Last Days of Sidney Lanier," *Sun* (Baltimore), February 4, 1968; Frederick Kelly, "Sidney Lanier at the Peabody Institute," *Peabody Bulletin* (Baltimore), 1976, 35–38; William Stump, "Man in the Street: Sidney Lanier," *Sun* (Baltimore), November 20, 1949; John C. French, "Sidney Lanier's Life in Baltimore: 'The Beautiful City' Has Yet to Discover Him Fully," *Sun* (Baltimore), September 6, 1931; Edward Lucas White, "Reminiscences of Sidney Lanier," *Johns Hopkins Alumni Magazine*, XVII, No. 4 (November 1928–June 1929), 329–331; and "Sidney Lanier Commemoration," *Johns Hopkins Alumni Magazine*, XIV, No. 5 (October 1925–June 1926), 480–505.

For PIB music conservatory directors, see Isabel L. Dobbin, "Asger Hamerik," *Peabody Bulletin* (Baltimore), April–May 1913, 2–4; "Asger Hamerik April 8, 1843–July 13, 1923," *Peabody Bulletin* (Baltimore), Fall 1923, 4–5; Mike Guiliano, "History of the Peabody Conservatory and Other Related Incidents," *Hopkins News-Letter*, LXXXI, No. 31 (February 11, 1977); [Asger Hamerik], *Peabody Bulletin* (Baltimore), May 1933; "Hamerik, Professor Asger," *Biographical Cyclopedia of Representative Men of Maryland and District of Columbia* (Baltimore: National Biographical Publishing Co., 1879), 84–86; "Hamerikana: To Asger Hamerik on his Seventieth Birthday. Congratulations and Loving Greetings from His Pupils and Friends" (with extracts from two letters from Sidney Lanier mentioning Hamerik), *Peabody Bulletin* (Baltimore), April–May 1913, 5; Otto T. Simon, Letter, "Thinks Asger Hamerik should be Honored by Some Memorial at the Peabody and That His Music Should be Frequently Heard There," *Sun* (Baltimore), April 15, 1922; Elizabeth Ellen Starr, "Asger Hamerik as I Knew Him as Teacher, Artist, Friend," *Peabody Bulletin* (Baltimore), Fall 1923, 6–7; Howard R. Thatcher, "A Teacher Glances Back—Notes on Music in Baltimore," *Evening Sun* (Baltimore), July 12, 1950; and Harold Randolph, "Asger Hamerik—An Appreciation," *Peabody Bulletin* (Baltimore), Fall 1923, 5–6.

Music directors continued: "The Man Who Brought Science into the Music Hall," *Baltimore Magazine*, LXXII, No. 8 (August 1979), 172, 170–171; [Otto Rudolph Ortmann], *Sun* (Baltimore), May 17, 1936; "Otto Ortmann," *Peabody Bulletin* (Baltimore), Fall 1941, 3–4; "Otto Ortmann," *Peabody Bulletin* (Baltimore), May 1936, 16; "Otto Ortmann," *Peabody Bulletin* (Baltimore), Fall 1941, 3+; P. J. B., [Otto Ortmann], *Sun* (Baltimore), November 11, 1934; "Three Goucher Faculty Members Retiring," *Evening Sun* (Baltimore), June 22, 1956; and "A Decade of Conservatory Activity," *Peabody Bulletin* (Baltimore), December 1938, 33–34. Ortmann's landmark books include *The Physical Basis of Piano Touch and Tone* (New York: E. P. Dutton, 1925) and *The Physiological Mechanics of Piano Technique* (New York: E. P. Dutton, 1929); paperback reprint, 1962.

Music directors continued: "Bon Voyage—Dr. Reginald Stewart," *Evening Sun* (Baltimore), June 24, 1958; "Conductor Makes Farewell Speech," *Sun* (Baltimore), March 13, 1952; "Director Change [Otto Ortmann, Reginald Stewart]," *Evening Sun* (Baltimore), August 5, 1941; "Little Orchestra Concerts to Continue Under Stewart," *Sun* (Baltimore), February 7, 1958; "Mr. Ortmann and His

Successor," *Gardens, Houses and People* (Baltimore), XVI, No. 8 (August 1941); "Progress at the Peabody," *Sun* (Baltimore), January 19, 1942; "Reginald Stewart Named Head of Peabody," *Evening Sun* (Baltimore), August 5, 1941; "Reginald Stewart, the New Director," *Peabody Bulletin* (Baltimore), Fall 1941, 1–3; "Reginald Stewart's Final Performance as Conductor," *Sun* (Baltimore), April 1, 1952; "Seventy of Symphony Urge Longer Season to Keep Stewart Here," *Sun* (Baltimore), January 31, 1952; "Stewart and the Peabody," *Gardens, Houses and People* (Baltimore), April 1952; "Stewart Defends Symphony Setup, Says He is Underpaid," *Sun* (Baltimore), November 24, 1951; "Stewart to Leave Peabody Conservatory Post in 1958," *Sun* (Baltimore), November 19, 1957; "Stewart's Move to Quit Accepted," *Sun* (Baltimore), February 2, 1952; "The Human Complexities of a Conductor's Job," *Sun* (Baltimore), February 4, 1952; and *Peabody Conservatory of Music* (Baltimore: Peabody Institute [1957]).

Peter Mennin as music director is in H. Donald Spatz, "Fire Engines, Cow Pastures and Music," *Forecast!* (Washington/Baltimore Entertainment Guide), XIV, No. 11 (January 1978), 60–61; George Kent Bellows, "Music Master: Whirlwind Tempo for Peabody Chief," *Evening Sun* (Baltimore), August 12, 1958; "Music . . . Mennin of the Peabody," *Gardens, Houses and People* (Baltimore), August 1958; [Peter Mennin], *Evening Sun* (Baltimore), April 8, 1958; Kathryn Geraghty, "Variations on a Theme in Blue, Green," *Sun* (Baltimore), December 31, 1961; and "Mennin Leaving as Peabody Head," *Sun* (Baltimore), June 11, 1962.

Charles Stanton Kent as music director is in "Succeeds Cooper: Peabody Conservatory Names Kent as Dean," *Baltimore News-Post*, May 19, 1961; "Peabody Names New Director," *Sun* (Baltimore), April 21, 1963; Peter Young, "New Peabody Director: Symphony Could Draw Teachers, He Believes," *Evening Sun* (Baltimore), May 9, 1963; Stephen A. Bennett, "Kent in Doubt, Peabody Scans Field for Director," *Sun* (Baltimore), February 7, 1968; "Illness Obliges Charles Kent to Leave Peabody," *Sun* (Baltimore), May 1, 1968; and [Charles Stanton Kent obituary], *Evening Sun* (Baltimore), June 2, 1969.

Raymond Edwin Robinson as interim music director: "Peabody Conservatory Lists R. E. Robinson as New Dean," *Sun* (Baltimore), July 2, 1963; and Ray E. Robinson, "A History of the Peabody Conservatory of Music" (D.M.Ed. diss., Indiana University, 1969).

Richard Franko Goldman as music director: "New Peabody Head Named," *Sun* (Baltimore), August 25, 1968; John Pappenheimer, "Goldman Wants Things to Happen," *Evening Sun* (Baltimore), August 27, 1968; Earl Arnett, "Richard Franko Goldman Found a Good School That Needed a Little Shaking Up," *Sun* (Baltimore), April 20, 1973, B-1; and Noel K. Lester, "Richard Franko Goldman: His Life and Works" (D.M.A. diss., Peabody Conservatory of Music of the Johns Hopkins University, 1984).

Other Conservatory of Music sources are "New Peabody Dean Named" [David S. Cooper], *Sun* (Baltimore), February 18, 1959; Richard W. Case, "How the Hopkins and Peabody Got Together," *Sun* (Baltimore), January 3, 1977;

"Peabody Students Getting in Tune for Transposition to Hopkins: Some Notes, Quotes, and Thoughts About New School," *Hopkins News-Letter*, LXXXI, No. 31 (February 11, 1977), 1–2; and Ulrike Huhs, "Peabody Conservatory Generates Sounds of the Future," *Asheville* (N.C.) *Citizen-Times*, November 28, 1992, C-4.

Peabody Museums, Harvard, Yale, and Salem, Massachusetts
    On Harvard's Peabody Museum of Archaeology and Ethnology see Frederic Ward Putnam, *The Archaeological Reports of Frederic Ward Putnam: Selected from the Annual Reports of the Peabody Museum of Archaeology and Ethnology, Harvard University 1875–1903* (New York: AMS Press, 1973, reprint), IX–XIII; and John O. Brew, ed., *One Hundred Years of Anthropology* (Cambridge: Harvard University Press, 1968).
    On Yale's Peabody Museum of Natural History and first director O. C. Marsh, see Charles Schuchert and Clara Mae LeVene, *O. C. Marsh, Pioneer in Paleontology* (New Haven: Yale University Press, 1940); Mark J. McCarren, *The Scientific Contributions of Othniel Charles Marsh: Birds, Bones, and Brontotheres* (New Haven: Peabody Museum of Natural History), 1993; Robert M. Schoch, "The Paleontological Collections of the Peabody Museum of Natural History," *Fossils Quarterly* (Fall/Winter 1984–1985), 4–14; Carl O. Dunbar, "Recollections on the Renaissance of Peabody Museum Exhibits, 1939–1959," *Discovery*, XII, No. 1 (Fall 1976), 17–35; Hugh S. McIntosh, "Marsh and the Dinosaurs," *Discovery*, I, No. 1 (1965), 31–37; Robert Plate, *The Dinosaur Hunters* (New York: David McKay Co., 1964); "Dedication of the Peabody Museum: Simple Exercises Mark the Laying of the Cornerstone of New Home for Notable Collections," *Yale Alumni Weekly* (July 6, 1923), 1249–1250; E.T.D., "Some Notes on the Beginnings of Peabody Museum," *Discovery*, II, No. 1 (Fall 1966), 33–35; "Carl O. Dunbar 1891–1979: An Appreciation," *Discovery*, XIV, No. 1 (1979), 44; and Cyril Bibby, *Scientist Extraordinary: The Life and Scientific Work of Thomas Henry Huxley, 1825–1895* (Oxford: Pergamon Press, 1972).
    For the O. C. Marsh-E. D. Cope rivalry see Nathan Reingold, ed., *Science in Nineteenth-Century America: A Documentary History* (New York: Hill and Wang, 1964), 236–241; George Gaylord Simpson, *George Gaylord Simpson: Concession to the Improbable, An Unconventional Autobiography* (New Haven: Yale University Press, 1978), 16–17, 40–41, 130–131, 270–271; Edwin Harris Colbert, *Men and Dinosaurs: The Search in Field and Laboratory* (New York: E. P. Dutton, 1968), 55, 66–97, 144–145; Edwin Harris Colbert, *The Great Dinosaur Hunters and Their Discoveries* (New York: Dover Publications, 1984); Edwin Harris Colbert, *Dinosaurs: Their Discovery and Their World* (New York: E. P. Dutton, 1961), 28–37, 70–71, 86–87, 118–119, 146–149, 277; Edwin Harris Colbert, *Dinosaurs: An Illustrated History* (Maplewood, New Jersey: Hammond, 1985), 24–27; Robert West Howard, *The Dawnseekers: The First History of American Paleontology* (New York: Harcourt Brace Jovanovich, 1975); Thomas F. Glick, ed., *Comparative Reception of Darwinism* (Austin: University of Texas Press, 1972), 192–213; Peter J. Bowler, *Fossils and Press: Paleontology and the Idea of Progressive Evolution in the Nineteenth Century* (New York:

Science History Publications, 1976), 130–141; Url Lanham, *The Bone Hunters* (New York: Columbia University Press, 1973), ix–xi, 79–164, 182–183, 218–267; Bernard Jaffe, *Men of Science in America: The Role of Science in the Growth of Our Country* (New York: Simon and Schuster, 1944), 279–306, 565; Stephen Jay Gould, *Bully for Brontosaurus: Reflections in Natural History* (New York: W. W. Norton, 1991), 86–93, 139, 160–163, 170–177, 416–433; Adrian J. Desmond, *The Hot-Blooded Dinosaurs: A Revolution in Palaeontology* (New York: Dial Press, 1976), 30–37, 106–117, 138–139, 174–177; Elizabeth Noble Shor, *Fossils and Flies: The Life of a Compleat Scientist Samuel Wendell Williston (1851–1918)* (Norman: University of Oklahoma Press, 1977), 3–7, 22–23, 64–71, 96–98, 117–123; Robert T. Bakker, *The Dinosaur Heresies: New Theories Unlocking the Mystery of the Dinosaurs and Their Extinction* (New York: William Morrow, 1986), 37–41, 164–165, 206–213, 298–305, 365–369; John H. Ostrom and John S. McIntosh, *Marsh's Dinosaurs: The Collections from Como Bluff* (New Haven: Yale University Press, 1966), v–vi, 6–11, 28–43; Bruce J. MacFadden, *Fossil Horses: Systematics, Paleobiology, and Evolution of the Family Equidae* (Cambridge: Cambridge University Press, 1992), 29–33; Martin J. S. Rudwick, *The Meaning of Fossils: Episodes in the History of Palaeontology.* 2nd ed. (New York: Neale Watson Academic Publications, 1976), 252–255; Diagram Group, *A Field Guide to Dinosaurs* (New York: Avon, 1983), 52–53, 146–147, 210–211, 218–223, 246–249; and Time-Life Books, *Emergence of Man: Life Before Man* (New York: Time-Life Books, 1972), 75–83.

Sources on the Peabody and Essex Museum of Salem, Massachusetts, include Ralph W. Dexter, "The Role of E. S. Morse, Director of the Peabody Academy of Science, in Bringing Zoology to Japan (1877–1883)," *Essex Institute Historical Collections*, CXXVI, No. 4 (October 1990), 254–260; and my article, "George Peabody and the Peabody Museum of Salem," *Curator*, X, No. 2 (1967), 137–153; Peabody Museum of Salem—Essex Institute News Release, May 19, 1992 [on creating Peabody and Essex Museum]; Peabody and Essex Museum Fact Sheet [1993]. Exhibit descriptions and current news are in Peabody and Essex Museum of Salem, *Annual Reports*, and its quarterly *Register*.

Sources of eulogies by Victor Hugo, Louis Blanc, and Elbert Hubbard are in my 1956 dissertation.

Sources of Extant Portraits, Photographs, and Illustrations

(arranged alphabetically by author's last name or by title of publication or repository)

Allen, Jack. "Peabody: A Tale of Two Centuries," *Peabody Reflector* XVIII, No. 2 (Spring 1986), 19–23.
  1. George Peabody photo in old age, seated, from waist up, p. 19.
  2. Four photos of George Peabody College for Teachers, pp. 21–23.

American Funeral Director, "Historical Funerals, George Peabody, 1795–1869, Philanthropist and Financier," LXXV, No. 5 (May 1952), 46–48.
  Drawings of funeral scenes, November 1869–February 1870.

Baltimore News, "Baltimore in Pictures," March 6, 1928. Photo of George Peabody's statue near Peabody Institute, Baltimore, copied after William W. Story's seated George Peabody statue near Royal Exchange, London. Given to Baltimore by Robert Garrett, April 7, 1890.

Brooke, Bissell. "Peabody Outwitted a Queen," *Sun* (Baltimore), February 13, 1955.
  George Peabody portrait, middle aged, from Enoch Pratt Free Library.

Bryan, Nelson. "The Life of a Philanthropist: George Peabody," *Peabody Reflector,* LXII, No. 2 (Winter 1994), 2–7. From archives of Peabody College of Vanderbilt University, Nashville.
  1. George Peabody photo in old age, head to waist, leaning on column, Contents page.
  2. Engraving of George Peabody in old age, head and shoulders, by W. H. Forbes, with Peabody's signature beneath, p. 3.
  3. Street scene sketch of sculptor W. W. Story's seated George Peabody statue, in Threadneedle Street, near Royal Exchange, London, p. 4; from Philip Whitwell Wilson, *George Peabody, Esq., An Interpretation.* Nashville: George Peabody College for Teachers, 1926.
  4. Sketch of Peabody Homes of London, p. 5.
  5. Sketch of funeral scene, carrying George Peabody's coffin aboard H.M.S. *Monarch,* p. 6.

6. Photo of first Peabody Education Fund Trustees, probably 1869: seated, left to right, George Peabody Russell, Massachusetts; William Alexander Graham, North Carolina; George Peabody; Robert Charles Winthrop, Massachusetts; William Cabell Rives, Virginia. Standing, left to right: George Washington Riggs, Washington, D.C.; George N. Eaton, Maryland; William Maxwell Evarts, New York; Edward A. Bradford, Louisiana; Charles Macalester, Pennsylvania; John Henry Clifford, Massachusetts; Admiral David Glasgow Farragut; Governor Hamilton Fish, New York; General Ulysses Simpson Grant; Governor William Aiken, South Carolina; Bishop Charles Pettit McIlvaine, Ohio; Samuel Wetmore, New York; p. 7.

7. Sketch of the first Peabody Institute, Peabody, Massachusetts, p. 9.

Burk, Kathleen. *Morgan Grenfell 1838–1988: The Biography of a Merchant Bank.* Oxford: Oxford University Press, 1989.

1. Photo of statue of George Peabody near Royal Exchange, London, frontispiece (*see* Bryan, #3).

2. Portrait of George Peabody (c.1854) by George Peter Alexander Healy, in National Portrait Gallery, Smithsonian Institution, Washington, D.C., facing p. 80.

3. Cartoon of George Peabody and John Bull from *Fun* (London), February 24, 1866, about Peabody Donation Fund, following p. 80.

4. Engraving of Peabody Square model dwellings on Blackfriars Road, London; from Morgan, Grenfell, following p. 80.

5. Junius S. Morgan portrait, from Morgan, Grenfell Group, following p. 80.

6. J. Pierpont Morgan portrait, from Bettman Archives, following p. 80.

Carosso, Vincent P. *The Morgans, Private International Bankers, 1854–1913.* Cambridge, Massachusetts: Harvard University Press, 1987, following p. 218, from Pierpont Morgan Library.

1. Photo of George Peabody seated.

2. Photo of Junius S. Morgan in 1881 at age 68.

3. Photo of J. Pierpont Morgan in 1889 at age 52.

Conkin, Paul K., *et al. Gone with the Ivy: A Biography of Vanderbilt University.* Knoxville: University of Tennessee Press, 1985.
Aerial photo of campus of George Peabody College for Teachers, Nashville, after World War II, p. 473.

Cullen, Tom A . "Peabody Pioneer: First Slum Push," *Austin American* (Texas), March 18, 1964.
Engraving of "Peabody's Apartment Houses" (London).

Curry, J. L. M. *A Brief Sketch of George Peabody, and a History of the Peabody Education Fund Through Thirty Years*. New York: Negro Universities Press, 1969; reprint of 1898 edition by John Wilson and Son.
Engraving of George Peabody in old age by W. H. Forbes, frontispiece (*see* Bryan, #2).

Dabney, Charles William. *Universal Education in the South. In Two Volumes. Volume I: From the Beginning to 1900*. Chapel Hill: University of North Carolina Press, 1936.
1. Photo of Robert E. Lee, George Peabody, and William W. Corcoran at White Sulphur Springs, West Virginia, August 1869, facing p. 83.
2. Photos of Barnas Sears, first agent of the Peabody Education Fund, facing p. 122, upper left; and Jabez Lamar Monroe Curry, second agent of the Peabody Education Fund, upper right.
3. Photo of the first Peabody Education Fund Trustees, 1867 (names in Bryan, #6), facing p. 123.
4. Illustration of Philip Lindsley, President of the University of Nashville, facing p. 287.

De Mare, Marie. *G. P. A. Healy, American Artist*. New York: David McKay Co., 1954.
Mentions 1862 exhibition of portraits by Healy, including his portrait of George Peabody (no illustration), p. 206.

Dorsey, John. *Mr. Peabody's Library: The Building, The Collection, The Neighborhood*. Baltimore: Enoch Pratt Free Library, 1978.
1. Engraving of George Peabody, head and shoulders, p. 4.
2. Interior of Peabody Institute Library, Baltimore, p. 2; Provost Nathaniel H. Morison, p. 6; and scenes of Mount Vernon Place and area.

Economist (London). "Victorian Yankee," February 2, 1972. Engraving of portrait of George Peabody in old age seated at desk, with head supported by right hand.

Frizzell, Mildred Armor. "George Peabody Cup," *Hobbies*, LXXXVI, No. 4 (June 1981), 41, 62.
Photo of George Peabody pressed-glass cup made in Sunderland, England.

Gwyn, Ann. "Changing Hands: Johns Hopkins Acquires Peabody Library," *Wilson Library Bulletin*, LVII, No. 5 (January 1983), 401–4.
Engraving of George Peabody, p. 401.

Hearn, Nicholas. *George Peabody (1795–1869) "One of the Poor's Greatest Benefactors?"* London: Peabody Donation Fund, 1980.
1. Engraving of George Peabody in old age, cover.

2. Lithograph of the U.S. display at the Great Exhibition of 1851, from a lithograph at the Queen's Library, Windsor Castle, p. 6.
3. Engravings of Peabody Homes of London buildings, pp. 20–21.
4. Engraving of unveiling of sculptor W. W. Story's George Peabody statue, near Royal Exchange, London, p. 24 (*see* Bryan, #3).
5. Engraving of George Peabody's funeral in Westminster Abbey, from *Illustrated London News* (November 1869), p. 26.
6. Engraving of George Peabody's remains being taken aboard H.M.S. *Monarch* at Portsmouth; from *Graphic* (December 25, 1869), p. 27.
7. Engraving of George Peabody's remains in mortuary chapel aboard H.M.S. *Monarch;* from Graphic (December 18, 1869), p. 28.

Hellman, Geoffrey T. "The First Great Cheerful Giver," *American Heritage,* XVII, No. 4 (1966), 28–33, 76–77; reprinted in *Peabody Reflector,* XL, No. 1 (January–February 1967), 4–11. (Page numbers below are in *Peabody Reflector.*)
1. Portrait in color of George Peabody in old age, seated, holding letter founding the Peabody Education Fund, front cover.
2. Engraving of George Peabody in middle age by J. C. Buttre from a daguerrotype, p. 4.
3. Photo of George Peabody in old age, with right hand resting inside jacket, p. 4.
4. Photo of George Peabody's bust by sculptor Hans Schuler unveiled 1926 at New York University Hall of Fame, p. 4.
5. Photo of George Peabody in old age holding glasses in right hand and letter in left hand, p. 5.
6. Engraving of sketch of Peabody Square model dwellings, London, p. 6.
7. Lithograph of street scene with welcoming arches on George Peabody's visit to Danvers (now Peabody), Massachusetts, 1856, p. 8.
8. Queen Victoria's miniature portrait done in 1867 by British artist F. A. Tilt, baked on porcelain with a frame of solid gold, given to George Peabody in 1867; original in Peabody Institute Library, Peabody, Massachusetts, p. 9.
9. Engraving of sketch of H.M.S. *Monarch* bearing George Peabody's remains, before docking in Portland, Maine, February 1870, p. 10.
10. Last photo of George Peabody taken by John Mayall, signed by George Peabody in 1868, with handwritten quotation from letter establishing the Peabody Education Fund, p. 11.

Hidy, Muriel E. "The George Peabody Papers," *Bulletin of the Business Historical Society,* XII, No. 1 (February 1938), 1–6.
George Peabody, "engraved by J. C. Buttre from a daguerrotype," with

signature, from "George Peabody," *Hunt's Merchants' Magazine*, XXXVI, No. 4 (April 1857), 428–37.

Hill, Eloise Wilkes. "The Peabody Influence. . . . A New Book," *Peabody Reflector*, XLII, No. 1 (January–February 1969), 15–16.
Photo of Peabody College President and Mrs. Henry H. Hill near sculptor W. W. Story's George Peabody statue, near Royal Exchange, London, in 1961, p. 16 (*see* Bryan, #3).

Hill, Ruth Henderson. *George Peabody "The Great Benefactor" 1795–1869, for the Centennial of the Peabody Institute, Peabody, Massachusetts*. Peabody, Massachusetts: Peabody Institute, 1953. Reprint. 1989.
1. Illustration of George Peabody holding letter, cover.
2. Other photos of the Peabody Institute Library, Peabody, Massachusetts, p. 4; birthplace of George Peabody, p. 8; tablet at birthplace, p. 10; Queen Victoria's miniature portrait done in 1867 by British artist F. A. Tilt, baked on porcelain with a frame of solid gold, given to George Peabody in 1867; original in Peabody Institute Library, Peabody, Massachusetts, p. 14; George Peabody's grave, Harmony Grove Cemetery, p. 16; and George Peabody memorial inscription, floor of Westminster Abbey, London.

Hoyt, Edwin P. *The Peabody Influence: How a Great New England Family Helped to Build America*. New York: Dodd, Mead and Co., 1968, facing p. 110.
1. Engraving of George Peabody in old age.
2. Drawing of George Peabody's birthplace.
3. Drawing of Peabody Square (Peabody Homes of London), Islington.

Kenin, Richard. *Return to Albion: Americans in England 1760–1940*. New York: Holt, Rinehart and Winston, 1979.
1. Portrait of George Peabody (c.1854) by George Peter Alexander Healy, in National Portrait Gallery, Smithsonian Institution, p. 94.
2. Portrait of Junius Spencer Morgan by Braga, p. 98.
3. George Peabody's 1862 founding letter offering housing for the poor of London; original in Peabody Institute Library, Peabody, Massachusetts, p. 100.
4. Photo of gold box with parchment granting George Peabody Freedom of the City of London, July 10, 1862; original in Peabody Institute Library, Peabody, Massachusetts, p. 102.
5. Photo of Queen Victoria's miniature portrait done in 1867 by British artist F. A. Tilt, baked on porcelain with a frame of solid gold; given to George Peabody in 1867; original in Peabody Institute Library, Peabody, Massachusetts, p. 103.
6. Photo of U. S. Congressional gold medal made by Starr and Marcus

Goldsmiths of New York, awarded to George Peabody in appreciation for his $2 million Peabody Education Fund, 1867; original in Peabody Institute Library, Peabody, Massachusetts, p. 104.

7. Photo of wood engraving of funeral of George Peabody in Westminster Abbey in *Illustrated London News*, November 20, 1869; original in Library of Congress, p. 105.

Kenyon, Paul. "Professor Tells How Peabody Pioneered in Giving Away Millions Constructively," *North Shore '71* (Gloucester, Massachusetts), VI, No. 50 (December 11, 1971), 1–2, 4+.

1. Enlarged photo of Queen Victoria's miniature portrait done in 1867 by British artist F. A. Tilt, baked on porcelain with a frame of solid gold, given to George Peabody in 1867. Below, from left to right, are Gold Box presenting membership in the Fishmongers' Company of London; Congressional Gold Medal awarded for the Peabody Education Fund; and Gold Box containing Freedom of the City of London; cover.

2. Portrait of George Peabody in middle age by John Neagle; original in Karolik Collection, Museum of Fine Arts, Boston, p. 2.

3. Photo of open vault, Peabody Institute Library, Peabody, Massachusetts, showing Queen Victoria's porcelainized miniature portrait, Congressional Gold Medal, and Gold Boxes containing membership in Fishmongers' Company and the Freedom of the City of London, p. 4.

4. Photo of George Peabody's birthplace, Peabody, Massachusetts, p. 4.

5. Photo of Shadwell Estate, 1935, Peabody Homes of London, p. 4.

6. Sketch of Peabody Square, Islington, Peabody Homes of London.

7. Photo closeup of Queen Victoria's porcelainized miniature portrait.

8. Photo closeup of Congressional Gold Medal.

Kocher, Alfred Lawrence, and Howard Dearstyne. *Shadows in Silver, a Record of Virginia, 1850–1900, in Contemporary Photographs taken by George and Huestis Cook with Additions from the Cook Collection.* New York: Charles Scribner's Sons, 1954.

1. Confederate leaders meeting at White Sulphur Springs, West Virginia, probably taken between August 15–19, 1869, p. 189.

2. Photo of George Peabody sitting alone, p. 190.

The same photos are also in the following books:

See Dabney #1.

Freeman, Douglas Southall, *Robert E. Lee, A Biography.* New York: Charles Scribner's Sons, 1947, IV, p. 438.

Meredith, Roy, *The Face of R. E. Lee.* New York: Charles Scribner's Sons, 1947, pp. 84–85.

Miller, Francis Trevelyan (ed.), *The Photographic History of the Civil War.* New York: Review of Reviews Company, 1911, X, p. 4.

Lane, William Coolidge, and Nina E. Brown, eds. *A.L.A. Portrait Index*. III.
New York: Burt Franklin, 1906, reprinted 1960, p. 1129, lists George Peabody illustrations in the following works:

1. *American Annual Cyclopedia*. VII. New York: Appleton, 1867, engraving
   by H. B. Hall, Jr., frontispiece.
2. *Appletons' Cyclopedia of American Biography*. IV. New York: Appleton,
   1888, engraving by H. B. Hall, Jr., p. 688.
3. Bolton, Sarah Knowles. *Lives of Poor Boys Who Became Famous*. New York:
   Crowell, 1885, frontispiece.
4. Buttre, Lillian C. *American Portrait Gallery*. New York: Buttre, 1877, I,
   plate 39, engraving by J. C. Buttre, after photo.
5. Duyckinck, Evart A. *Portrait Gallery of Eminent Men and Women of Europe
   and America*. II. New York: Johnson, 1873, photo, p. 291.
6. *Harper's New Monthly Magazine*, LXVIII (1884). Illustration of sculptor
   W. W. Story's seated George Peabody statue, near Royal Exchange,
   London, p. 773 (*see* Bryan, #3).
7. *Harper's Weekly*, VI (1862), woodcut, p. 309. X (1866), woodcuts, pp. 221
   and 701. XI (1867), woodcut of group, p. 228. XIII (1869), woodcut, pp.
   749 and 808.
8. Harrison, Frederick G. *Biographical Sketches of Preeminent Americans*. II.
   Boston: Walker, 1892, plate 22.
9. Loubat, J. F. *Medallic History of the U. S. 1776–1876* New York: Loubat,
   1880. II, etching of U.S. Congressional medal by Jules Jacquemart,
   plate 78.
10. *Magazine of Art* (London). XIII (1890), J. M. Johnstone's engraving of
    George Peabody portrait by G. F. Watts, p. 49.
11. *Massachusetts Historical Society Proceedings*, IX (1866), W. H. Forbes en-
    graving of George Peabody, frontispiece.
12. *New England Magazine New Series*, XXII (1900), p. 227.

Law, Frederick Houk. Great Americans. New York: Globe, 1953, 391–96.
Portrait of George Peabody, p. 389.

Marney, Betty. "Fascinating Life of Great Philanthropist," *Nashville Banner* (Tennessee), December 10, 1971, 56. Photo of engraving of George Peabody in
old age.

Maryland Historical Society, Prints and Photographs Division, 201 West Monument St., Baltimore, Maryland 21201, Phone (301) 685-3750.
1. Uncatalogued extensive photos and prints of George Peabody, including
   1866 photo of George Peabody and various dignitaries on the steps of the
   Peabody Institute of Baltimore watching parade.
2. Photos of Peabody Conservatory of Music of Baltimore.

Maryland History Notes, "Baltimore's 150th Birthday," V, No. 3 (November 1947), 1–2.
1. George Peabody portrait painted by James R. Lambdin, 1857 (original at Maryland Historical Society) is mentioned on p. 1.
2. George Peabody portrait, "Painted during the early years of his maturity" (probably in his early thirties) by Chester Harding (original in Maryland Historical Society, oil on canvas, 30" x 25", in oval frame), received from Mrs. Charles R. Weld (née Frances Eaton, who died March 13, 1947), p. 1.

New York University. Hall of Fame for Great Americans. *Hall of Fame for Great Americans at New York University: Official Handbook.* New York: New York University Press, 1962.
Portrait of George Peabody.

Parker, Franklin. "Founder Paid Debt to Education," *Peabody Post* (George Peabody College for Teachers), VIII, No. 8 (February 10, 1955), 1.
Portrait of George Peabody, seated, holding letter founding the Peabody Education Fund.

————. *George Peabody, A Biography.* Nashville: Vanderbilt University Press, 1971.
1. Engraving of photo of George Peabody, with his signature, holding letter founding the Peabody Education Fund, facing title page.
2. Copy of profile of George Peabody as a young man, made for dust jacket, after an original by Gary Gore, design and promotion manager, Vanderbilt University Press; his design was awarded Gold Medal by the Art Directors' Club, Nashville, 1971. This profile also appears in: Herbert A. Kenny, "The Old Tycoons," Globe (Boston), December 17, 1971; and *Nashville Banner,* December 9, 1971, p. 39.

————. "George Peabody and the Peabody Museum of Salem," *Curator,* X, No. 2 (1967). Illustrations:
1. Full figure photo of George Peabody, standing, one hand tucked inside front of coat, p. 134.
2. Fig. 2, George Peabody's birthplace; and Fig. 3, artist's sketch of Peabody Homes in London, p. 139.
3. Fig. 4, Westminster Abbey scene of George Peabody's November 12, 1869, funeral; and Fig. 5, H.M.S. *Monarch* leaving Portsmouth Harbor with George Peabody's remains aboard, p. 141.
4. Fig. 6, photo of the Peabody Museum of Salem (now Peabody and Essex Museum), p. 147.
5. Fig. 7 and Fig. 8, photos inside East India Marine Hall (now Peabody and Essex Museum), Salem, p. 149.

6. Fig. 9 and Fig. 10, photos of exhibits, Peabody and Essex Museum, Salem, Massachusetts, p. 151.

————. "George Peabody and the Spirit of America," *Peabody Reflector*, XXIX, No. 2 (February 1956), 26–27.

1. Photo of bronze doors with tableaux depicting the Spirit of America designed by Louis Amateis, featuring as part of the design the head of George Peabody; doors intended for U.S. Capitol Building, p. 26.
2. Photo of enlarged portion of above featuring George Peabody's face on right end of transom, p. 27.

————. *George Peabody (1795–1869), Founder of Modern Philanthropy.* Nashville: George Peabody College for Teachers, 1955 (pamphlet, Founders Day Address, February 18, 1955, Peabody College).

1. Color portrait of George Peabody, head and chest, cover.
2. Handwritten copy of last part of February 7, 1867, letter founding the Peabody Education Fund, with George Peabody's signature, inside front cover.
3. Photo of Queen Victoria's porcelainized miniature portrait (*see* Hellman, #8) and accompanying letter dated March 1866; given to George Peabody in 1867; original in Peabody Institute Library, Peabody, Massachusetts; Queen's gift to thank George Peabody for his Homes of London Donation, p. 7.
4. Photo of George Peabody's bust by sculptor Hans Schuler unveiled 1926 at New York University Hall of Fame, p. 11.
5. Photo of the original Trustees of Peabody Education Fund, probably 1869, including George Peabody (names in Bryan, #6), p. 13.
6. Photo of George Peabody's statue near Peabody Institute, Baltimore, copied after William W. Story's seated George Peabody statue near Royal Exchange, London (*see* Bryan, #3). Given by Robert Garrett of Baltimore, April 7, 1890, p. 16.
7. Photo of Queen Victoria's miniature portrait done in 1867 by British artist F. A. Tilt, baked on porcelain with a frame of solid gold, given to George Peabody in 1867; original in Peabody Institute Library, Peabody, Massachusetts; p. 19 (*see* Hellman, #8).
8. Photo of sculptor W. W. Story's seated George Peabody statue, near Royal Exchange, London, unveiled 1869, p. 25.

————. "The Girl George Peabody Almost Married," *Peabody Reflector*, XXVIII, No. 8 (October 1955), 215, 224–25; reprinted in *Peabody Notes*, XVII, No. 3 (Spring 1964), 10–14.
Portrait of Esther Hoppin Lardner by Thomas Sully, completed December 3, 1840. Original (20" x 24") in Frick Art Reference Library, New York. *Peabody Reflector*, p. 215.

————. "Maryland's Yankee Friend, George Peabody, Esq.," *Maryland Teacher*, XX, No. 5 (January 1963), 6–7, 24.
1. Sketch of George Peabody (head and chest) in old age, p. 6.
2. Sketch of Baltimore street scene of victory arches honoring George Peabody during his 1856 visit to the U.S., p. 7.
3. Sketch of George Peabody's coffin being received aboard H.M.S. *Monarch* in Portsmouth harbor, England, for transport to the United States, p. 7.

————. "Pantheon of Philanthropy: George Peabody," *National Society of Fundraisers Journal*, I, No. 1 (December 1976), 16–20.
Portrait of George Peabody in old age, head and shoulders. p. 17.

————. "To Live Fulfilled: George Peabody, 1795–1869, Founder of George Peabody College for Teachers," *Peabody Reflector*, XLIII, No. 2 (Spring 1970), 50–53.
Portrait of George Peabody, with February 7, 1867, letter founding Peabody Education Fund, p. 51.

The Peabody: An Illustrated Guide. Baltimore: Peabody Institute of the Johns Hopkins University, 1977.
1. Life-size photo of George Peabody by London photographer John Mayall; was painted over by Queen Victoria's portrait painter, A. Arnoult, to resemble an oil painting; first exhibited at the Royal Pavilion, Brighton, 1867; original in Peabody Institute of Baltimore art collection, facing p. 3.
2. Photo of George Peabody seated, White Sulphur Springs, West Virginia, with Robert E. Lee to his right and Turkish Minister to the U.S. Blacque Bey; seated to his left are W. W. Evans and James Lyons; standing (left to right): Generals Martin W. Gary, J. B. Magruder, Robert B. Lilley, P. G. T. Beauregard, Alexander R. Lawton, Governor Henry A. Wise, and Generals Joseph L. Brent and James Conner, summer 1869, p. 4 (*see* Dabney and Kocher).
3. Black and white etching of George Peabody's burial in Salem, Massachusetts, p. 7.
4. Photo of George Peabody's statue near Peabody Institute, Baltimore, copied after William W. Story's George Peabody statue near Royal Exchange, London; p. 19 (*see* Bryan, #3).
5. Photo of George Peabody and crowd outside Peabody Institute Building, Baltimore, at dedication, October 25, 1866; inside back cover.

Peabody and Essex Museum, Salem, Massachusetts. Holdings of George Peabody illustrations:
1. Oil portrait of George Peabody by A. Bertram Schell.
2. Three photos of George Peabody in old age.

3. One engraved portrait of George Peabody.
4. Menus for George Peabody London dinners: October 27, 1851, and July 4, 1856.
5. Two photos of George Peabody's birthplace, 205 Washington Street, Peabody, Massachusetts.
6. Photo closeup of birthplace marker, Peabody, Massachusetts, placed June 13, 1902.

Peabody Institute Library. Peabody, Massachusetts: Peabody Institute Library, n.d., unpaged.
1. Color portrait of George Peabody in old age, leaning on table, right hand in jacket, left hand holding letter; front cover.
2. Color photo of Queen Victoria's miniature portrait done in 1867 by British artist F. A. Tilt, baked on porcelain with a frame of solid gold, given to George Peabody in 1867 [p. 8] (*see* Hellman, #8).
3. Engraving of Peabody Institute Library, Peabody, Massachusetts, 1854 [p. 10].
4. Broadside notice of dedication of the Peabody Institute Library, Peabody, Massachusetts, 1854 [p. 11].
5. Engraving of Peabody Institute Library, Peabody, Massachusetts, after George Peabody's death, 1869 [p. 13].
6. Portrait of George Peabody in old age, black and white, reduced from cover portrait, inside back cover [p. 15].

Peabody Reflector, XXXVIII, No. 1 (January–February 1965), cover.
Portrait (black and white) of George Peabody holding Peabody Education Fund founding letter addressed to the Honorable Robert C. Winthrop, February 7, 1867.

————, XLI, No. 4 (Fall 1971).
Copy of silhouette of a young George Peabody, taken from dust jacket of Franklin Parker, George Peabody, A Biography. Nashville: Vanderbilt University Press, 1971, back cover.

————, LII, No. 4 (Winter 1980).
Engraving of George Peabody in old age, cover.
(*See also* these authors of articles in *Peabody Reflector:* Allen, Bryan, Hellman, Hill, Parker.)

Peabody Trust. *Peabody Trust 1862–1987: 125 Years Caring for Londoners.* London: Peabody Trust, 1987.
1. Illustration of George Peabody in old age, cover.
2. Portrait in color of George Peabody holding letter founding the Peabody Donation Fund, facing p. 1.

3. Portrait of George Peabody on cover of music score, "Good George Peabody," p. 2.
4. Drawing of Peabody Homes at Spitalfields, London, p. 2.
5. Engraving of George Peabody's funeral in Westminster Abbey, p. 2.

Pollard, Michael. *People Who Care*. Ada, Oklahoma: Garrett Educational Corp., 1992, 12–13.
Portrait of George Peabody.

Rauch, Henry C. "Tale of Two Cities," *Sun* (Baltimore), May 2, 1948.
1. Photo of sculptor W. W. Story's George Peabody statue, near Royal Exchange, London (*see* Bryan, #3).
2. Photo of George Peabody's statue near Peabody Institute, Baltimore; copied after William W. Story's George Peabody statue near Royal Exchange, London (*see* Bryan, #3). Given by Robert Garrett of Baltimore, April 7, 1890.

Rogers, Tom. "Londoners' Homes Peabody Legacy," *Tennessean* (Nashville), November 28, 1976, F-3.
1. Photo of of W. W. Story's statue of George Peabody on Threadneedle Street near Royal Exchange, London (*see* Bryan, #3).
2. Photos of outside of two apartment blocks, part of the Peabody Homes of London.
3. Photo of interior of one apartment, Peabody Homes of London, with resident couple.

Salem Evening News (Salem, Massachusetts), "A World Benefactor is Peabody's Pride," August 31, 1963, 3.
1. Photo of Queen Victoria's porcelainized miniature portrait, given to George Peabody in 1867; original in Peabody Institute Library, Peabody, Massachusetts (*see* Hellman, #8).
2. Photo of sculptured bust of George Peabody.
3. Photo of George Peabody's birthplace, 205 Washington Street, Peabody, Massachusetts.
4. Photo of Peabody Institute Library, Peabody, Massachusetts.

Salem News (Salem, Massachusetts), "New Book on Life of George Peabody," November 4, 1971.
Portrait of George Peabody in old age.

Salisbury, Lynne Trowbridge. *Peabody Museum of Natural History: A Guide to the Exhibits*. New Haven, Connecticut: Yale University, 1961, 6.
1 Photo of George Peabody, head and shoulders, in old age.
2. Photo of paleontologist Othniel Charles Marsh, head, in old age (George Peabody's nephew).

Schaaf, Elizabeth, compiler. *Guide to the Archives: The Peabody Institute of the City of Baltimore, 1857–1977.* Baltimore: Archives of the Peabody Institute of the Johns Hopkins University, 1987.
1. Drawing of the exterior of the Peabody Institute of Baltimore building, front cover.
2. 1870s aerial photo of Peabody Institute Building on Mount Vernon Place, Baltimore; photo from steeple of nearby church, facing p. 1.
3. Life-size photographic portrait of George Peabody by John Mayall. In 1866 the 8-ft. print was overpainted in oil and is in the Peabody Institute of Baltimore art collection; p. 8.
4. Reduced size photo of George Peabody seated and the trustees of the Peabody Education Fund, probably 1867, p. 11 (*see* Dabney and Kocher).
5. Peabody Square (Peabody Homes of London), Spitalfields, p. 12.
6. Photo of George Peabody standing amid crowd outside Peabody Institute of Baltimore building at dedication, October 25, 1866, p. 14.
7. Drawing of 6 levels of stacks inside library building, Peabody Institute of Baltimore, p. 16.

Southern Education Foundation Annual Report 1986–87. *Toward Equity and Excellence; A 50 Year Commitment, 1937–1987.* Atlanta: Southern Education Foundation, 1987.
1. Illustration of George Peabody in old age, p. 8.
2. Related illustrations of John L. Slater, p. 9; Anna T. Jeanes, p. 10; and others concerned with the history of the Southern Education Foundation.

Stump, William. "Man in the Street: Peabody," *Sun* (Baltimore), January 25, 1953.
Photo of portrait of George Peabody in middle age, from Enoch Pratt Free Library.

Sun (Baltimore), "At the Maryland Historical Society," November 4, 1971, B-2.
Portrait of George Peabody in old age.
(*See also* these authors for articles in the *Sun:* Brooke, Rauch, Stump.)

Virginia Journal of Education, "George Peabody Fund," LVII (September 1963), 32–40.
Portrait of George Peabody.

Welch, Allen Howard. "George Peabody's Funeral Voyage: A Tarnished Homecoming," *Essex Institute Historical Collections,* CIX, No. 2 (April 1973), 116–37. The four illustrations below, in the Peabody and Essex Museum, are pp. 128–29.

1. Drawing, "Reception of Mr. Peabody's Remains on Board H.M.S. *Monarch* at Portsmouth [England]."
2. Drawing of H.M.S. *Monarch* at Portsmouth [England].
3. H.M.S. *Monarch* with George Peabody's remains off Portland Light, Maine; oil painting by H. Brown of Portland.
4. Drawing of funeral ships in Portland, Maine, harbor, with crowds watching.

Welcome to—Peabody, Massachusetts: 'The World's Largest Leather City' (tri-fold pamphlet). Peabody, Massachusetts: Chamber of Commerce and Peabody Historical Society, n.d.

1. Portrait of George Peabody, seated, holding letter founding Peabody Institute, Peabody, Massachusetts, with signature.
2. Photo of Queen Victoria's porcelainized miniature portrait (*see* Hellman #8).

Williams, David A. "George Peabody," *McGraw Hill Encyclopedia of World Biography*. New York: McGraw Hill, 1973, VIII, 334. Engraving of George Peabody in mid life, from Library of Congress.

Bibliography

(Arranged by author's last name, repository, or title)

MANUSCRIPTS, DISSERTATIONS, AND THESES

Boston Public Library, Rare Book Room, Manuscript Collection, Boston. George Peabody Papers.

British Museum Manuscript Division, London. William Ewart Gladstone Papers. George Peabody Papers.

Brouillette, Joseph Walter. "The Third Phase of the Peabody Education Fund, 1904–1914." Ph.D. diss., George Peabody College for Teachers, 1940.

Clothworkers' Company of London. "Court Orders of the Clothworkers' Company, London, July 2, 1862."

Corporation of London, Guildhall Record Office, London. "Journals of the Court of Common Council," July 10, 1862.

Cullum, Edward Neely. "George Peabody College for Teachers, 1914–1937." Ed.D. diss., George Peabody College for Teachers, 1963.

Drake, Thomas Michael. "The Impact of the Peabody Education Fund on the Development of Tax-Supported Education in Tennessee, 1867–1880." Ed.D. diss., Tennessee State University, 1990.

Enoch Pratt Free Library, Maryland Room, Baltimore. George Peabody Folder. Picture File Index.

General Register Office, Somerset House, London. Death Certificate of George Peabody, November 4, 1869, DA 176659.

Guildhall Library, London. Minutes of the Committee for Erecting a Statue to Mr. George Peabody, 1866–1870, Manuscript 192.

Hidy, Muriel Emmie. *George Peabody, Merchant and Financier, 1829–1854.* Ph.D. diss., Radcliffe College, 1939; published: New York: Arno Press, 1978.

J. P. Morgan Information Resource Center (formerly Morgan Guaranty Trust of New York).

Kahn, Roseann. "A History of the Peabody Institute Library, Baltimore, Maryland, 1857–1916." Master's thesis, Catholic University of America, 1953. Published as ACRL Microcard Series No. 16 (Rochester, N.Y.:

University of Rochester Press for the Association of College and Reference Libraries, 1954).

Kasprzak, John F. "George Peabody and the Peabody Education Fund: A
Study in Reconciliation." Master's thesis, American University, 1966.

Lester, Noel K. "Richard Franko Goldman: His Life and Works." D.M.A.
diss., Peabody Conservatory of Music, Peabody Institute of the Johns
Hopkins University, 1984.

Lewis, William J. "The Educational Speaking of Jabez L. M. Curry." Ph.D.
diss., University of Florida, 1955.

Library of Congress Manuscript Division, Washington, D.C. William
Wilson Corcoran Papers. Hamilton Fish Papers. Garrett Family Papers.
Andrew Johnson Papers. Benjamin Moran Papers and Diaries. George
Peabody Papers. Riggs Family Papers.

Maine State Library, Augusta. Executive Council, "Register of the Council,"
XXXIV (1870).

Maryland Historical Society, Baltimore. Corner Collection, MS. 1242. John
Pendleton Kennedy Papers, MS. 1336. George Peabody Papers.

Massachusetts Historical Society, Boston. George Peabody Papers. Horatio
Gates Somerby Papers. Robert Charles Winthrop Papers.

Morgan, Grenfell and Co., Ltd., London. Archives.

National Archives, Washington, D.C. "Admirals and Commodores' Letters."
"Dispatches from United States Ministers, Great Britain." Naval
Records. Log of U.S.S. *Plymouth*. Veterans' Records of the War of 1812.

Parker, Franklin. "George Peabody, Founder of Modern Philanthropy." 3
vols. Ed.D. diss., George Peabody College for Teachers, 1956; ab-
stracted in *Abstracts of Dissertations for the Year, 1956* (Nashville: George
Peabody College for Teachers, 1956), 181–188; and *Dissertation Abstracts*,
XVII, No. 8 (August 1957), 1701–1702. (Contains extensive bibliography, listing all locatable relevant British and U.S. newspaper accounts.
More recent newspaper accounts are listed in Bibliography, in An Essay
on Sources, and in Sources of Extant Portraits, Photographs, and Illustrations of this volume.)

Peabody and Essex Museum, Salem, Mass. George Peabody Papers and
Newspaper Albums. Riggs, Peabody & Co. Papers and Account Books.
Peabody, Riggs & Co. Papers and Account Books. George Peabody &
Co. Papers and Account Books. Fitch Poole's Diary. George Peabody
Russell Papers.

Peabody Historical Society, Peabody, Mass. George Peabody Papers.

Peabody Library Archives of the Johns Hopkins University Library. John
Pendleton Kennedy Papers and Journals. George Peabody Papers and
Newspaper Albums.

Peabody Museum of Yale University, New Haven, Conn. Othniel Charles
Marsh Papers.

Peck, Richard Connelley. "Jabez Lamar Monroe Curry: Educational Crusader." Ph.D. diss., George Peabody College for Teachers, 1942.

Pierpont Morgan Library, New York. John Pierpont Morgan Papers. Junius Spencer Morgan Papers. George Peabody Papers.

Public Record Office, London. Admiralty Papers. Home Office, Alien Entry Lists. Foreign Office Papers. Log of H.M.S. *Monarch*.

Robinson, Ray E. "A History of the Peabody Conservatory of Music." D.M.Ed. diss., Indiana University, 1969.

Royal Archives, Windsor Castle, Windsor, England.

Turner, Howard. "Robert M. Lusher, Louisiana Educator." Ph.D. diss., Louisiana State University, 1944.

University of Rochester, Rochester, New York. Thurlow Weed Collection.

West, Earle H. "The Life and Educational Contributions of Barnas Sears." Ph.D. diss., George Peabody College for Teachers, 1961.

Westminster Abbey, London. Arthur Penrhyn Stanley, "Recollections by Dean Stanley of Funerals in Westminster Abbey 1865–1881." Westminster Abbey Muniments, "Funeral Fee Book 1811–1899."

Worshipful Company of Fishmongers of London, Fishmongers' Hall, London. "Extracts from Court Minutes, April 19, 1866."

Yale University Manuscript Division, New Haven, Conn. George Peabody Papers. O. C. Marsh Papers.

BOOKS, PAMPHLETS, GOVERNMENT DOCUMENTS, AND SERIALS

Allen, Frederick Lewis. *The Great Pierpont Morgan*. New York: Harper and Brothers, 1949.

Allen, Jack. "Peabody: A Tale of Two Centuries," *Peabody Reflector*, LVIII, No. 2 (Spring 1986), 19–23.

―――. "The Peabody Saga," *Peabody Reflector*, LIII, No. 2 (Summer 1980), 4–13.

Annual Message of the Executive to the General Assembly of Maryland. December Session, 1847, Document A.

Arnett, Earl. "Richard Franko Goldman Found a Good School That Needed a Little Shaking Up," *Sun* (Baltimore), April 20, 1973, B-1.

"Asger Hamerik April 8, 1843–July 13, 1923," *Peabody Bulletin* (Baltimore), Fall 1923, 4–5.

"At the Maryland Historical Society," *Sun* (Baltimore), November 4, 1971, B-2.

Ayres, Leonard P. *Seven Great Foundations*. New York: Russell Sage Foundation, 1911.

Bakker, Robert T. *The Dinosaur Heresies: New Theories Unlocking the Mystery of the Dinosaurs and Their Extinction*. New York: William Morrow, 1986.

Baldwin, Leland D. *The Stream of American History.* 2 vols. New York: American Book Co., 1952.

"Baltimore's 150th Birthday," *Maryland History Notes,* V, No. 3 (November 1947), 1–2.

Barnes, Thurlow Weed. *Memoirs of Thurlow Weed by His Grandson.* 2 vols. Boston: Houghton, Mifflin and Co., 1884.

Barrett, Francis T. "A Great Catalogue, Being an Appreciation of the Catalogue of the Library of the Peabody Institute, Baltimore," *The Library,* VI (1894), 69–73.

Beasley, Wallace. *The Life and Educational Contributions of James D. Porter.* Nashville: Bureau of Publications, George Peabody College for Teachers, 1950.

Bellows, George Kent. "Music Master: Whirlwind Tempo for Peabody Chief," *Evening Sun* (Baltimore), August 12, 1958.

Bennett, Stephen A. "Kent in Doubt, Peabody Scans Field for Director," *Sun* (Baltimore), February 7, 1968.

Bibby, Cyril. *Scientist Extraordinary: The Life and Scientific Work of Thomas Henry Huxley, 1825–1895.* Oxford: Pergamon Press, 1972.

"Boards Vote Peabody Merger," *Vanderbilt Gazette,* No. 111 (May 16, 1979), 1, 12.

Bohner, Charles H. *John Pendleton Kennedy: Gentleman from Baltimore.* Baltimore: Johns Hopkins Press, 1961.

Bolton, Sarah K. *Famous Givers and Their Gifts,* 1896. Reprint. Freeport, N.Y: Books for Libraries Press, 1971.

"Bon Voyage–Dr. Reginald Stewart," *Evening Sun* (Baltimore), June 24, 1958.

Bond, Horace Mann. *The Education of the Negro in the American Social Order.* Rev. ed. New York: Octagon Books, 1966.

————. *Negro Education in Alabama: A Study in Cotton and Steel.* New York: Octagon Books, 1969.

Bowler, Peter J. *Fossils and Press: Paleontology and the Idea of Progressive Evolution in the Nineteenth Century.* New York: Science History Publications, 1976.

Boyd, William K. "Some Phases of Educational History in the South Since 1865," *Studies in Southern History and Politics.* New York: Columbia University Press, 1915.

Branscomb, Harvie. *Purely Academic: An Autobiography.* Nashville: Vanderbilt University, 1978.

Bready, James H. "Peabody Institute Library," *Sun* (Baltimore), January 6, 1952.

————. "What's Ahead for Peabody Library Now That Hopkins Owns It?" *Sun* (Baltimore), July 4, 1982.

Breen, Robert G. "A Carroll Colloquy: College Left Its Cachet," *Sun* (Baltimore), February 8, 1952.

Brew, John O., ed. *One Hundred Years of Anthropology*. Cambridge, Mass.: Harvard University Press, 1968.

Bright, John. *The Diaries of John Bright*. London: Cassell and Co., 1930.

Brooke, Bissell. "Peabody Outwitted a Queen," *Sun* (Baltimore), Feb. 13, 1955.

Brown, Hugh Victor. *A History of the Education of Negroes in North Carolina*. Raleigh, N.C.: Irving Swain Press, 1961.

Bryan, Nelson. "The Dean and the Decade: Willis Hawley, Completing His Deanship, Reflects on Peabody's First Ten Years as a School of Vanderbilt University," *Peabody Reflector*, LXI, No. 1 (Fall 1989), 12–15.

_____. "The Life of a Philanthropist: George Peabody," *Peabody Reflector*, LXII, No. 2 (Winter 1994), 2–7.

Buck, Paul H. *The Road to Reunion, 1865–1900*. Boston: Little, Brown and Co., 1937.

Bullock, Henry Allen. *A History of Negro Education in the South From 1619 to the Present*. Cambridge, Mass.: Harvard University Press, 1967.

Burk, Kathleen. *Morgan Grenfell 1838–1988: The Biography of a Merchant Bank*. Oxford: Oxford University Press, 1989.

"Campus Links to National, Metro K–12 Alliances," *Vanderbilt Register* (September 17 and 21, 1992), 1, 6.

Carnegie, Andrew. *Autobiography of Andrew Carnegie*. New York: Doubleday, Doran and Co., 1933.

Carosso, Vincent P. *The Morgans, Private International Bankers, 1854–1913*. Cambridge, Mass.: Harvard University Press, 1987.

Carus, William, ed. *Memorials of the Right Reverend Charles Pettit McIlvaine, Late Bishop of Ohio in the Protestant Episcopal Church of the United States*. London: Elliot Stock, 1882.

Case, Richard W. "How the Hopkins and Peabody Got Together," *Sun* (Baltimore), January 3, 1977.

Catalogue of the Library of the Peabody Institute of the City of Baltimore. Baltimore: Peabody Library, 1883–1893.

Centennial Celebration at Danvers, Mass. June 16, 1852. Boston: Dutton and Wentworth, 1852.

"Centuries of Influence: A Celebration of Library Science at Peabody," *Peabody Reflector*, LIX, No. 2 (Fall 1987), 9, 11.

Chapman, Stanley. *The Rise of Merchant Banking*. London: George Allen & Unwin, 1984.

Clark, Thomas D. *The Southern Country Editor*. New York: Bobbs–Merrill Co., 1948.

Colbert, Edwin Harris. *Dinosaurs: An Illustrated History*. Maplewood, N.J.: Hammond, 1985.

_____. *Dinosaurs: Their Discovery and Their World*. New York: E. P. Dutton, 1961.

————. *The Great Dinosaur Hunters and Their Discoveries*. New York: Dover Publications, 1984.

————. *Men and Dinosaurs: The Search in Field and Laboratory*. New York: E. P. Dutton, 1968.

"The Committee of Visitors," *Peabody Reflector*, LII, No. 3 (Autumn 1979), 10, 12.

Commonwealth of Virginia. *Journal of the Senate of the Commonwealth of Virginia, Begun and Held at the Capitol in the City of Richmond, On Wednesday, December 5 1895*. Richmond: Superintendent of Public Printing, 1895.

"Conductor Makes Farewell Speech," *Sun* (Baltimore), March 13, 1952.

Congressional Globe 40th Congress, 1st Session, March 4–December 2 1867. LXXIX. Washington, D.C.: U.S. Congress.

Conkin, Paul K., *et al. Gone with the Ivy: A Biography of Vanderbilt University*. Knoxville: University of Tennessee Press, 1985.

Corcoran, William Wilson. *A Grandfather's Legacy; Containing a Sketch of His Life and Obituary Notices Of Some Members Of His Family, Together with Letters From His Friends*. Washington, D.C.: Henry Polkinhorn, 1879.

Corey, Lewis. *The House of Morgan: A Social Biography of the Masters of Money*. New York: G. Howard Watt, 1930.

Coulter, E. Merton. *The South During Reconstruction, 1855–1877*. Baton Rouge: Louisiana State University Press, 1947.

[Courtenay, William Ashmead]. "A Memoir of George Peabody," *Proceedings of the General Assembly of South Carolina, Proposing Concerted Action by the Southern States, for Placing a Statue of the Philanthropist in the Capitol at Washington*. Charleston, S.C.: Lucas and Richardson Co., 1896.

Crawford, Jean. "Learning with Jasper," *Peabody Reflector*, LXI, No. 2 (Summer 1990), 26–27.

Cullen, Tom A. "Peabody Pioneer: First Slum Push," *Austin* (Tex.) *American*, March 18, 1964.

Cummings, Richard O. "The Growth of Technical Cooperation with Governments Abroad, 1849–1853," *Pacific Historical Review*, XVIII, No. 2 (May 1949), 199–212.

Curry, Jabez Lamar Monroe. *A Brief Sketch of George Peabody and a History of the Peabody Education Fund Through Thirty Years*. 1898. Reprint. New York: Negro Universities Press, 1969.

————. "The Peabody Education Fund," *Educational Review*, XIII (March 1897), 226.

Dabney, Charles W. *Universal Education in the South*. 2 vols. Chapel Hill: University of North Carolina Press, 1936.

"Decade of Conservatory Activity." *Peabody Bulletin* (Baltimore), December 1938, 33–34.

"Dedication of the Peabody Museum: Simple Exercises Mark the Laying of the Cornerstone of New Home for Notable Collections," *Yale Alumni Weekly* (July 6, 1923), 1249–1250.

De Mare, Marie. *G. P. A. Healy, American Artist.* New York: David McKay Co., 1954.

Desmond, Adrian J. *The Hot-Blooded Dinosaurs: A Revolution in Palaeontology.* New York: Dial Press, 1976.

Dexter, Ralph W. "The Role of E. S. Morse, Director of the Peabody Academy of Science, in Bringing Zoology to Japan (1877–1883)," *Essex Institute Historical Collections*, CXXVI, No. 4 (October 1990), 254–260.

Diagram Group. *A Field Guide to Dinosaurs.* New York: Avon, 1983.

[Dielman, Louis Henry, Retires as Peabody Librarian]. *Baltimore News-Post,* May 30, 1942.

"Dielman, Louis Henry," *Maryland History Notes*, XVII, No. 1 (May 1959), 2.

Dillingham, George A. *The Foundation of the Peabody Tradition.* Lanham, Md.: University Press of America, 1989.

"Director Change," *Evening Sun* (Baltimore), August 5, 1941.

Dobbin, Isabel L. "Asger Hamerik," *peabody Bulletin* (Baltimore), April–May 1913, 2–4.

Dodge, Ernest S. "Manuscripts Relating to Maritime Business Activities in the Peabody Museum of Salem," *Explorations in Entrepreneurial History,* II, No. 3 (1965), 227–231.

———. "Marion Vernon Brewington," *Massachusetts Historical Society Proceedings*, LXXXVI (1974), 95–98.

Dodgson, Charles Lutwidge. *The Diaries of Lewis Carroll.* 2 vols. Edited by Roger Green. New York: Oxford University Press, 1954.

Dorsey, John. *Mr. Peabody's Library: The Building, The Collection, The Neighborhood.* Baltimore: Enoch Pratt Free Library, 1978.

———., ed. *On Mencken.* New York: Alfred A. Knopf, 1980.

Dunbar, Carl O. "Recollections on the Renaissance of Peabody Museum Exhibits, 1939–1959," *Discovery*, XII, No. 1 (Fall 1976), 17–35.

"Dunbar, Carl O., 1891–1979: An Appreciation," *Discovery*, XIV, No. 1 (1979), 44.

E. T. D. "Some Notes on the Beginnings of Peabody Museum," *Discovery*, II, No. 1 (Fall 1966), 33–35.

Eaton, John. *First Report of the Superintendent of Public Instruction in the State of Tennessee, Ending Thursday, October 7, 1869.* Nashville: George Edgar Grishman, 1869, appendix T.

[Evans, May Garrettson]. "Baltimore," in Ishbel Ross, *Ladies of the Press: The Story of Women in Journalism by an Insider.* New York: Harper and Brothers, 1936.

[Evans, May Garrettson, Retires from Peabody Conservatory]. *Evening Sun* (Baltimore), November 29, 1934.

Farr, R. R. *Report of the Superintendent of Public Instruction of Virginia.* Richmond: Superintendent of Public Printing, 1885, Part II.

"Fifty Turn Out for First Sunday Open-Day at Peabody Library," *Sun* (Baltimore), January 14, 1952.

Flexner, Abraham, with collaborator Esther S. Bailey. *Funds and Foundations: Their Policies Past and Present.* New York: Harper and Brothers, 1952.

Force, William W. *Payne of Peabody: An Apostle of Education.* Nashville: privately printed, 1985.

————. *A Short History of George Peabody College for Teachers, 1974–1979.* Nashville: Williams Printing Co., 1986.

Forney, John Wien. *Letters From Europe.* Philadelphia: T. B. Peterson and Co., 1867.

Foundation Directory. 2nd ed. New York: Russell Sage Foundation, 1964.

Freeman, Douglas Southall. *Robert E. Lee: A Biography.* 4 vols. New York: Charles Scribner's Sons, 1947.

French, John C. "Sidney Lanier's Life in Baltimore: 'The Beautiful City' Has Yet to Discover Him Fully," *Sun* (Baltimore), September 6, 1931.

Frizzell, Mildred Armor. "George Peabody Cup," Hobbies, LXXXVI, No. 4 (June 1981), 41, 62.

Galkin, Elliott. "The Man Who Brought Science into the Music Hall," *Baltimore Magazine,* LXXII, No. 8 (August 1979), 172, 170–171.

Garland, Eric. "Has Baltimore Put Its Library on the Shelf?" *Baltimore Magazine,* LXXVI, No. 2 (February 1983), 46–51, 102–106.

Garrett, John W. *Address Delivered on the 30th of January, 1883 before the Young Men's Christian Association of Baltimore on the Occasion of Their Thirtieth Anniversary.* Baltimore: News Steam Printing Office, 1883.

Genzmer, George Harvey. "Morris, John Gottlieb (Nov. 14, 1803–Oct. 10, 1895)," *Dictionary of American Biography.* Edited by Dumas Malone. New York: Charles Scribner's Sons, 1934.

"George Peabody," *Hunt's Merchants' Magazine,* XXXVI, No. 4 (April 1857), 428–437.

"George Peabody," *Leisure Hour Monthly Library,* XV, No. 761 (1866), 471–475.

George Peabody & Co., J.S. Morgan & Co., 1838–1958. Oxford: Oxford University Press, 1958.

George Peabody College for Teachers. *Design for the Future: A Report from the Select Committee on Peabody's Second Century to President John Dunworth and the Board of Trustees.* Nashville: George Peabody College for Teachers, 1974.

"George Peabody Fund," *Virginia Journal of Education,* LVII (September 1963), 32–40.

Geraghty, Kathryn. "Variations on a Theme in Blue, Green," *Sun* (Baltimore), December 31, 1961.

"Gifts to the Peabody Double Last Year's," *Sun* (Baltimore), July 7, 1978.

Gilman, Daniel Coit. "Five Great Gifts," *Outlook*, LXXXVI, No. 13 (July 27, 1907), 645–657.

————. *The Launching of a University and Other Papers; A Sheaf of Remembrances*. New York: Dodd, Mead and Co., 1906.

————. "Thirty Years of the Peabody Education Fund," *Atlantic Monthly*, LXXIX (February 1897), 161–166.

Gilmore, P. S. *History of the National Peace Jubilee and Great Music Festival Held in the City of Boston, June, 1869 to Commemorate the Restoration of Peace throughout the Land*. Boston: Lee and Shepard, 1871.

Glick, Thomas F., ed. *Comparative Reception of Darwinism*. Austin: University of Texas Press, 1972.

Gould, Stephen Jay. *Bully for Brontosaurus: Reflections in Natural History*. New York: W. W. Norton, 1991.

Green, Samuel Swett. *The Public Library in the United States, 1853–1893*. Boston: Boston Book Co., 1913.

Guiliano, Mike. "History of the Peabody Conservatory and Other Related Incidents," *Hopkins News-Letter*, LXXXI, No. 31 (February 11, 1977).

Gutman, Arthur Joseph. Letter, "Peabody Library," *Morning Sun* (Baltimore), June 14, 1966.

Gwyn, Ann. "Changing Hands: Johns Hopkins Acquires Peabody Library," *Wilson Library Bulletin*, LVII, No. 5 (January 1983), 401–404.

[Hamerik, Asger, His Children in Music]. *Peabody Bulletin* (Baltimore), May 1933.

"Hamerik, Professor Asger," *Biographical Cyclopedia of Representative Men of Maryland and District of Columbia*. Baltimore: National Biographical Publishing Co., 1879.

"Hamerikana: To Asger Hamerik on his Seventieth Birthday. Congratulations and Loving Greetings from His Pupils and Friends" (with extracts from two letters from Sidney Lanier mentioning Hamerik), *Peabody Bulletin* (Baltimore), April–May 1913, 5.

Hanaford, Phebe Ann. *The Life of George Peabody*. Boston: B. B. Russell, 1870.

Hanna, Hugh Sisson. *Financial History of Maryland, 1789–1848*. Johns Hopkins University Studies in History and Political Science, 25th Series, Numbers 8–10. Baltimore: Johns Hopkins University Press, 1907.

Harlow, Alvin F. "Stewart, Alexander Turney (October 12, 1803–April 10, 1867)," *Dictionary of American Biography*. Edited by Dumas Malone. New York: Charles Scribner's Sons, 1936.

Harris, James Morrison. *Address by the Hon. J. Morrison Harris, upon the Occasion of the Celebration of the Fiftieth Anniversary of the Organization of the Maryland Historical Society, Delivered March 12, 1894*. Baltimore: J. Murphy and Co., 1897.

Hart, Richard H. *Enoch Pratt, the Story of a Plain Man.* Baltimore: Enoch Pratt Free Library, 1935.

Harvard University. *Baccalaureate Sermon, and Oration and Poem, Class of 1867.* Cambridge, Mass.: John Wilson and Son, 1867.

Harvard University. *Quinquentennial Catalogue of the Officers and Graduates of Harvard University, 1636–1905.* Cambridge, Mass.: Harvard University Press, 1905.

Hawley, Willis D. "From the Dean," *Peabody Reflector,* LVIII, No. 2 (Spring 1986), 2; and *Peabody Reflector,* LIX, No. 2 (Fall 1987), 2.

"Head Start Program Marks Anniversary: Has Peabody History," *Peabody Reflector,* LXII, No. 1 (Spring 1991), 7.

Healy, George P. A. *Reminiscences of a Portrait-Painter.* Chicago: A. C. McClurg and Co., 1894.

Heard, Alexander. "A Vanderbilt Perspective on the Merger," *Peabody Reflector,* LII, No. 2 (Summer 1979), 4–5.

Hearn, Nicholas. *George Peabody (1795–1869): "One of the Poor's Greatest Benefactors?"* London: Peabody Donation Fund, 1980.

Hellman, Geoffrey. "The First Great Cheerful Giver," *American Heritage,* XVII, No. 4 (1966), 28–33, 76–77.

Hidy, Muriel Emmie. *George Peabody, Merchant and Financier, 1829–1854.* New York: Arno Press, 1978.

————. "The George Peabody Papers," *Bulletin of the Business Historical Society,* XII, No. 1 (February 1938), 1–6.

Hidy, Ralph W. *The House of Baring in American Trade and Finance; English Merchant Bankers at Work 1763–1861.* Cambridge, Mass.: Harvard University Press, 1949.

Hiles, Bill. "A New Era Dawns . . . ," *Peabody Reflector,* LII, No. 1 (Spring 1979), 4–5.

Hill, Eloise Wilkes. "The Peabody Influence. . . . A New Book," *Peabody Reflector,* XLII, No. 1 (January—February 1969), 15–16.

Hill, Ruth Henderson. *George Peabody, "The Great Benefactor," 1795–1869.* Peabody, Mass.: Peabody Institute, 1953.

"Historical Funerals, George Peabody, 1795–1869, Philanthropist and Financier," *American Funeral Director,* LXXV, No. 5 (May 1952), 46–48.

Hoffschwelle, Mary S. "The Science of Domesticity: Home Economics at George Peabody College for Teachers, 1914–1939," *Journal of Southern History,* LVII, No. 4 (1991), 659–680.

Hollis, Ernest Victor. *Philanthropic Foundations and Higher Education.* New York: Columbia University Press, 1938.

Hovey, Carl. *The Life Story of J. Pierpont Morgan.* New York: Sturgis and Calton Co., 1911.

"How Students See the Merger," *Peabody Reflector,* LII, No. 3 (Autumn 1979), 13–14.

Howard, Robert West. *The Dawnseekers: The First History of American Paleontology.* New York: Harcourt Brace Jovanovich, 1975.

Hoyt, Edwin P. *The Peabody Influence: How a Great New England Family Helped to Build America.* New York: Dodd, Mead and Co., 1968.

Huhs, Ulrike. "Peabody Conservatory Generates Sounds of the Future," *Asheville* (N.C.) *Citizen-Times* , November 28, 1992, C-4.

"The Human Complexities of a Conductor's Job," *Sun* (Baltimore), February 4, 1952.

"Illness Obliges Charles Kent to Leave Peabody," *Sun* (Baltimore), May 1, 1968.

Illustrated London News, XLVIII, No. 1368 (April 28, 1866), 409.

Ingalls, Zoë. "The Soaring Splendor of the Peabody Library," *Chronicle of Higher Education*, XL, No. 15 (December 1, 1993), B-5.

Ingersoll, Ernest. "The Peabody Museum of American Archaeology," *Lippincott's Magazine*, X (November 1885), 474–487.

Jacob, Kathryn A. "Mr. Johns Hopkins," *Johns Hopkins Magazine*, XXV, No. 1 (January 1974), 13–17.

Jaffe, Bernard. *Men of Science in America: The Role of Science in the Growth of Our Country.* New York: Simon and Schuster, 1944.

"Johns Hopkins, Bachelor Father to a Great University," *Sun* (Baltimore), December 23, 1973.

Johnson, Gerald W. Letter, "The Real Question About the Library," *Sun* (Baltimore), April 22, 1966.

Johnson, Kenneth R. "The Peabody Fund: Its Role and Influence in Alabama," *Alabama Review*, XXVII, No. 2 (April 1974), 101–126.

Jones, Frank N. *George Peabody and the Peabody Institute.* Baltimore: Peabody Institute Library, 1965.

Jones, Weimer. "The Last Days of Sidney Lanier," *Sun* (Baltimore), February 4, 1968.

Josephson, Matthew. *The Robber Barons.* New York: Harcourt, Brace and Co., 1934.

Journal of Proceedings of the House of Delegates of the State of Maryland. Annapolis, Md.: Riley and Davis, 1847.

Journal of the United States Senate, 40th Congress, 1st and Special Session, 1867. Washington, D.C.: U.S. Congress.

Kellman, Naomi. "Mr. Peabody's Pet Project," *Sun* (Baltimore), February 9, 1947.

Kelly, Frederick. "Sidney Lanier at the Peabody Institute," *Peabody Bulletin* (Baltimore), 1976, 35–38.

Kenin, Richard. *Return to Albion: Americans in England, 1760–1940.* New York: Holt, Rinehart and Winston, 1979.

Kennedy, John Pendleton. "Sketch of the Peabody Institute, Baltimore," *Occasional Addresses; and the Letters of Mr. Ambrose on the Rebellion.* New York: G. P. Putnam and Son, 1872.

[Kent, Charles Stanton, obituary]. *Evening Sun* (Baltimore), June 2, 1969.

Kenyon, Paul. "Professor Tells How Peabody Pioneered in Giving Away Millions Constructively," *North Shore '71* (Gloucester, Mass.), VI, No. 50 (December 11, 1971), 1–2, 4+.

"Kerr Gets Post in Annapolis," *Evening Sun* (Baltimore), October 31, 1960.

Knight, Edgar W. *Education in the United States*. New York: Ginn and Co., 1951.

_____. *Public Education in the South*. New York: Ginn and Co., 1922.

Kocher, Alfred Lawrence, and Howard Dearstyne. *Shadows in Silver, A Record of Virginia, 1850–1900, in Contemporary Photographs Taken By George and Huestis Cook with Additions from the Cook Collection*. New York: Charles Scribner's Sons, 1954.

Lane, William Coolidge, and Nina E. Browne, eds. *A.L.A. Portrait Index*. 1906. Reprint. New York: Burt Franklin, 1960.

Lanham, Url. *The Bone Hunters*. New York: Columbia University Press, 1973.

"Lanier, Sidney," *appletons' Cyclopaedia of American Biography*. Edited by James Grant Wilson and John Fiske. New York: D. Appleton and Co., 1888.

Larson, Henrietta M. *Guide to Business History*. Cambridge, Mass.: Harvard University Press, 1948.

Laubat, Joseph Florimund. *Medallic History of the United States, 1776–1876*. 2 vols. New York: J. W. Bouton, 1878.

Law, Frederick Houk. *Great Americans*. New York: Globe, 1953.

Leavell, Ullin Whitney. *Philanthropy in Negro Education*. Nashville: George Peabody College for Teachers, 1930.

Letters of H. L. Mencken; Selected and Annotated by Guy J. Forgue. Boston: Northeastern University Press, 1981.

Leyda, Jay. *The Melville Log, a Documentary Life of Herman Melville, 1819–1891*. New York: Harcourt, Brace and Co., 1951.

"Little Orchestra Concerts to Continue Under Stewart," *Sun* (Baltimore), February 7, 1958.

London, Corporation of. *London's Roll of Fame, 1757–1884*. London: Cassell and Co., Ltd., 1884.

Luckett, Margie H. "May Garrettson Evans," *Maryland Women*. Baltimore: 1937.

Ludington, Townsend. *John Dos Passos: A Twentieth Century Odyssey*. New York: E. P. Dutton, 1980.

Macauley, James, ed. *Speeches and Addresses of H.R.H. the Prince of Wales: 1863–1888*. London: John Murray, 1889.

McCarren, Mark J. *The Scientific Contributions of Othniel Charles Marsh: Birds, Bones, and Brontotheres*. New Haven, Conn.: Peabody Museum of Natural History, 1993.

MacCracken, Henry Mitchell. *The Hall of Fame*. New York: G. P. Putnam's Sons, 1901.

McCrank, Lawrence J. "The Centennial Celebration of the Foundation of the Peabody Library, Baltimore, Maryland: A Report and Review," *Journal of Library History*, XIV, No. 2 (Spring 1979), 183–187.

MacFadden, Bruce J. *Fossil Horses: Systematics, Paleobiology, and Evolution of the Family Equidae*. Cambridge: Cambridge University Press, 1992.

McGinty, Brian. "A Shining Presence: Rebel Poet Sidney Lanier Goes to War," *Civil War Times Illustrated*, XIX, No. 2 (May 1980), 25–31.

McIntosh, Hugh S. "Marsh and the Dinosaurs," *Discovery*, I, No. 1 (1965), 31–37.

Manchester, William. *Disturber of the Peace: The Life of H. L. Mencken*. New York: Harper & Brothers, 1950.

Marney, Betty. "Fascinating Life of Great Philanthropist," *Nashville Banner*, December 10, 1971, 56.

Maryland Historical Society. *Maryland Historical Society and the Peabody Institute Trustees. A Report from a Special Committee of the Maryland Historical Society, Read and Adopted at the Society's Monthly Meeting, April the 5th, 1866*. Baltimore: John Murphy and Co., 1866.

Massachusetts Historical Society Proceedings, X (1867–1869).

Melville, Herman. *Journal of a Visit to London and the Continent*. Cambridge, Mass.: Harvard University Press, 1948.

"Mennin Leaving as Peabody Head," *Sun* (Baltimore), June 11, 1962.

[Mennin, Peter, Named Director of Peabody Conservatory]. *Evening Sun* (Baltimore), April 8, 1958.

Meredith, Roy. *The Face of R. E. Lee*. New York: Charles Scribner's Sons, 1947.

Miller, Francis Trevelyan, ed. *The Photographic History of the Civil War*. 10 vols. New York: Review of Reviews Company, 1911.

Mims, Edwin. *Chancellor Kirkland of Vanderbilt*. Nashville: Vanderbilt University Press, 1940.

————. *History of Vanderbilt University*. Nashville: Vanderbilt University Press, 1946.

Mitchell, Broadus. "Hopkins, Johns," *Dictionary of American Biography*. Edited by Dumas Malone. New York: Charles Scribner's Sons, 1943, IX.

"Morison, Nathaniel Holmes." *Biographical Cyclopedia: Representative Men of Maryland and District of Columbia*. Baltimore: National Biographical Publishing Co., 1879.

[Morison, Nathaniel Holmes, Biographical Sketch]. *Peabody Bulletin* (Baltimore), May 1936.

Morison, Samuel Eliot. *Nathaniel Holmes Morison, 1815–1890: Provost of the Peabody Institute of Baltimore, 1867–1890, An Address . . . February 12, 1957*. Baltimore: Peabody Institute Library, 1962.

Morris, John G. *Life Reminiscences of an Old Lutheran Minister.* Philadelphia: Lutheran Publication Society, 1896.

"Morris, John Godlove," *National Cyclopedia of American Biography.* New York: James T. White & Co., 1893.

Mortuary Honors to the Late George Peabody in Portland, Maine. Portland, Me.: Loring, Short and Harmon, 1870.

Mowat, Robert B. *Americans in England.* 1935. Reprint. New York: Houghton Mifflin, 1969.

"Mr. Ortmann and His Successor," *Gardens, Houses and People* (Baltimore), XVI, No. 8 (August 1941).

"Music . . . Mennin of the Peabody," *Gardens, Houses and People* (Baltimore), August 1958.

Myers, Gustavus. *History of the Great American Fortunes.* New York: Modern Library, 1936.

"New Book on Life of George Peabody," *Salem* (Mass.) *News*, November 4, 1971.

"New Initiatives Strengthen VU/Metro Ties," *Peabody Columns*, III, No. 5 (January 1993), 2.

"New Library Director," *Sun* (Baltimore), June 17, 1957.

"New Peabody Dean Eager to Help State Change Face of Education," *Tennessean* (Nashville), December 26, 1991, 3-B.

"New Peabody Dean Named" [David S. Cooper], *Sun* (Baltimore), February 18, 1959.

"New Peabody Head Named," *Sun* (Baltimore), August 25, 1968.

"New Peabody Librarian," *Gardens, Houses and People* (Baltimore), July 1957.

New York University. Hall of Fame for Great Americans. *Hall of Fame for Great Americans at New York University: Official Handbook.* New York: New York University Press, 1962.

New York University. *Handbook of the Hall of Fame.* New York: Hall of Fame, 1951.

Oberholtzer, Ellis Paxton. *A History of the United States Since the Civil War.* 5 vols. New York: Macmillan Co., 1917.

Olson, Sherry H. *Baltimore: The Building of an American City.* Baltimore: The Johns Hopkins University Press, 1980.

Ortmann, Otto. *The Physical Basis of Piano Touch and Tone.* New York: E. P. Dutton, 1925.

————. *The Physiological Mechanics of Piano Technique.* 1929. Reprint. New York: E. P. Dutton, 1962.

[Ortmann, Otto Rudolph, Made President of Middle Atlantic Branch of American Musicological Society]. *Sun* (Baltimore), May 17, 1936.

Ostrom, John H., and John S. McIntosh. *Marsh's Dinosaurs: The Collections from Como Bluff.* New Haven, Conn.: Yale University Press, 1966.

"Otto Ortmann," *Peabody Bulletin* (Baltimore), Fall 194, 3+.

"Otto Ortmann," *Peabody Bulletin* (Baltimore), May 1936, 16.

Oxford University Calendar, 1868. Oxford: James Parke and Co., 1868.

P. J. B. [Otto Ortmann], *Sun* (Baltimore), November 11, 1934.

Pappenheimer, John. "Goldman Wants Things to Happen," *Evening Sun* (Baltimore), August 27, 1968.

Parker, Franklin. "Abraham Flexner, 1866–1959," *History of Education Quarterly*, II, No. 4 (December 1962), 199–209.

————. "Abraham Flexner (1866–1959) and Medical Education," *Journal of Medical Education*, XXXVI, No. 6 (June 1961), 709–714.

————. "Educational Philanthropist George Peabody (1795–1869): Photos and Related Illustrations in Printed Sources and Depositories," *CORE (Collected Original Resources in Education)*, XVIII, No. 2 (June 1994), Fiche 1 D1Z.

————. "Founder Paid Debt to Education," *Peabody Post* (George Peabody College for Teachers), VIII, No. 8 (February 10, 1955), 1.

————. "The Funeral of George Peabody," *Essex Institute Historical Collections*, XCIX, No. 2 (April 1963), 67–87.

————. *George Peabody, A Biography.* Nashville: Vanderbilt University Press, 1971.

————. "George Peabody and Maryland," *Peabody Journal of Education*, XXXVII, No. 4 (November 1959), 150–157.

————. "George Peabody and the Peabody Museum of Salem," *Curator*, X, No. 2 (1967), 137–153.

————. "George Peabody and the Search for Sir John Franklin, 1852–1854," *American Neptune*, XX, No. 2 (April 1960), 104–111.

————. "George Peabody and the Spirit of America," *Peabody Reflector*, XXIX, No. 2 (February 1956), 26–27.

————. *George Peabody (1795–1869), Founder of Modern Philanthropy.* Nashville: George Peabody College for Teachers, 1955 (pamphlet, Founders Day Address, February 18, 1955, Peabody College).

————. "George Peabody's Influence on Southern Educational Philanthropy," *Tennessee Historical Quarterly*, XX, No. 2 (March 1961), 65–74.

————. "The Girl George Peabody Almost Married," *Peabody Reflector*, XXVII, No. 8 (October 1955), 215, 224–225; reprinted in *Peabody Notes*, XVII, No. 3 (Spring 1964), 10–14.

————. "Influences on the Founder of the Johns Hopkins University and the Johns Hopkins Medical School," *Bulletin of the History of Medicine*, XXXIV, No. 2 (1960), 148–153.

————. "Maryland's Yankee Friend—George Peabody Esq.," *Maryland Teacher*, XX, No. 5 (January 1963), 6–7, 24; reprinted in *Peabody Notes* (Spring 1963), 4–7, 10.

————. "Pantheon of Philanthropy: George Peabody," *National Society of Fundraisers Journal*, I, No. 1 (December 1976), 16–20.

————. "To Live Fulfilled: George Peabody, 1795–1869, Founder of George Peabody College for Teachers," *Peabody Reflector*, XLIII, No. 2 (Spring 1970), 50–53.

————, and Walter Merrill. "William Lloyd Garrison and George Peabody," *Essex Institute Historical Collections*, XCV, No. 1 (January 1959), 1–20.

Parker, John. "Reminiscences of Fifty Years in the Library of the Peabody Institute of the City of Baltimore," *Peabody Bulletin* (Spring 1922), 4–8.

Parker, John, et al. *Second Catalogue of the Library of the Peabody Institute of the City of Baltimore, including the Additions made Since 1882*. 8 vols. Baltimore: Peabody Institute, 1896–1905.

Parker, Wyman. *Henry Stevens of Vermont: American Rare Book Dealer in London, 1845–1886*. Amsterdam: N. Israel, 1963.

Payne, Bruce Ryburn. *George Peabody*. Founder's Day Address. February 18, 1916. Nashville: George Peabody College for Teachers, 1916.

The Peabody: An Illustrated Guide. Baltimore: Peabody Institute of the Johns Hopkins University, 1977.

"Peabody Conservatory Lists R. E. Robinson as New Dean," *Sun* (Baltimore), July 2, 1963.

Peabody Conservatory of Music. Baltimore: Peabody Institute [1957].

Peabody Conservatory of Music, Academic Years 1993–95. Baltimore: Peabody Institute of the Johns Hopkins University, 1993, and later issues.

Peabody Donation. London: E. Couchman and Co., 1862.

Peabody Donation Fund, 1862–1962. London: George Berridge and Co., Ltd., 1962.

Peabody Donation Fund. *Mr. Peabody's Gift to the Poor of London*. London: Spottiswood and Co., 1865.

Peabody Education Fund. *Proceedings of the Trustees of the Peabody Education Fund 1867–1915*. 6 vols. Boston: John Wilson and Son, 1875 to 1916.

"Peabody gets $80,000 Grant," *Vanderbilt Register* (December 8, 1989), 7.

The Peabody Institute and Its Future. Baltimore: Peabody Institute [1957].

Peabody Institute, Baltimore Library. *Alphabetical Catalogue of Books Proposed to be Purchased for the Library of the Peabody Institute, Baltimore*. Baltimore: J. D. Toy, 1861.

"Peabody Institute, Baltimore," *The International Cyclopedia of Music and Musicians*. Edited by Oscar Thompson. New York: Dodd, Mead and Co., 1975.

Peabody Institute of Baltimore. *The Founder's Letters and Papers Relating to its Dedication and its History Up to the 1st of January, 1868*. Baltimore: William K. Boyle, 1868.

"Peabody Library," *Sun* (Baltimore), July 5, 1982.

"Peabody Library Returns," *Peabody News* (Baltimore), August/September 1982, 4.

"Peabody Library Starts 260,000-Card Index," *Evening Sun* (Baltimore), January 10, 1952.

Peabody Museum of Salem–Essex Institute News Release, May 19, 1992 [on creating Peabody and Essex Museum].

"Peabody Names New Director," *Sun* (Baltimore), April 21, 1963.

"Peabody Preparatory School Founder to be Honored Sunday," *Sun* (Baltimore), May 21, 1947.

"Peabody Students Getting in Tune for Transposition to Hopkins: Some Notes, Quotes, and Thoughts About New School," *Hopkins News-Letter*, LXXXI, No. 31 (February 11, 1977), 1–2.

"Peabody to Join Hopkins," *Sun* (Baltimore), December 21, 1976, A-1 (c. 1), A-8 (c. 2–c. 5).

"Peabody Top Choice in Education," *Peabody Columns* (Nashville), I, No. 7 (March 1991), 2.

Peabody Trust. *Peabody Trust 1862–1987: 125 Years Caring for Londoners.* London: Peabody Trust, 1987.

"Peabody-Vanderbilt Merger Information," *Peabody Reflector*, Special Section, LI, No. 4 (Winter 1979), 98 a–h.

"Pellegrino Announces Faculty Searches in Each Department," *Peabody Columns*, II, No. 45 (January 1992), 1.

Pellegrino, James. "From the Dean," *Peabody Reflector*, LXIII, No. 2 (Fall 1992), inside front cover.

Perkinson, Henry J. *The Imperfect Panacea: American Faith in Education 1865–1990.* New York: McGraw Hill, 1991.

Plate, Robert. *The Dinosaur Hunters.* New York: David McKay Co., 1964.

Pollard, Michael. *People Who Care.* Ada, Okla.: Garrett Educational, 1992.

Poole, Lynn D. "Mantle of Success," *Sun* (Baltimore), May 16, 1948.

"Pratt Takes Over Peabody," *News American* (Baltimore), July 3, 1966, B-9.

"President Claunch Dies," *Peabody Reflector*, LXII, No. 1 (Spring 1991), 2.

Proceedings At the Reception and Dinner in Honor of George Peabody, Esq., of London by the Citizens of the Old Town of Danvers, October 9, 1856. Boston: H. W. Dutton and Son, 1856.

Proceedings of the 23rd Congress, 1st Session, House of Representatives, Tuesday, August 1, 1854. Washington, D.C.: U.S. Congress.

"Progress at the Peabody," *Sun* (Baltimore), January 19, 1942.

Putnam, Alice L. "The Peabody Celebration in Danvers. From a Letter in Possession of Col. Eben Putnam," *The Historical Collections of the Danvers Historical Society*, XX (1932), 63–64.

Putnam, Elizabeth. "George Peabody—Pioneer in Civic Giving," *The Historical Collections of the Danvers Historical Society*, XXXIV (1946), 12–22.

Putnam, Frederic Ward. *The Archaeological Reports of Frederic Ward Putnam: Selected from the Annual Reports of the Peabody Museum of Archaeology and Ethnology, Harvard University 1875–1903.* Reprint. New York: AMS Press, 1973.

Randolph, Harold. "Asger Hamerik: An Appreciation," *Peabody Bulletin* (Baltimore), Fall 1923, 5–6.

Range, Willard. *The Rise and Progress of Negro Colleges in Georgia 1865–1949.* Athens: University of Georgia Press, 1951.

Rauch, Henry C. "Tale of Two Cities," *Sun* (Baltimore), May 2, 1948.

Redlich, Fritz. *The Molding of American Banking: Men and Ideas.* New York: Johnson Reprint Corporation, 1968.

Reed, Charles E. B. *Memoir of Charles Reed.* London: Macmillan and Co., 1883.

"Reginald Stewart Named Head of Peabody," *Evening Sun* (Baltimore), August 5, 1941.

"Reginald Stewart, the New Director," *Peabody Bulletin* (Baltimore), Fall 1941, 1–3.

"Reginald Stewart's Final Performance as Conductor," *Sun* (Baltimore), April 1, 1952.

Reingold, Nathan, ed. *Science in Nineteenth-Century America: A Documentary History.* New York: Hill and Wang, 1964.

Reniers, Perceval. *The Springs of Virginia; Life, Love and Death at the Waters 1775–1900.* Chapel Hill: University of North Carolina Press, 1941.

Report of the Centennial Celebration of the Birth of George Peabody, Held at Peabody, Mass., Monday, February 18, 1895. Cambridge, Mass.: Riverside Press, 1895.

"Resumption in Maryland," *Bankers' Magazine and State Financial Register,* III, No. 7 (January 1849), 394–397.

Riggs, John Beverley. *Riggs Family of Maryland; A Genealogical and Historical Record, incl. a Study of the Several Families in England.* Brookeville, Md.: privately printed, 1939.

"Rinehart, William Henry," *Appletons' Cyclopaedia of American Biography.* Edited by James Grant Wilson and John Fiske. New York: D. Appleton and Co., 1888, V.

[Rinehart, William Henry, Biographical Sketch]. *Sun* (Baltimore), January 5, 1936.

Robertson, Marcelle. "New Dean to Work for 'Answers,'" *Vanderbilt Hustler,* CIV, No. 1 (January 14, 1992), 1, 11.

Rodgers, George. "Some of Peabody Library Books Set for Disposal," *Evening Sun* (Baltimore), June 23, 1966.

Rogers, Tom. "Londoners' Homes Peabody Legacy," *Tennessean* (Nashville), November 28, 1976, 3-F.

Rosen, F. Bruce. "The Influence of the Peabody Fund on Education in Reconstruction Florida," *Florida Historical Quarterly,* LV, No. 3 (1977), 310–320.

Rudwick, Martin J. S. *The Meaning of Fossils: Episodes in the History of Palae-ontology.* 2nd ed. New York: Neale Watson Academic Publications, 1976.

Rusk, William S. "Notes on the Life of William Henry Rinehart, Sculptor," *Maryland Historical Magazine*, XIX, No. 4 (December 1924), 309–338.

————. "Rinehart, William Henry," *Dictionary of American Biography.* Edited by Dumas Malone. New York: Charles Scribner's Sons, 1943, XV.

Russell, John Dale. *Report of the Study of Closer Cooperation Between George Peabody College for Teachers and Vanderbilt University.* Nashville: 1962.

Rutledge, Anna Wells, compiler. *List of Works of Art in the Collection of the Peabody Institute, Baltimore, Md.* Baltimore: Peabody Institute, 1949.

Salisbury, Lynne Trowbridge. *Peabody Museum of Natural History: A Guide to the Exhibits.* New Haven, Conn.: Yale University, 1961.

Sandburg, Carl. *Abraham Lincoln, The War Years.* 4 vols. New York: Harcourt, Brace and Co., 1939.

Satterlee, Herbert. *The Life of J. Pierpont Morgan.* New York: privately printed, 1937.

Schaaf, Elizabeth. "Baltimore's Peabody Art Gallery," *The Archives of the American Art Journal*, XXIV, No. 4 (1984), 9–14.

————. "From Idea to Tradition: The Peabody Prep," *Music Educators Journal*, LXXII, No. 1 (September 1985), 38–43.

———— (compiler). *Guide to the Archives of the Peabody Institute of the City of Baltimore 1857–1977.* Baltimore: Archives of the Peabody Institute of the Johns Hopkins University, 1987.

Schoch, Robert M. "The Paleontological Collections of the Peabody Museum of Natural History," *Fossils Quarterly* (Fall/Winter 1984–85), 4–14.

Schuchert, Charles, and Clara Mae LeVene. *O. C. Marsh, Pioneer in Paleontology.* New Haven, Conn.: Yale University Press, 1940.

Sears, Jesse Brundage. *Philanthropy in the History of American Higher Education.* Bulletin No. 26. Washington, D.C.: United States Bureau of Education, 1922.

"Seventy of Symphony Urge Longer Season to Keep Stewart Here," *Sun* (Baltimore), January 31, 1952.

Sherer, Robert G. *Subordination or Liberation? The Development and Conflicting Theories of Black Education in Nineteenth Century Alabama.* University: University of Alabama Press, 1977.

Shor, Elizabeth Noble. *Fossils and Flies: The Life of a Compleat Scientist Samuel Wendell Williston (1851–1918).* Norman: University of Oklahoma Press, 1977.

"Sidney Lanier Commemoration," *Johns Hopkins Alumni Magazine*, XIV, No. 5 (October 1925–June 1926), 480–505.

Simon, Otto T. Letter, "Thinks Asger Hamerik Should be Honored by

Some Memorial at the Peabody and That His Music Should be Frequently Heard There," *Sun* (Baltimore), April 15, 1922.

Simpson, George Gaylord. *George Gaylord Simpson: Concession to the Improbable, An Unconventional Autobiography.* New Haven, Conn.: Yale University Press, 1978.

Sioussat, St. George L. "Notes of Colonel W. G. Moore, Private Secretary to President Johnson, 1866–1869," *American Historical Review,* XIX, No. 1 (October 1913), 98–132.

Smith, Philip Chadwick Foster. "Ernest Stanley Dodge, Museum Builder," *Sea History,* XVII (1980), 35.

Snyder, William T., Jr. "Peabody Institute of Baltimore," *Baltimore,* XXXVI, No. 6 (March 1943), 37–38.

Somerville, Frank P. L. "Peabody-Pratt Tie-Up Weighed," *Sun* (Baltimore), January 22, 1966.

————. "Peabody's Shift of Books Fought," *Sun* (Baltimore), October 1, 1966.

————. "Pratt Board is Silent on Peabody Plan," *Sun* (Baltimore), January 22, 1966.

"Soot Hides Treasures. Peabody Library Spruced Up," *Sun* (Baltimore), February 19, 1977.

South Carolina. *Acts and Resolutions of the General Assembly of the State of South Carolina Passed at the Regular Session of 1896.* Columbia, S.C.: Charles A. Calvo, Junior, State Printer, 1896.

————. *Journal of the House of Representatives of the General Assembly of the State of South Carolina Being the Regular Session Beginning January 14, 1896.* Columbia, S.C.: Charles A. Calvo, Junior, State Printer, 1896.

————. *Journal of the Senate of the General Assembly of the State of South Carolina Being the Regular Session Beginning January 14, 1896.* Columbia, S.C.: Charles A. Calvo, Junior, State Printer, 1896.

Southern Education Foundation Annual Report 1986–87. Toward Equity and Excellence; A 50 Year Commitment, 1937–1987. Atlanta: SEF, 1987.

Spatz, H. Donald. "Fire Engines, Cow Pastures and Music," *Forecast!* (Washington/Baltimore Entertainment Guide), XIV, No. 11 (January 1978), 60–61.

Spivey, Donald. *Schooling for the New Slavery: Black Industrial Education, 1868–1915.* Contributions in Afro-American and African Studies, No. 38. Westport, Conn.: Greenwood Press, 1978.

"SR Building to Return as Focal Point for Campus," *Peabody Columns* (Nashville), III, No. 7 (March 1993), 1–2; *Vanderbilt Register,* May 3–16, 1993, 1, 5.

Starr, Elizabeth Ellen. "Asger Hamerik as I Knew Him as Teacher, Artist, Friend," *Peabody Bulletin* (Baltimore), Fall 1923, 6–7.

Stevens, Henry (compiler). *An Account of the Proceedings at the Dinner Given by*

Mr. George Peabody to the Americans Connected with the Great Exhibition, at the London Coffee House, Ludgate Hill, on the 27th October, 1851. London: William Pickering, 1851.

"Stewart and the Peabody," *Gardens, Houses and People* (Baltimore), April 1952.

"Stewart Defends Symphony Setup, Says He is Underpaid," *Sun* (Baltimore), November 24, 1951.

"Stewart to Leave Peabody Conservatory Post in 1958," *Sun* (Baltimore), November 19, 1957.

"Stewart's Move to Quit Accepted," *Sun* (Baltimore), February 2, 1952.

Stump, William. "Man in the Street: Sidney Lanier," *Sun* (Baltimore), November 20, 1949.

"Succeeds Cooper: Peabody Conservatory Names Kent as Dean," *Baltimore News-Post*, May 19, 1961.

Tate, William Knox. "Elementary Education in the South," *The South in the Building of a Nation, A History of the Southern States.* Richmond, Va.: Southern Historical Publication Society, 1909.

Taylor, Hoy. *An Interpretation of the Early Administration of the Peabody Education Fund.* Contributions to Education No. 114. Nashville: George Peabody College for Teachers, 1933.

"Technology Can Reconstruct Classroom Instruction," *Vanderbilt Register*, December 8, 1989, n.p.

Thatcher, Howard R. "A Teacher Glances Back—Notes on Music in Baltimore," *Evening Sun* (Baltimore), July 12, 1950.

"Three Goucher Faculty Members Retiring," *Evening Sun* (Baltimore), June 22, 1956.

Time-Life Books. *Emergence of Man: Life Before Man.* New York: Time-Life Books, 1972.

"Uhler, Philip Reese," *Appletons' Cyclopaedia of American Biography.* Edited by James Grant Wilson and John Fiske. New York: D. Appleton and Co., 1889, VI.

"Uhler, Philip Reese," *Biographical Cyclopedia of Representative Men of Maryland and District of Columbia.* Baltimore: National Biographical Publishing Co., 1879.

"Uhler, Philip Reese," *Dictionary of American Biography.* Edited by Dumas Malone. New York: Charles Scribner's Sons, 1943, XIX.

"Uhler, Philip Reese," *National Cyclopaedia of American Biography Being the History of the United States.* New York: James T. White and Co., 1900, VIII.

"Uhler, Philip Reese," *Who Was Who in America.* Chicago: A. N. Marquis Co., 1943, I.

United States Senate Document No. 610 (1840), 174–194. Washington, D.C.: U.S. Senate.

Vanderbilt University. *Vanderbilt University Centennial: The Program and Ad-*

dresses Given on October 3, 1975, Celebrating the One Hundredth Anniversary of the Ceremonies that Opened the University. Nashville: Vanderbilt University, 1976.

Vaughn, William P. "Partners in Segregation: Barnas Sears and the Peabody Fund," *Civil War History,* X, No. 3 (1964), 260–274.

————. *Schools for All: The Blacks and Public Education in the South, 1865–1877.* Lexington: University Press of Kentucky, 1974.

"Victorian Yankee," *Economist* (London), February 2, 1972.

Virginia Museum of Fine Arts, Richmond, Va. *A Souvenir of the Exhibition Entitled Healy's Sitters.* Richmond: Virginia Museum of Fine Arts, 1950.

"VU's Peabody Holds Top Ranking Again," *Nashville Banner,* February 18, 1991, B-5.

W. S. R. "Rinehart, William Henry," *Dictionary of American Biography.* Edited by Dumas Malone. New York: Charles Scribner's Sons, 1943, XV.

Wallace, Sarah Agnes, and Frances Elma Gillespie, eds. *The Journal of Benjamin Moran 1857–1865.* Chicago: University of Chicago Press, 1948.

Ward, Humphrey. *History of the Athenaeum, 1824–1925.* London: William Clowes and Sons, 1926.

Weed, Thurlow. *Autobiography of Thurlow Weed.* 2 vols. Edited by Harriet A. Weed. Boston: Houghton, Mifflin and Co., 1884.

————. "The Late George Peabody; A Vindication of his Course During the Civil War," *The Historical Collections of the Danvers Historical Society,* XIX (1931), 9–15.

Welch, Allen Howard. "George Peabody's Funeral Voyage: A Tarnished Homecoming," *Essex Institute Historical Collections,* CIX, No. 2 (April 1973), 116–137.

"Welcome to—Peabody, Massachusetts: 'The World's Largest Leather City'" (tri-fold pamphlet). Peabody, Mass.: Chamber of Commerce and Peabody Historical Society, n.d.

Wertheimer, Gunther. "Disgrace at the Peabody," *Evening Sun* (Baltimore), June 9, 1989.

West, Earle H. "The Peabody Fund and Negro Education, 1867–1880," *History of Education Quarterly,* VI (Summer 1966), 3–21.

White, Andrew Dickson. *Autobiography of Andrew Dickson White.* 2 vols. New York: Century Co., 1906.

White, Edward Lucas. "Reminiscences of Sidney Lanier," *Johns Hopkins Alumni Magazine,* XVII, No. 4 (November 1928–June 1929), 329–331.

Wilcoxon, Hardy C. "Continuing Our Mission," *Peabody Reflector,* LII, No. 2 (Summer 1979), 2–3.

Williams, David A. "George Peabody," *McGraw Hill Encyclopedia of World Biography.* New York: McGraw Hill Book Co., 1973, VIII.

Williams, Harold A. *Robert Garrett & Sons Incorporated: Origin and Development: 1840–1965.* Baltimore: 1965.

Willoughby, Charles G. "The Peabody Museum of Archaeology and Ethnology, Harvard University," *The Harvard Graduates' Magazine*, XXXI, No. 124 (June 23, 1923), 495–503.

Wilson, Philip Whitwell. *George Peabody, Esq., An Interpretation*. Nashville: George Peabody College for Teachers, 1926.

Winkler, John K. *Morgan the Magnificent*. New York: Vanguard Press, 1930.

Winthrop, Robert Charles. *Addresses and Speeches on Various Occasions from 1852–1886*. 4 vols. Boston: Little, Brown and Co., 1852 to 1886.

————. *Eulogy Pronounced at the Funeral of George Peabody, at Peabody, Mass., February 8, 1870*. Boston: John Wilson and Son, 1870.

————. *Reminiscences of Foreign Travel; A Fragment of Autobiography*. Boston: John Wilson and Son, 1894.

Wish, Harvey. *Society and Thought in Modern America*. 2 vols. New York: Longmans Green and Co., 1952.

"A World Benefactor Is Peabody's Pride," *Salem* (Mass.) *Evening News*, August 31, 1963, 3.

Young, Peter. "Back to the Stacks: Lloyd Brown to Assemble Historical Annapolis Data," *Evening Sun* (Baltimore), November 30, 1960.

————. "New Peabody Director: Symphony Could Draw Teachers, He Believes," *Evening Sun* (Baltimore), May 9, 1963.

Index